国际汇兑与结算

International Exchange and Settlement

主编　胡　凌　郭晓晶

哈尔滨工程大学出版社
Harbin Engineering University Press

内容简介

本书由南京工业职业技术大学国际汇兑与结算课程团队会同行业企业专家共同编写。全书共设计了3个能力模块、9个学习任务，每个学习任务都以"展示案例"开头，针对案例"提出问题"，针对案例及问题详细介绍"相关知识"，最终"分析案例"、解决问题。

本书既可作为高职高专院校、中等职业技术学校、本科院校国际商务专业和其他相关财经类专业学生的教学及实训用书，也可作为相关涉外企业业务人员培训用书，同时也适合有志从事进出口贸易、国际物流、商务英语等相关工作的人员使用。

图书在版编目(CIP)数据

国际汇兑与结算/胡凌，郭晓晶主编. —哈尔滨：哈尔滨工程大学出版社，2020.8
ISBN 978-7-5661-2758-7

Ⅰ.①国… Ⅱ.①胡… ②郭… Ⅲ.①汇兑结算-国际结算 Ⅳ.①F830.73

中国版本图书馆CIP数据核字(2020)第155312号

选题策划 田 婧
责任编辑 王俊一 张如意
封面设计 刘长友

出版发行 哈尔滨工程大学出版社
社 址 哈尔滨市南岗区南通大街145号
邮政编码 150001
发行电话 0451-82519328
传 真 0451-82519699
经 销 新华书店
印 刷 哈尔滨市石桥印务有限公司
开 本 787 mm×1 092 mm 1/16
印 张 15.5
字 数 512千字
版 次 2020年8月第1版
印 次 2020年8月第1次印刷
定 价 46.50元
http://www.hrbeupress.com
E-mail:heupress@hrbeu.edu.cn

Curriculum guidance

1. The orientation and objectives of the course

International Exchange and Settlement is mainly offered for international business majors. To meet the new demands of international economic development, higher vocational schools aim to train business majors into high skilled technical talents mastering basic theories of international trade, professional knowledge, and fundamental skills and possessing strong abilities in business English communication, international marketing, implementing import and export contracts, operating international cargo clearance and transportation, preventing and transferring foreign exchange risks, among which, the core capabilities center on business English communication, international marketing, implementing import and export contracts, operating international cargo clearance and transportation, preventing and transferring foreign exchange risks. To cultivate these fundamental competence, our school has developed corresponding courses such as international trade practice, business English, foreign trade documents, international marketing, customs declaration, international freight forwarding, and international exchange and settlement. In the above courses, international trade practice focuses on how to complete the whole process of import and export according to relevant international trade practices and legal knowledge, while the course of foreign trade documents deals with how to make out and transfer documents in different steps of international trade.

This course attempts to solve the following problems:

(1) How to handle foreign exchange and exchange rate is essential in international trade practices. The calculation of the exchange rate and application of the skills can affect the success rate of transactions and even the trade income. The trend of exchange rate determines the quoted price, and its fluctuation indicates the risks involved in international trade. Therefore, the correct calculation of international exchange rates constitutes the fundamental capabilities of international business talents.

(2) Every step in international trade is full of risks, therefore, how to shelter from risks, safeguard against risks, and transfer risks become key capabilities of international business talents.

(3) No matter involved in international trade or internal trade, enterprises must settle accounts in the end. Guaranteeing their remittance collection is one of the important goals for exporters in international trade. Consequently, the ability to conduct international settlement, including the application of instruments of settlement, choice of settlement methods, is an important capability of international business talents. Meanwhile, knowing how to deal with capital in circulation before making international trade and how to input capital in reproduction when the fund is in float after the shipment is also necessary abilities for international business talents.

Therefore, *International Exchange and Settlement* aims to settle financial problems in international trade and improve students' abilities of properly using international finance instruments in international trade.

After learning this course, students will master relevant basic concepts, theories, and methods concerning international exchange and settlement, be able to analyze the status quo of international trade and engaged in international trade practice by applying international finance techniques, way of thinking and taking reference to an actual situation so that they can apply theories to practice, enhance their practical skills and develop work habits of being adept at observation, innovation, and standardized operation. Meanwhile, work ethics and work qualities strengthened through flexible teaching activities will help place a solid foundation for comprehensively promoting students' professional qualities.

2. The framework of the course

International Exchange and Settlement focuses on three capability modules: the capability of analyzing and applying the exchange rate, the capability of preventing and transferring foreign exchange rate risks, and the capability of operating and financing international settlement (the framework of the course).

3. Teaching methods

(1) Teaching philosophy

①Emphasize students' initiative, focus on students' abilities

This course is open to all major international students. Teachers should both highlight academic theories, methods, skills related to this course, and quality education so as to stimulate students' interests. Students are encouraged to digest all the relevant theories and methods independently so as to improve their thinking and practical skills, enhance their ability to combine theory and practice, facilitates their innovation.

This course tries to focus on the students' initiative from setting the learning objective, the process of teaching, course evaluation, developing teaching resources to cultivating students' practical skills and abilities. Learning this course is a process for them to construct knowledge, promote skills, enhance thinking, and broaden their visions.

②Respect individual difference, center on process evaluation

Teachers should encourage students to learn independently by inspiring them to think and analyze practical situations and advocating free expression based on respecting individual differences. Composed of both formative assessment and summative assessment, the whole evaluation system is established to develop students' interests and self-study ability. Teachers ought to give priority to formative assessment to help facilitate students' motivation and confidence, while summative assessment serves as a way to test students' knowledge application ability. The evaluation is conducive to both the advancement of students' knowledge application ability and the healthy development of their personality. The basic idea is to set up a two-way promotion mechanism to promote individual development through the process cultivation and to evaluate the teaching process by students' sustainable development ability.

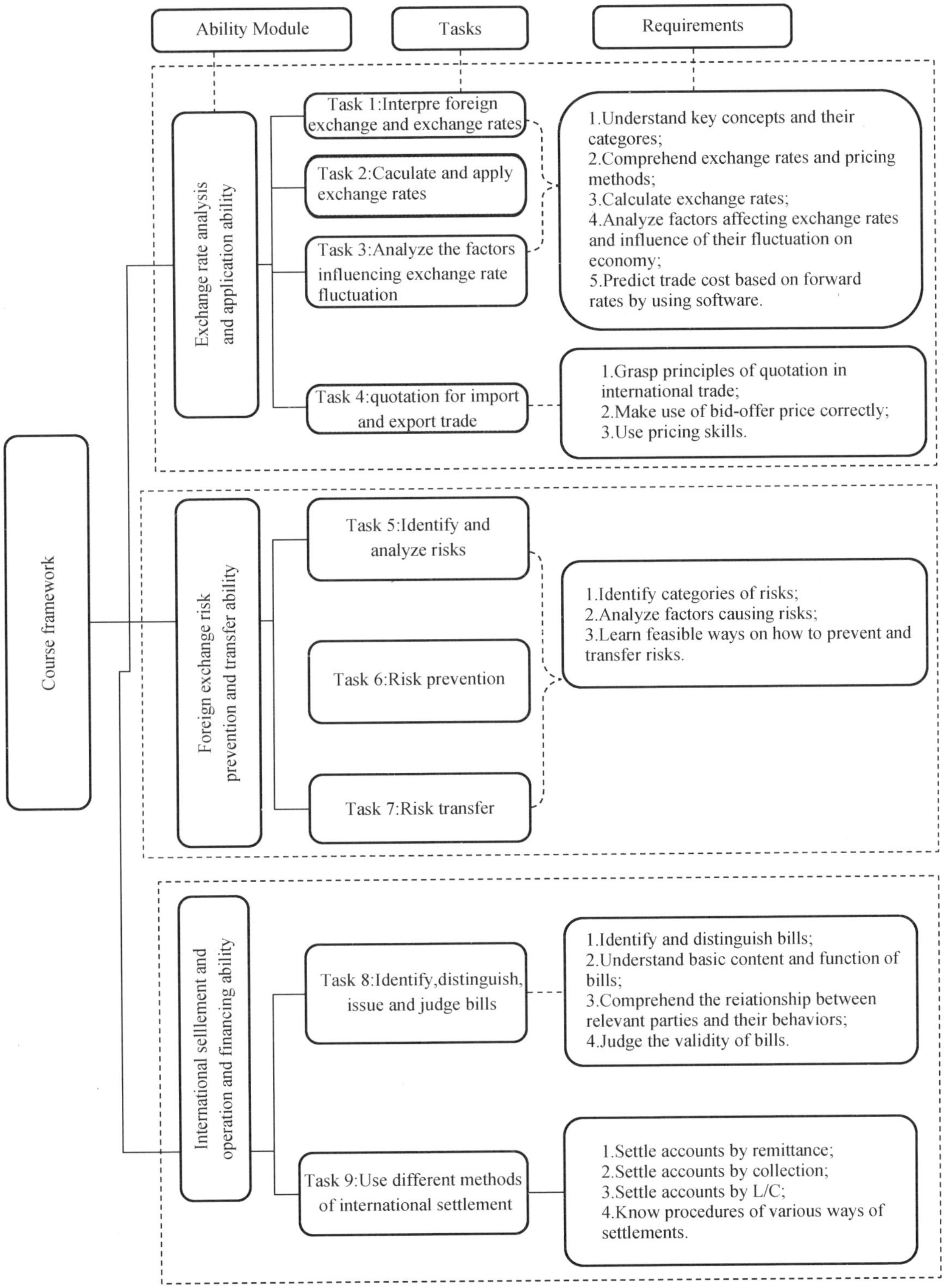

The framework of the course

③Integrate course resources, improve teaching methods and expand learning channels

In the course of teaching, teachers are supposed to remind students to pay attention to various economic phenomena in life and encourage them to put forward questions or assumptions based on the familiar examples of exchange and trade settlement in practice. Under the guidance of teachers, students can reach a conclusion and make summarization by themselves through analytical reasoning so that their understanding of basic theories of international finance can be strengthened. Case for demonstration, case for aralysis, and other activities like social investigation, classroom lecturing, and classroom discussion are designed to increase students' comprehension of academic theories and develop their practical skills. Modern teaching methods, advanced teaching tactics exemplified by organizing students to learn fresh materials through the multimedia network, audio-visual materials, highlighting the analysis of typical cases, using interactive teaching to make students get simulation training, all help much greatly to improve their abilities to find problems, analyzing problems and solving problems.

(2) Basic teaching tactics

This course mainly cultivates students' ability of analysis and application, preventing and transferring foreign exchange risks, operating international settlement in international business activities as well as cultivates their methodology and social competence, therefore various teaching methods, such as role playing, case analysis, network searching, workshop, debate, simulation operation, software, scenario simulation, interaction, task setting, video, charts illustration, samples demonstration, multimedia presentation are encouraged to be combined to carry out teaching activities flexibly. It enables students to learn in a happy atmosphere. Consequently, not only their professional skills are improved, but also they learn how to deal with various social relations in a harmonious way, reflecting the students centered classroom teaching philosophy with the teacher as the guide.

International exchange and settlement is a course updated along with the social progress, therefore, when stressing the ability of practice, teachers should also pay attention to modern educational technology to create an open learning environment for students. Students are encouraged to observe phenomena with up-to-date and broad views, analyze reasons behind these phenomena, put forward their own methods and ideas and take an active part in social practice.

A flexible teaching schedule can be established to encourage students to make full use of professional software, modern educational technology, and network teaching resources to learn independently, so that teaching quality can be guaranteed.

Last but not least, teachers should guide students to improve their work ethics and cultivate their spirits of abiding by disciplines, cherishing their posts, being honest and trustworthy, and contributing to society.

4. Evaluation

This course aims to cultivate students' ability of international exchange and settlement, so both process evaluation and result evaluation should be emphasized.

The assessment of this course can be conducted in two ways: formative assessment and summative assessment, with the former accounting for 70% of the total score, while the later accounting for 30% of the total score.

Contents

Module 1 Exchange rate analysis and application

Task 1　An illustration of foreign exchange and exchange rate

【Objectives】

(1) Understand foreign exchange and its classification;

(2) Be familiar with the physical form of different currencies around the world and their standard currency codes and names;

(3) Grasp the exchange rate and pricing methods.

【Tasks】

(1) Distinguish standard codes and names for currencies frequently used in the world;

(2) Summarize the concepts concerning foreign exchange and classify them;

(3) Understand the foreign exchange rate.

【Requirements】

(1) Identify the physical form and standard code and name of currencies commonly used;

(2) Understand foreign exchange and its classification;

(3) Understand the exchange rate and its pricing methods.

Task 1.1　Foreign currency

Every country in modern society needs to conduct monetary and economic exchanges with other countries in some way or another. The trade of commodities, the exchange of capital, the international transfer of capital, and the settlement and payment of claims and debts among different countries must ultimately be made through currency and currency exchange between domestic countries and overseas countries. Foreign exchange and exchange rate are always closely linked with the former dealing with the instruments for the exchange, while the latter handling the proportion of the exchange. Foreign exchange and exchange rate is one of the core issues in international economic and financial activities, therefore mastering basic knowledge and skills on foreign exchange and the exchange rate is the foundation for handling international business.

How to understand foreign exchange correctly? We can get the answer from the following discussions.

【Case for demonstration】

(1) Case 1.1　Li Lin is a new employee of Jiangsu Guosheng Import and Export Trading

Company. He may often go abroad for businesses. In order to identify foreign currencies, he has exchanged for some banknotes from different countries(figure 1.1). Li Lin believes this is what people often call foreign exchange.

Figure 1.1 Currencies from different countries

Case 1.2 On March 21, 2018, Jiangsu Guosheng Import and Export Trading Company signed an export contract for electronic components with AAA ELECTRONICS INC. According to the contract, accounts should be settled through Bank of America and Bank of China Nanjing branch. The basic process of settlement is shown in figure 1.2.

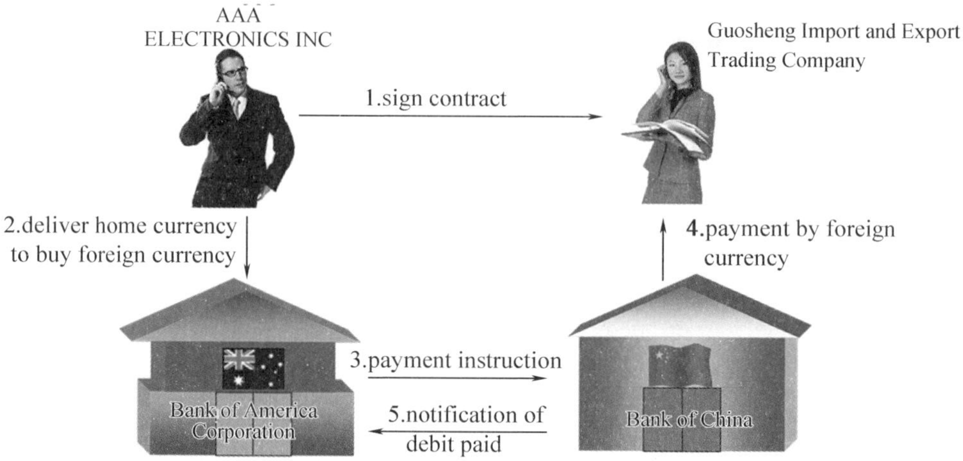

Figure 1.2 The basic process of trade settlement for Guosheng company

【Questions】

(1) Which country's currency is demonstrated by Li Lin in case 1.1?

(2) Is Li Lin right in case 1.1?

(3) What does the figure 1.2 inform us?

【Relevant knowledge】

(1) Concept of foreign exchange

Foreign exchange is a means of payment and a credit voucher presented in foreign currency, including convertible foreign currencies (foreign currency notes and foreign currency deposits); documents of payment (bills of exchange, promissory notes, cheques, etc.) presented in freely convertible foreign currencies; securities presented in convertible foreign currency, etc. This is what we usually refer to as foreign exchange, which is also a static concept of foreign exchange.

Article 3 of *the Regulations of the People's Republic of China on the Administration of Foreign Exchange* stipulates that foreign exchange refers to the means of payment and assets expressed in foreign currencies that can be used for international settlement, as listed below:

①Foreign currency, including banknotes and coins;

②Foreign currency payment instruments, including bills, bank deposit certificates, postal savings certificates, etc.;

③Securities denominated in foreign currencies, including government bonds, corporate bonds, stocks, etc.;

④Special drawing rights(SDRs);

⑤Other foreign exchange assets, mainly consist of all kinds of foreign currency investment income, such as stock dividends, interest, debt service, bonus, and so on.

(2) Role of foreign exchange

①It makes the purchasing power of each country's currency convertible and makes the currency circulation among countries possible. Currency is the carrier and expression of purchasing power, whose conversion is possible with foreign exchange.

②It greatly facilitates international settlement and promotes international trade. Bills of exchange in convertible currencies are the most convenient and principal means of payment for international settlement.

③It has regulated the international flow of funds and accelerated the process of world economic integration. As the value carrier of alleviating funds surplus and shortage and the unique way of international investment, foreign exchange accelerates the international flow of capital.

④It serves as official reserves to achieve the balance of payments. With foreign exchange, the balance of payments can be reached by returning the overcharge and demanding payment of the shortage.

(3) Classification of foreign exchange

Foreign exchange can be classified according to different standards:

①Based on whether it can be freely converted, foreign exchange can be divided into convertible foreign exchange and accounting foreign exchange.

Convertible currency refers to foreign currencies and payment vouchers that can be freely converted into the currencies of other countries or regions without the approval of the issuing country when they are used and can also be settled and paid to a third country.

Accounting foreign exchange, also known as the non-convertible currency or bilateral foreign exchange, refers to the foreign currencies and payment vouchers that cannot be freely converted into currencies of other countries or regions without the approval of the issuing country when used.

Accounting foreign exchange shall only be used between two countries upon their agreement.

② Foreign exchange can be classified into trade foreign exchange, non-trade foreign exchange, and financial foreign exchange according to their sources and purposes.

Trade foreign exchange, also known as physical foreign exchange, refers to foreign exchange derived from or used in import and export trade. It's an international means of payment formed by the international circulation of commodities.

Non-trade foreign exchange refers to all foreign exchange except trade foreign exchange, that is, all foreign exchange that is not derived from or used in import and export trade, such as labor exchange, overseas remittance, and donated foreign exchange.

Different from the above two exchanges, financial foreign exchange is a kind of financial asset foreign exchange. For example, foreign exchange bought and sold among banks is neither derived from visible trade or invisible trade, nor used for visible trade, but for the management and manipulation of various currency positions. The transfer of capital among countries also takes the form of money. Both indirect investment and direct investment develop from financial assets flowing among countries. In particular, hot money, due to its large amount, frequent transactions and strong impact, has been attracting more and more attentions. Trade foreign exchange, non'trade foreign exchange and financial foreign exchange are essentially all foreign exchanges. There does not exist an impassible gap among them. Instead they can often be converted into one another.

③By the market trend of the foreign exchange rate, foreign exchange can be divided into hard foreign exchange and soft foreign exchange.

Foreign exchange, in terms of its characteristics and significance, is always represented by specific currencies. For instance, United States dollar foreign exchange refers to foreign exchange using United States dollar as the means of international payment; pound foreign exchange refers to foreign exchange using Great Britain Pound as an international means of payment and yen foreign exchange refers to foreign exchange using yen as the means of international payment, etc. In the international foreign exchange market, due to various reasons, the value of various currencies changes frequently, consequently the exchange rate often changes. Therefore, on the basis of the trend of currency value and exchange rate, we can classify various currencies into hard currency and soft currency, or strong currency and weak currency. Hard currency is a kind of freely convertible currency with a strong value, strong purchasing power, and a rising exchange rate. Because of the ever-changing economic and political conditions at home and abroad, hard currency is not fixed into certain currencies. It can be commonly seen that currency was hard yesterday but today becomes weak and vice versa.

(4) Major foreign exchanges

In foreign exchange trading, a currency must experience continuous buying and selling before it becomes a foreign exchange. Here are three conditions listed below: ①The holder has faith in its store value. ②This currency can serve as a measure of value in international trade. ③This currency can serve as a medium of exchange. Currently, among more than 150 countries in the world, about 30 currencies are active currencies. For each of the 30 currencies, there are 29 different exchange rates with others, so there are 435 different exchange rates. At present, the basic pattern of key foreign exchanges in the world market is that United States dollar dominates the basic pricing relationship among most currencies. The domineering role of United States dollar is achieved by the strong power of the United States and promoted by the formation and development of the international exchange rate system. Japan's economic boom has dramatically contributed to the stabilization and expansion of Japanese yen's important position. Though newly born, the euro is bound to become another crucial currency dominating the foreign exchange market together with United States dollar and Japanese yen in the 21st century because of its potential power from the unified policy and inherent economic strength of the eurozone.

①United States dollar

The issuance of United States dollar is authorized by US Treasury, but is handled by US Federal Reserve Bank. There are seven denominations of United States dollar paper currency in circulation, namely \$100, \$50, \$20, \$10, \$5, \$2, and \$1. \$1 equals to 100 cents. The current banknotes in circulation in the United States are the 1928, 1934, 1935, 1950, 1953, 1963, 1966, 1969, 1974, 1977, 1981, 1985, and 1996 editions. For all denominations, the notes are in sizes of 15.6 cm × 6.6 cm. The front of each paper note is printed with the name of the notes, the United States of America, the seal of the United States Treasury, and the signature of a Treasury Official. The bill has a portrait of a well-known figure in American history on the front and a picture on the back. The 500-dollar-note and paper notes over 500 dollars have no pictures on the back with very limited circulation. Since 1963 "IN GOD WE TRUST" was added on the back of each edition. In 1996 the United States began to issue notes with new security features. The letters and Arabic numbers in the center of United States dollar bill represent the names of 12 Federal Reserve Banks in the United States.

Among the global foreign exchange transactions, United States dollars account for 86%, therefore, become the most important foreign exchange in the international foreign exchange market at present.

The face of United States dollar bill is a famous figure in American history, see table 1.1.

Table 1.1 Historical figures represented by dollar bills

Denomination	Front	Back	Pictures on both sides
1 dollar	Washington	"ONE" in the center with big seals on the left and the right	 

Table 1.1(continued)

Denomination	Front	Back	Pictures on both sides
2 dollars	Jefferson	Independence Declaration in 1776	 
5 dollars	Lincoln	Lincoln Memorial	 
10 dollars	Hamilton	Treasury Department of the United States	 
20 dollars	Jackson	the White House	 

②Euro

The euro was officially launched on January 1, 1999. Eleven countries, except Britain, Greece, Sweden, and Denmark, became the first members of the Euro Club in 1998. The euro grew out of Doyle's plan proposed in 1989. Since the launch of the euro mechanism by the Maastricht Treaty on December 11, 1991, by early 1999, most EU countries had linked their currencies to the euro at a fixed exchange rate. Under the Maastricht treaty, Europe's single currency is called the ECU. In December 1995, the European Commission decided to rename the single European currency as the euro. The euro officially entered into circulation at 0:00 on January 1, 2002. From then on, all incomes and expenditures, including payroll income and taxes, etc. are calculated in Euros. On March 1, 2002, the old name of the European currency disappeared with the official circulation of euro.

Euro notes are issued by the European Central Bank, which is mandated by the central banks of the participating countries. The governments of participating countries issue euro coins . Different issuers coordinate with each other. The underlying intention of EU politicians pushing for the euro is to end the "tyranny of the dollar". In December 1996, the European Monetary Agency in Frankfurt Germany announced that the design of the euro—the European Union common currency in 1999, had been selected through an open ballot. Austrian paper money designer Robert Calina won the bid. In his design scheme, there are seven denominations of the euro, namely 5, 10, 20, 50, 100, 200, and 500 euros. The larger the denomination, the larger the size of the note. The front of each bill features doors and windows, symbolizing the EU's spirit of co-operation and openness. On the backside of the bill are all kinds of bridges, including small bridges in ancient times and suspension Bridges in modern time, symbolizing the bond between Europe and countries in other parts of the world. Euro coins come in eight denominations, including 1, 2, 5, 10, 20, 50 euro cent, 1 euro and 2 euro. The strong economic strength of the EU will facilitate the rising status of the euro in the world.

③Japanese yen

Japanese yen is issued by the bank of Japan. Notes issued in Japan are in denominations of 100 000, 5 000, 1 000, 500, 100, 50, 10, 5, 1 in addition to 500,100,50,10,5,1yen coins. Japanese banknotes are all written in Chinese characters on the front (arranged from left to right) with "Bank of Japan Notes" at the top of the middle. All banknotes have no issuing date. The person in charge of the issuing unit uses seals. "President's Seal" and "Chief Officer's Seal" are printed on the bill.

④Great Britain pound

The Great Britain Pound is the British standard monetary unit issued by the Bank of England. On October 15, 1971, the Bank of England introduced a new currency system with the subsidiary unit changed to the New Penny. A pound is equal to 100 New pence. Currently, there are 5, 10, 20, and 50 pound notes in circulation, plus 1, 2, 5, 10, 50 new pence, and 1 pound coin.

Britain officially adopted the gold standard in 1821, when the Great Britain Pound became the standard monetary unit of Britain, containing 7.322 38 pure gold per pound. When World War I broke out in 1914, Britain abandoned the gold standard, consequently, gold coins ceased to circulate, and Britain stopped exchanging gold. The result is the British pound evolved into notes that could not be redeemed. However, due to the need of exchange control, Britain still set the gold content of Great Britain Pound at 3.581 34 grams a pound on December 18, 1946. On July 15, 1947, Britain announced the implementation of the free convertibility of Great Britain Pound. However, due to the rapid loss of foreign exchange reserves, the exchange control was restored in August of the same year. After the floating of United States dollar on August 15, 1971, the British pound began to fix its value against the dollar on the basis of its constant gold content. After the official depreciation of United States dollar on December 18 of the same year, the new official exchange rate of the British pound against United States dollar rose to US $2.605

7 per pound, while the real exchange rate fluctuated within the limit of US $2.547 1 to US $2.664 3, with a fluctuation range of about 4.5%. On March 9, 1973, the eight western European, countries formed a joint floating group, nevertheless Britain did not participate but continued to float alone. On October 8, 1990, Great Britain Pound joined the European monetary system with 6% fluctuation rate against other currencies within the monetary system. On September 16, 1992, Britain announced that the British pound was temporarily out of the European monetary system.

⑤Hong Kong dollar

Hong Kong dollar is mainly issued by the British Bank HSBC, Hong Kong's Standard Chartered Bank, and Bank of China. The Hong Kong dollar notes currently in circulation in Hong Kong are: $1 000, $500, $100, $50, $20, $10, $5, in addition to 1 cent note, 5, 2, 1 dollar coins and 5, 2, 10 cent coins. One Hong Kong dollar is equal to ten dimes, and one dime is equal to 10 cents. Hong Kong dollar is pegged to United States dollar, with the exchange rate of them fluctuating around 1:7.8.

⑥Australian dollar

Australian dollar is the legal tender of Australia and is issued by the Reserve Bank of Australia. There are 5, 10, 20, 50, and 100 notes in circulation in Australia in addition to 1, 2, 5, 10, 20 and 50 cent coins. One Australian dollar equals 100 cents. All coins feature Queen Elizabeth II on the front. New Australian dollars are plastic banknotes, put into use after nearly 30 years of research and development. Made of polyester material instead of paper, they are wear-resistant, not easy to be fold, and able to withstand rubbing and washing with impressive counterfeiting effects, therefore boasting long cycle of usage.

⑦Canadian dollar

Canadian dollar is issued by the Bank of Canada. Canadian banknotes come in eight denominations: 1, 2, 5, 10, 20, 50, 100, and 1 000 dollars with coins in denominations of 1 dollar, 1 cent, 5 cents, 10 cents, 25 cents and 50 cents. One dollar equals 100 cents. The first Canadian banknotes bearing the image of George V were issued in 1935. A 1937 version of the banknote featured the image of King George VI. The 1954 edition of the banknote had the image of Queen Elizabeth II. Since August 1970, the 1937 edition of the banknote bearing the image of King George VI has been issued. New notes have been issued since August 1970. Both the old and new versions of the notes are available. The coin has Queen Elizabeth II on the front and the word "CANADA" cast on the back. Canadian residents are mainly the descendants of English and French immigrants, clustering in English and French areas, so the bill is in both English and French languages.

⑧Singapore dollar

Singapore dollar is issued by the Singapore monetary authority. At present, the currency circulated in Singapore has its official values of 10 000, 1 000, 500, 50, 20, 10, 5, 1 dollar respectively, plus coins in denomination of 1 dollar and 50,20,10,5,1 cent. One dollar equals to 100 cents. Among all the bills, the 20, 25, 500 and 10 000 Singapore dollar notes have one version respectively, while 1, 5, 10, and 50 dollar notes are available in two versions respectively and 100, 1 000 dollar notes in three versions respectively. One version is characterized by Orchid, while another version features birds and the third type of banknotes are the $100 and $1 000 notes issued since 1984 with the main design featuring a variety of different ships. The word "SINGAPORE" is printed markedly on the front and the back of all denominations of banknotes. And the front also with a picture of a lion standing up to support a shield of stars and moon. Old and new banknotes are in mixed circulation.

⑨ Swiss franc

Swiss franc is issued by the Swiss National Bank. One Swiss franc is equal to 100 centimes. The notes are in denominations of 10, 20, 50, 100, 500 and 1 000 Swiss francs. Coins are in denominations of 1, 2, 5 Swiss francs and 1, 5, 10, 20, 50 centimes. Because of pursuing a policy of neutrality and nonalignment, Switzerland is considered to be the safest place in the world, therefore Swiss franc is also known as traditional safe-haven currency. The Swiss government protection policies on finance, foreign exchange result in a lot of foreign exchange in Switzerland. All these explain why Swiss franc has become one of the safest and most popular international settlements and foreign exchange currencies.

(5) Some major foreign exchange codes and symbols

To make the foreign exchange market more efficient, each currency needs a standard code and symbol. These codes are defined by the International Organization for Standardization (ISO), and consist of three English letters. Table 1.2 shows ISO codes and symbols of several foreign currencies commonly used in payment and settlement in China.

Table 1.2 Foreign exchange codes and symbols

Currency	Full name in English	ISO	Conventional money symbol
United States dollar	United States dollar	USD	US $
Japanese yen	Japanese yen	JPY	¥
Great Britain Pound	Great Britain Pound	GBP	£
Hongkong dollar	Hong Kong dollar	HKD	HK $
euro	euro	EUR	€

(6) Requirements of foreign exchange

In general, to become a foreign exchange, the currency of a country should meet the following two requirements in addition to the strong economic strength of the issuing country, its integration into the world economic system and the relative stability of the currency value:

①Foreign exchange must be foreign assets denominated in foreign currency. For example, American importers use United States dollars to buy Japanese goods. This means of payment is not foreign exchange for Americans, because dollars are local currencies for them, but for Japanese exporters, it is foreign currency.

②Foreign exchange must be a foreign currency asset or a payment document that is freely convertible and can be accepted internationally. For example, the Thai baht is not a foreign currency for China, because although it is presented in a foreign currency, it is not freely convertible, so it is not foreign currency.

③Foreign exchange must be financial claims in foreign currencies that can be paid internationally. Those that cannot be freely exchanged or paid internationally, such as rubber checks or dishonored bills of exchange, cannot be regarded as foreign exchanges. Because otherwise, the process of international exchange cannot be carried out. At the same time, under the multilateral settlement system, it is obvious that the international debt that cannot be repaid cannot be used to pay off the debts of a third country.

【Case for analysis】

(1) In case 1.1, the banknotes displayed by Li Lin is shown in (figure 1.3).

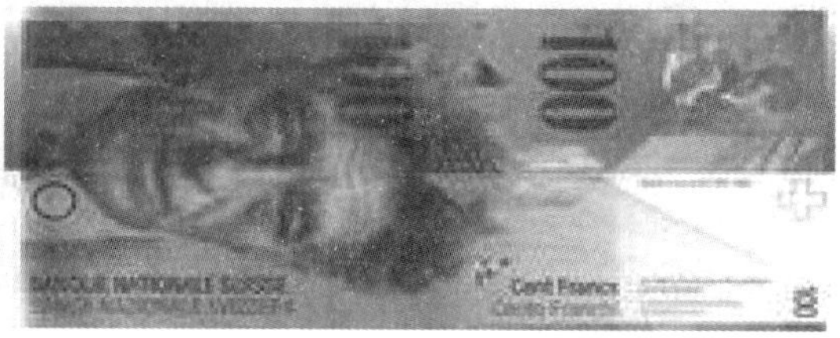

(a) Swiss franc 100
(2004 front)
sculptor and master painter
Alberto Giacometti

(b) Swiss franc 100
(2004 back)
Giacometti's magnum opus:
the statue of the advancing man

(c) United States dollar 20
(2003 front)
Andrew Jackson
7th President of the United States

(d) United States dollar 20
(2003 back)
the White House

Figure 1.3 Banknotes

(e) Great Britain pound 10

(1992 front)

British Queen Elizabeth Ⅱ

(f) Great Britain pound 10

(1992 back)

Charles Dickens, British writer

(g) Australian dollar 100 (front)

Australian soprano Melba

(h) Australian dollar 100 (back)

Sir Monash,

Australia's pre-eminent military general

(i) Singapore dollar 100 (front)

Singapore's first President Yusuf

(j) Singapore dollar 100 (back)

Singapore youth

(k) Japanese yen 10,000 (front)

Fukuzawa Yoshi,

one of the three most outstanding people

in Meiji time

(l) Japanese yen 10,000 (back)

the phoenix sculpture on the roof

of the phoenix hall of the equality

institute in Japan

Figure 1.3 (Continued)

(m) Euro 200 (front)
steel and glass architecture

(n) Euro 200 (back)
the bridge symbolizing the close ties
among European countries

(o) Hongkong dollar 100(front)
issued by Bank of China in 2006
Bank of China tower, Bank of China
logo and lotus

(p) Hongkong dollar 100(back)
issued by Bank of China in 2006
Bronze lion head watermark

(q) Vietnamese dong 50 (front)
President of the state of Vietnam
Ho Chi Minh

(r) Vietnamese dong 50 (back)
the office building of the
National Bank of Vietnam

Figure 1.3(Continued)

(2) In case 1.1, Li Lin's idea is not comprehensive enough, because foreign exchange refers to foreign currencies, means of payment and credit instruments in a foreign currency, including convertible foreign currencies (foreign currency notes and foreign currency deposits), documents of payment (bills of exchange, promissory notes, cheques, etc.) expressed in freely convertible foreign currencies and securities in convertible foreign currencies, etc. What Li Lin said is only one part of the content. Foreign currency notes do not represent all foreign exchanges.

(3) Case 1.2 shows an international trade settlement procedure, namely:

①The importer shall apply for telegraphic transfer of United States dollar 500 000 to the exporter at bank A (remitting agent bank).

②The remitting bank issues a receipt after receiving the payment.

③The remitting bank issues a telegraphic transfer notice (sealed), a cable or a telex to the exporter's agent (bank B).

④Foreign exchange must be reimbursable internationally.

The whole process reflects the dynamic meaning of foreign exchange. Dynamic foreign exchange refers to a kind of specialized business activity in which the currency of one country is converted into the currency of another country so as to pay off international debts. In this sense, foreign exchange is also equivalent to international settlement or foreign exchange trading activities, as a currency collection and payment process. In real international settlements, people do not transport different currencies between different countries, but mainly carry on international transmissions through international credit instruments such as foreign exchange bills so as to concentrate various debts to the bank account to offset and transfer to achieve the final payment.

Task 1.2 Exchange rate and pricing method

Within one country, money is the general equivalent and acts as a medium for all kinds of economic transactions, however, in international economic exchanges, each country has its own currency, so it is impossible for a currency of one country to circulate in another country. Therefore, foreign exchange and exchange rate are the primary problems to be solved in international transactions.

【Case for demonstration】

To familiarize himself with foreign exchange rates, Lin clicks on the relevant websites below:

http://www.123cha.com/hl/

http://www.baidu.com/s?tn=haokan123&wd=%BB%E3%C2%CA%BB%BB%CB%E3

http://www.123cha.com/hl/?q=100&from=USD&to=CHF&s=USDCHF#symbol=USDCHF=X;range=1y

http://www.njcb.com.cn/

http://www.99fob.com/html/tool/currency/

http://www.99fob.com/html/tool/exchangerate/

http://www.icbc.com.cn/icbc/%E7%BD%91%E4%B8%8A%E6%B1%87%E5%B8%82/7.

http://www.boc.cn/sourcedb/whpj/

From the website of Bank of China, the website of Industrial and Commercial Bank of China and the interface of foreign exchange websites, Li Lin sees the following information concerning foreign exchange rate(figure 1.4 to figure 1.6).

中国银行 BANK OF CHINA

服务热线：95566　信用卡热线：40066 95566　请输入检索关键词

首页　公司金融　个人金融　银行卡　金融市场　电子银行　投资者关系　关于中行

首页 > 金融市场 > 外汇牌价

网银登录

中国银行外汇牌价

打印

起始时间：　结束时间：　牌价选择：选择货币

货币名称	现汇买入价	现钞买入价	现汇卖出价	现钞卖出价	中行折算价	发布日期	发布时间
阿联酋迪拉姆		182.37		195.59	189.25	2018-10-26	15:52:08
澳大利亚元	486.94	471.81	490.52	491.59	491.87	2018-10-26	15:52:08
巴西里亚尔		179.8		196.65	187.66	2018-10-26	15:52:08
加拿大元	526.7	510.07	530.58	531.74	531.76	2018-10-26	15:52:08
瑞士法郎	692.07	670.71	696.93	698.67	695.07	2018-10-26	15:52:08
丹麦克朗	105.43	102.17	106.27	106.49	105.93	2018-10-26	15:52:08
欧元	787.14	762.68	792.94	794.52	790.36	2018-10-26	15:52:08
英镑	886.42	858.88	892.95	894.91	891.26	2018-10-26	15:52:08
港币	88.35	87.65	88.71	88.71	88.66	2018-10-26	15:52:08
印尼卢比		0.044		0.0472	0.0457	2018-10-26	15:52:08
印度卢比		8.9015		10.0379	9.4975	2018-10-26	15:52:08
日元	6.173	5.9812	6.2184	6.2184	6.1853	2018-10-26	15:52:08
韩国元	0.606	0.5847	0.6108	0.633	0.6113	2018-10-26	15:52:08
澳门元	85.95	83.07	86.29	89.06	86.22	2018-10-26	15:52:08
林吉特	167.28		168.79		166.68	2018-10-26	15:52:08
挪威克朗	82.72	80.16	83.38	83.55	83.28	2018-10-26	15:52:08
新西兰元	447.75	433.93	450.89	456.42	453.51	2018-10-26	15:52:08
菲律宾比索	12.88	12.48	12.98	13.59	12.94	2018-10-26	15:52:08
卢布	10.54	9.89	10.62	11.02	10.6	2018-10-26	15:52:08
沙特里亚尔		179.91		189.27	185.3	2018-10-26	15:52:08
瑞典克朗	75.72	73.38	76.32	76.48	76.25	2018-10-26	15:52:08
新加坡元	500.16	484.73	503.68	504.93	503.23	2018-10-26	15:52:08
泰国铢	20.94	20.29	21.1	21.75	21.11	2018-10-26	15:52:08
土耳其里拉	122.44	116.44	123.42	139.26	123.34	2018-10-26	15:52:08

Figure 1.4　Bank of China exchange rate

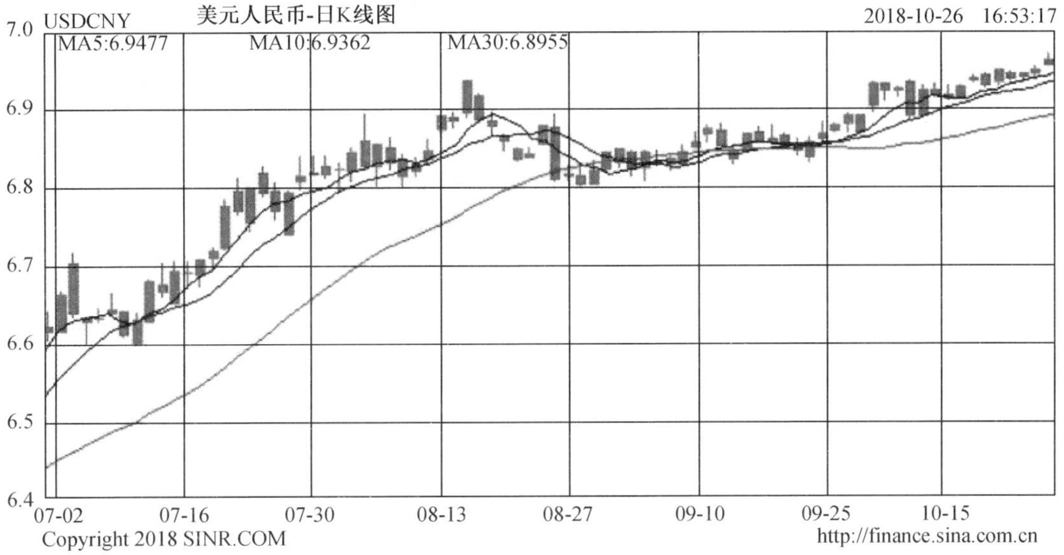

Figure 1.5 Chart of the exchange rate of United States dollar to RMB

中国工商银行人民币即期外汇牌价

按日期查询（****-**-**） 日期 [ ] 查询

按货币查询（日期范围为一个月） 货币名称 所有类别 起始日期 2011-05-10 截至日期 2011-06-09 查询

日期：2011年06月09日 星期四 单位：人民币/100外币

币种	汇买、汇卖中间价	现汇买入价	现钞买入价	卖出价	发布时间
美元(USD)	647.60	646.30	641.12	648.90	16:31:13
港币(HKD)	83.19	83.02	82.36	83.36	04:54:03
日元(JPY)	8.0597	8.0275	7.7696	8.0919	04:54:03
欧元(EUR)	939.73	935.97	905.90	943.49	04:54:03
英镑(GBP)	1059.93	1055.69	1021.77	1064.17	04:54:03
瑞士法郎(CHF)	769.49	766.41	741.79	772.57	04:54:03
加拿大元(CAD)	665.50	662.84	641.54	668.16	04:54:03
澳大利亚元(AUD)	687.75	685.00	662.99	690.50	04:54:03
新加坡元(SGD)	525.91	523.81	506.98	528.01	04:54:03
丹麦克朗(DKK)	126.00	125.50	121.46	126.50	04:54:03
挪威克朗(NOK)	119.45	118.97	115.15	119.93	04:54:03
瑞典克朗(SEK)	103.82	103.40	100.08	104.24	04:54:03
澳门元(MOP)	81.10	80.94	80.29	81.26	04:54:03
新西兰元(NZD)	534.01	531.87	514.79	536.15	04:54:03
韩元(KRW)	0.5980	--	0.5669	0.6291	20:33:40
卢布(RUB)	23.40	23.31	22.56	23.49	20:33:34
林吉特(MYR)	214.33	213.47	214.33	215.19	20:33:34

备注：此汇率为我行初始报价，成交价以各地分行实际交易汇率为准

Figure 1.6 Industrial and Commercial Bank of China exchange rate

【Questions】

(1) What is shown in figure 1.4, figure 1.5 and figure 1.6?

(2) Why are spot and cash not equivalent to each other in the above exchange rate tables?

(3) How will the exchange rate move in figure 1.5?

【Relevant knowledge】

(1) Definition of exchange rate

Foreign exchange rate, also known as exchange rate or foreign exchange price, refers to the ratio or price ratio of one country's currency converted into the currency of another country, that is, the price of the currency unit of one country expressed by the currency unit of another country.

In general, countries do not allow foreign currency to circulate in their own countries. Residents engaged in international trade and investment activities must convert their local currencies into foreign exchange at foreign exchange banks or designated non-bank financial institutions permitted by the government to handle foreign exchange. Export earnings remitted home and imported foreign investments shall also be converted into local currencies through designated foreign exchange banks and relevant institutions. Different from domestic finance, international finance, where different currencies are exchanged with each other and selling and purchasing, are accounted on a different basis, which is much more complicated technically.

Since currencies from different countries need to be exchanged among each other, here comes a question of quantity and price in currency exchange. In a complete market economy, the state does not limit the amount of foreign exchange. Therefore the exchange rate between currencies is determined by the market, nevertheless, in a planned economy, the state controls the amount of foreign exchange and sets exchange rate standards, and all are subject to the examination and approval of administrative departments. Thus, there are multiple foreign exchanges and exchange rate systems between the extremes of planning and marketing.

In international exchange, different currencies can indicate each other's prices. Foreign exchange features bi-directional indication, in terms that the price of a foreign currency can be indicated by the local currency and vice versa. Therefore, when indicating the exchange rate, we should first determine which country's currency is taken as the standard. Due to the difference in standards, the pricing method of exchange rate is also different. At present, the international exchange rate has three basic pricing methods, namely direct quotation, indirect quotation and US dollar quotation.

(2) Direct quotation

Direct quotation, also known as giving quotation, is a method taking a fixed amount of the foreign currency (1, 100, 1 000, 10 000) as the standard to calculate the amount of the domestic currency to be paid. Namely, the calculation on how many local currencies should be paid for buying a certain number of foreign currencies is based on foreign currencies. At present, except the United Kingdom, the United States, and the Euro zone countries, the vast majority of countries in the world have adopted direct quotation. For example, the exchange rate of Japanese yen to United States dollar is 89.74, meaning that one United States dollar is traded at 89.74 yen. The diagram of direct quation is shown in figure 1.7.

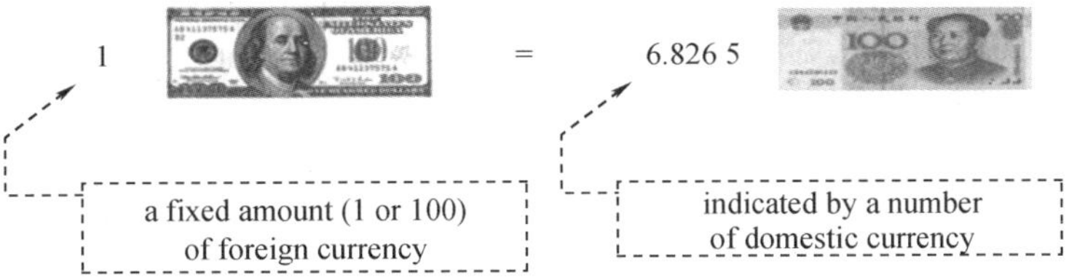

Figure 1.7 The diagram of direct quotation

Under the direct quotation, the amount of foreign currency is fixed, and the change of foreign exchange rate is presented by the changing amount of domestic currency. The fluctuation of foreign exchange rate and that of local currency prices move in the same direction. If the amount of domestic currency measured by a fixed amount of foreign currency increases compared to the previous period, it indicates that the foreign currency appreciates while the domestic currency depreciates, which is called the rise of foreign exchange rate. On the contrary, less local currency converted to the same amount of foreign currency indicates foreign currency devaluation and domestic currency appreciation, which is called the decline of foreign exchange rate. That is, the value of foreign currency is in direct proportion to the rise and fall of the exchange rate.

China's RMB also adopts the direct quotation method, announcing two kinds of quotations. The former is the price at which Bank of China purchases foreign currency, and the latter is the price at which Bank of China sells foreign currency. The difference is the bank's handling charge for foreign exchange. The average of the two is the median price, used to analyze the exchange rate level.

The quotation on the foreign exchange market is a bi-directional quotation. Bidders quote both their bid and offer prices. It is up to the customer to decide the direction of buying and selling. The smaller the spread between the bid price and the offer price, the lower the cost is for investors. The diagram of understand direct quotation is shown in figure 1.8.

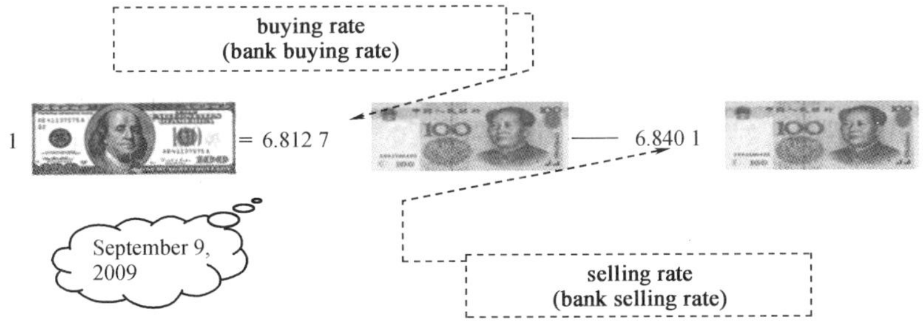

Figure 1.8 The diagram of understand direct quotation

The direct quotation method has the following characteristics:

①The base currency is a foreign currency, also known as the based currency, while the quote currency is the domestic currency, also known as the quoted currency.

②The change of foreign exchange rate (its rise and fall) is indicated by the increase and decrease of the local currency bidding price.

③In the bidding prices of the local currency, the former is the buying price and the latter is the selling price. The buying price refers to the price at which the bank buys foreign currency and the selling price refers to the price at which the bank sells foreign currency. The sum of the bid price and the offer price is divided by two, and the result is the middle price.

④With the direct quotation method, the fluctuation of foreign exchange rate and that of the local currency move in the same direction. Specifically speaking, when the price of the domestic currency increases, the foreign exchange rate rises (the exchange rate of the home currency declines), which indicates that the foreign currency appreciates and the domestic currency depreciates. When the price of the domestic currency decreases, the foreign exchange rate drops (or the exchange rate of domestic currency rises), which indicates that the foreign currency depreciates and the home currency appreciates.

(3) Indirect quotation

Indirect quotation, also known as the receivable quotation, is a calculation method in which the domestic currency of certain units (e. g., 1 or 100 units) is taken as the standard and converted into a number of foreign currencies. That is, the domestic currency is taken as the standard to calculate the receivable units of the foreign currency, thus called the receivable pricing method. The dollar is still directly priced against the pound. At present, indirect quotation is mainly used by the British pound, United States dollar, the Australian dollar and the Euro. For example, the exchange rate of Euro against US \$ is 1.501 0, that is to say one Euro is equal to \$1.501 0. The diagram of indirect qutation is shown in figure 1.9.

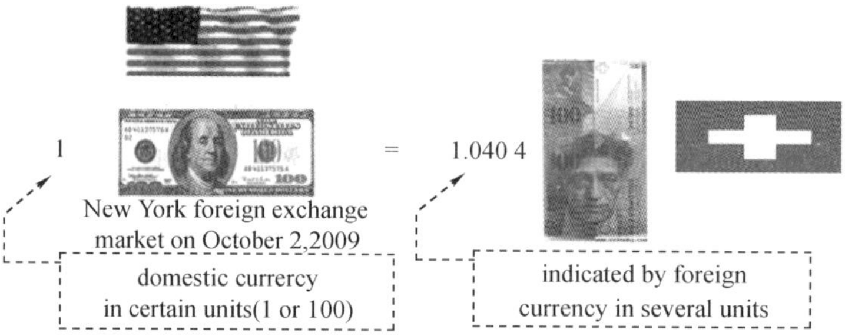

Figure 1.9 The diagram of indirect qutation

In indirect quotation, the amount of domestic currency is fixed, and the change of foreign exchange rate is expressed indirectly through the changing amount of foreign currency. The exchange rate moves in the opposite direction with the foreign currency. If the amount of foreign currency that can be exchanged based on a certain unit of domestic currency decreases than in the previous time, it indicates that the foreign currency appreciates while the domestic currency depreciates, namely, the foreign exchange rate rises. On the other hand, if the amount of foreign currency that can be exchanged for by a certain unit of domestic currency increases than the previous period, it indicates that the foreign currency depreciates while the domestic currency appreciates, namely, the foreign exchange rate declines. It can be seen that the rise and fall of the exchange rate are reflected "indirectly" through the rise and fall of the local currency exchange rate, so it is called the indirect quotation.

Between direct quotation and indirect quotation, a reciprocal relationship is exhibited in the foreign exchange rate. In indirect quotation, the former price is the price at which the bank sells foreign currency, and the latter price is the price at which the bank buys a foreign currency. For example, in London Foreign Exchange Market, 1 pound = 1.591 6 – 1.591 9 United States dollar. 1.591 6 United States dollar is the selling price, and 1.591 9 United States dollar is the buying price (see figure 1.10).

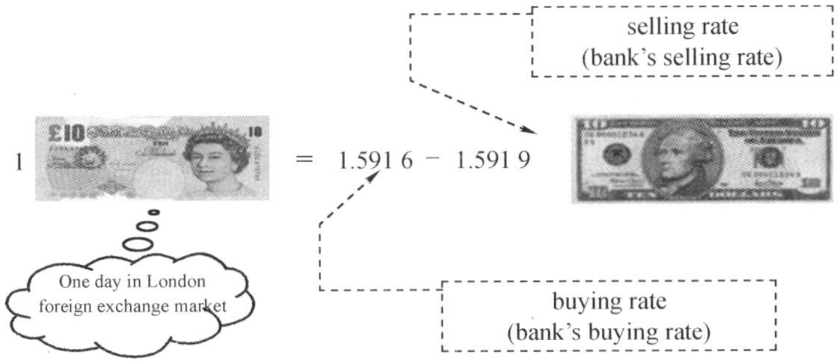

Figure 1.10 Understand indirect quotation

The indirect quotation has the following characteristics:

①Base currency is the domestic currency, also known as the benchmark currency. The counter currency is a foreign currency, also known as the quoted currency.

②The change of foreign exchange rate (rise and fall) is expressed by the change of the foreign currency quoted price.

③Among the foreign currency quoted prices, the former is the selling price, and the latter is the buying price.

④In indirect quotation, the foreign exchange rate goes in the opposite direction with the quoted price of foreign currency, and the value of the foreign exchange is inversely proportional to the rise and fall of the exchange rate. That is, when the quoted price of foreign currency increases, the foreign exchange rate drops (the exchange rate of the domestic currency rises), namely, the foreign currency depreciates and the domestic currency appreciates. When the quoted price of a foreign currency decreases, the foreign exchange rate rises (the domestic currency exchange rate falls), that means the foreign currency appreciates and the domestic currency depreciates.

Direct quotation and indirect quotation have no real differences between them, but are measured in different ways. However, generally speaking, the rise and fall of the exchange rate are consistent with the increase and decrease of the amount of the quote currency. In direct quotation, quote currency is domestic currency, while in indirect quotation, quote currency is foreign currency, therefore in these two quotations, the rise and fall of exchange rate have the opposite meanings, that is, rising (falling) exchange rate in direct quotation means the decline (rise) of the value of the domestic currency against foreign currency; while rising (falling) exchange rate rise in indirect quotation indicates an increase (decrease) of the value of the domestic currency against foreign currency. Therefore, when we quote a certain currency and explain the tendency of its exchange rate, we must make clear which foreign exchange market its exchange rate comes from, namely which quotation is adopted, so as to avoid confusion.

(4) United States dollar quotation

United States dollar quotation is a quotation in the foreign exchange market whereby the value of the American dollar is stated as a per-unit measure of foreign currency.

In foreign exchange transactions, for either party, both direct quotation and indirect quotation can only indicate the exchange rate between domestic currency and foreign currency. But sometimes it is possible that neither of the two currencies involved in a transaction is a domestic currency. For example, if Bank of China conducts a foreign exchange transaction with a bank in Japan, and the currencies bought and sold are United States dollars and euros respectively. Then it is difficult to make a comparison with either direct quotation or indirect quotation. After the World War Ⅱ, due to the prominent role taken by United States dollar in the international foreign exchange market, in order to facilitate foreign exchange transactions, the international foreign exchange market uses United States dollar as the benchmark currency to express the price of each country's currency, which has become a habit up to now, hence comes United States dollar quotation. The foreign exchange quotations published by the international banks in the world's financial centers are all based on the exchange rate between United States dollar and other major currencies. The exchange rate between non-United States dollars is calculated by the exchange rate between United States dollar and each other as the basis of quotation. As in the case of Bank of China and Bank of Japan, the deal between them has to be done with United States dollar quotation. United States dollar quotation is helpful to compare the exchange rate of different foreign exchange markets and facilitate the transaction.

According to market practice, the quoted price of a foreign exchange rate is usually composed of five significant digits. From right to left, the first digit is called "X point", which is the smallest unit of an exchange rate. And the second is called "X ten points", and so on.

For example, 1 euro = $1.501 0; 1 dollar = 89.74 yen.

Euro against United States dollar increasing from 1.501 0 to 1.501 5 is called Euro against United States dollar was up 5 points.

United States dollar against Japanese yen decreasing from 89.74 to 89.00 is called United States dollar against Japanese yen fell 74 points.

【Case for demonstration】

(1) Figure 1.4, figure 1.5 and figure 1.6 all indicate exchange rates. Figure 1.4 shows the RMB spot exchange rate quoted by Bank of China. Figure 1.5 is the exchange rate chart demonstrating the

trend of United States dollar against RMB from July 2, 2018 to October 26, 2018. Figure 1.6 shows the RMB spot foreign exchange quotation of Industrial and Commercial Bank of China.

(2) In the exchange rate table in figure 1.4 and figure 1.6, the selling price of spot exchange is the same as that of cash, while the buying price of cash is lower than that of spot exchange. Cash mainly refers to the convertible foreign currency brought in from abroad or held individually. In brief, it refers to the foreign banknotes held individually, such as dollar, yen, pound note, etc. Spot exchange refers to foreign currency bills and vouchers brought in and sent in from abroad. Those that we can frequently contact in our daily lives are overseas remittances and traveler's checks.

Because RMB is China's legal currency, foreign cash can't circulate in China but can only circulate outside China. Banks need to transport foreign cash to the issuing countries. Because the delivery of foreign currency cash costs a certain amount of money in transportation and insurance, the bank receives foreign currency cash with the exchange rate slightly lower than the foreign exchange buying rate. Because spot exchange is a foreign exchange on books, transferring it out of the country only needs to be done on the books. In the foreign exchange quotations announced by banks, cash and spot exchange are not equal, the buying rate for cash is lower than that for spot exchange.

(3) Figure 1.5 shows the trend of United States dollar/RMB from July 2, 2018 to October 26, 2018 released by China foreign exchange trading center, from which we can see that the RMB against United States dollar is in continuous decline. There are two reasons behind this phenomenon: on the one hand, United States dollar index is in a strong phase, which is especially supported by various strong economic datum in USA and the rhythm that the Federal Reserve System raises interest rate is relatively stable, which promotes United States dollar in a stronger cycle; on the other hand, big differences begin to appear between the monetary policies of China and that of the United States. The yield on 10-year Treasury Bonds between China and the US has narrowed to 0.4 percentage points, which is the fundamental domestic factor behind the recent continuous depreciation of the exchange rate of RMB.

Task 1.3 Extracurricular exercise

(1) Compare dynamic foreign exchange with static foreign exchange and analyze the differences between them.

(2) Please fill in the blanks (Table 1.3) with names of relevant countries and currencies corresponding to the currencies below.

Table 1.3 Practice

Name of country/region	Name of currency	Currency symbol	ISO standard money code
		RMB ¥	CNY
			EUR
		£	GBP
		SF	CHF
		SKR	SEK
		US $	USD
		CAN $	CAD
		J ¥	JPY
		S $	SGD
		HK $	HKD
		A $	AUD

(3) In March, an import and export company in our country signs and issues a draft to a foreign importer, demanding an unconditional and immediate 500 000 pound payment for the exported commodity.

Question: Does the draft in Great Britain Pound belong to the category of foreign exchange? Why or why not?

(4) Is pound a foreign exchange for Britain? Is Thai baht a foreign exchange for China? It has been argued that the possession of payment vouchers in Burmese dollars and dollar notes equals to the possession of foreign exchange. Do you think so? Why?

(5) It is known that the Canadian foreign exchange market adopts the direct quotation method. The exchange rate between United States dollar and Canadian dollar is: 1 United States dollar = 1.051 6 – 1.052 1 Canadian dollars, and the exchange rate of the next day is: 1 United States dollar = 1.052 6 – 1.053 0 Canadian dollars. Please explain the quoted prices of these two days.

(6) If the Canadian foreign exchange market with a direct quotation in question (5) is changed to the New York foreign exchange market with other conditions remain unchanged, please illustrate the above two quotes and explain why?

Task 2 Calculation and application of the exchange rate

【Objectives】

(1) Understand the concepts of buying rate and selling rate, and can use them properly;

(2) Understand the concepts of base rate and cross rate and calculate the cross rate correctly according to the base rate;

(3) Understand the relationship between spot rate and forward rate and can calculate the forward rate according to the spot rate.

【Tasks】

(1) Calculate the exchange rate;

(2) Classify exchange rates according to certain criteria;

(3) Use different exchange rates to solve real problems.

【Requirements】

(1) Master basic calculation methods concerning exchange rates;

(2) Inquire about exchange rates through different channels (methods of obtaining exchange rate information);

(3) Use different exchange rates to solve practical problems.

Task 2.1 Calculation and application of buying rate and selling rate

【Case for demonstration】

Case 2.1 On September 2, 2009, Jiangsu Guosheng Import and Export Trading Company, exported a shipment of stuffed bears and obtained foreign exchange income of United States dollar 44 278. Considering the financial crisis and the instability of United States dollar, the company decided to sell the foreign exchange to the bank. The exchange rate on that day was one United States dollar was bought at 6.817 1 yuan and sold at 6.844 5 yuan. Li Lin, the company's new salesman, calculated the transaction as revenue of 303 000 yuan and recorded it in the business log.

【Questions】

Is Li Lin correct? Why? How will you calculate it?

【Relevant knowledge】

(1) Buying rate

In real foreign exchange trading business, the exchange rate marked by the bank dealing with foreign exchange business has two parallel figures. One shows the buying rate, the other indicates the selling rate.

The buying rate, also known as bid price, is the price at which foreign exchange banks buy foreign exchanges from customers. Generally, the exchange rate at which foreign currency is converted into a smaller amount of local currency is the buying rate, which indicates how much it costs to buy a certain amount of foreign currency. Because the clients are mainly exporters, the bid price is often called the "export rate".

In direct quotation, the rate at which a given amount of foreign currency is converted into a smaller amount of local currency is the buying price, which precedes the selling price, while in the indirect quotation, the case is the opposite. The rate at which a given amount of local currency is converted into a larger amount of foreign currency is the buying price, which comes after the selling price.

(2) Selling rate

The selling rate, also called offer price, is the rate at which a bank sells foreign exchange to its customers. Generally, the rate at which foreign currency is converted into a larger amount of local currency is the selling rate, which indicates how much domestic currency the bank needs to take back after selling a certain amount of foreign currency. Because the clients are mainly importers, the selling rate is often referred to as the "import rate".

Whether the price is bid price or offer price is determined by whether the client is a buyer or seller in the foreign exchange transaction. Companies, enterprises, and other clients shall use selling rate when buying foreign exchange from the bank and use buying rate when selling foreign exchange to the bank. In the process of foreign exchange trading, banks, as a service institution, mainly make profits by buying at a low price and selling at a high price. Therefore, the criteria for using buying rate or selling rate are: first, from the bank's perspective; second, for foreign exchange; third, buy low and sell high. Therefore, the exchange rate at which foreign currency is converted into a smaller amount of domestic currency is the buying rate, while the exchange rate at which foreign currency is converted into a larger amount of domestic currency is the selling rate.

With direct quotation method, the exchange rate at which a certain amount of foreign currency is converted into more local currency is the selling rate, which means the amount of local currency that the bank should charge the counterparty when selling foreign currency and comes after the buying price. With the indirect quotation method, a certain amount of local currency is converted into foreign currency, and the smaller amount is the selling rate, indicating the amount of foreign currency payable to the counterparty when the bank sells foreign currency and coming before the buying price.

The difference between the buying price and the selling price of foreign exchange is the income earned by the bank from buying and selling foreign exchanges, called exchange earning, which varies with the bank's trading strategy, the types of foreign currencies bought and sold, the volume of transactions, the changes in the foreign exchange market and the objects of sale, generally ranging from 1‰ to 5‰.

(3) Middle rate

Middle rate is the average of the bid price and the offer price. Newspapers often use middle rate for currency news.

The middle rate is generally suitable for foreign exchange transactions between banks but not for general customers. The purpose of calculating the middle rate is firstly to facilitate the analysis of the exchange rates in the foreign exchange market, secondly to facilitate news reports from the press and the radios, and thirdly to serve as the basis for the calculation of the cross rate.

【Case for analysis】

In case 2.1, the buying price is the buying rate, which refers to the price at which the foreign exchange bank buys foreign currency, and the selling price is the price at which the foreign exchange bank sells foreign currency. Before calculating, it should be clear which exchange rate should be used, 6.817 1 yuan or 6.844 5 yuan. The bank's client (Jiangsu Guosheng Import and Export Trading Company) sells its earned dollars to the bank. It seems that using selling price is appropriate, but from the perspective of the bank, it is the bank that buys the foreign currency (United States dollars). Therefore, using buying rate is reasonable. As a result, the company should receive 301 800 yuan of foreign exchange instead of 303 000 yuan for the income of 44 278 United States dollar. Li Lin calculated wrong and got the wrong result.

Task 2.2 Calculation and application of basic rate and cross rate

【Case for demonstration】

Case 2.2 Jiangsu Guosheng Import and Export Trading Company, imported a shipment of watches from Switzerland in March 2009. The company planned to pay the exporter 1 million Swiss francs by the contract.

Its salesman Li Lin found out that at that time, the exchange rates of United States dollar to Swiss franc and United States dollar to RMB are listed bellow: 1.00 USD = 1.142 6 CHF, 1.00 USD = 6.836 0 CNY. At that exchange rate, Li paid out 5 982 800 yuan in exchange costs and made the payment.

【Question】

How did Li Lin of Guosheng Company determine the cost of foreign exchange?

【Relevant knowledge】

There are many kinds of foreign currencies. When a country sets its exchange rate, it does not independently set the exchange rate between its own currency and other foreign currencies, because this is bound to cause great differences between the exchange rate set by the country and the exchange rate of various currencies in the international foreign exchange market, and aggravate international arbitrage activities. Therefore, when a country sets the exchange rate, it should first select a country's currency (key currency) as the main object. A key currency is a currency that is the most commonly used in a country's balance of payments, occupies the largest proportion of its foreign exchange reserves, can be freely convertible, and is internationally accepted.

(1) Basic rate

The basic rate, also known as the Basic Rate of Exchange, is the exchange rate set by a country between its domestic currency and its base currency (often the key currency). At present, many countries usually take United States dollar as the key currency and take the exchange rate of their currencies against United States dollar as the basic rate.

The basic rate of RMB is published by the People's Bank of China on the basis of the weighted average price of United States dollar against RMB formed in the inter-bank foreign exchange market of the previous day. The basic rate of major trading currencies (United States dollar, Japanese yen and Hong Kong dollar) against RMB on the day are published, namely the market price midpoint.

(2) Cross rate

Cross rate, also known as the Cross Rate of Exchange. It is the ratio between the domestic currency and non-key currencies calculated on the basis of the basic rate. After the establishment of the base rate, the exchange rate of each country's currency against currencies from other countries needs to be calculated through the base rate, referring to the exchange rate of key currencies against the domestic currency of that country in the international foreign exchange market.

The RMB exchange rate is set first by determining the basic rate of RMB against United States dollar, and then by calculating the exchange rate of it against other currencies.

(3) The calculation of cross rate

According to the position of the intermediate money in the exchange rate of the two currencies, the calculation of the cross rate is divided into three types.

Suppose United States dollar is the intermediate currency. There are three positions it possibly takes in the exchange rate of two currencies: first, United States dollar acts as the base currency in the exchange rates of both currencies; second, it acts as the quoted currency in the exchange rates of both currencies; third, it acts as the base currency in the exchange rate of one currency and the quoted currency in the exchange rate of another currency. The calculation of cross rate in the above three cases is as follows.

①When United States dollar acts as the base currency, the method of cross division is advisable.

Given: USD/SFR = 1.624 0 – 1.624 8, USD/EUR = 0.811 0 – 0.811 8.

Calculate the exchange rate of EUR/SFR.

To do cross division, two problems need to be solved: one is the confirmation of the numerator and denominator, the other is to determine whether it's in the numerator or the denominator. When United States dollar is the base currency, the previously given exchange rate containing the base currency and at the position of the base currency is the denominator in the cross rate. The previously given rate of exchange with the quoted currency is the numerator. The denominator crosses.

In the above example, it is required to calculate the EUR/SER exchange rate. USD/EUR = 0.811 0 – 0.811 8 should be taken as the denominator, and should be crossed. While USD/SFR = 1.624 0 – 1.624 8 should be taken as the numerator. The buying rate of EUR/SFR is 1.624 0/0.811 8 = 2.000 5, and the selling rate is 1.624 8/0.811 0 = 2.003 5. The cross rate is EUR/

SFR = 2.000 5 - 2.003 5.

The above mentioned cross calculation can be analyzed from the customer's point of view. In the given conditions, United States dollar is the base currency. In the cross rate EUR/SFR, EUR is the base currency, SFR is the quoted currency. When a customer sells euros and buys dollars, the bank buys euros and sells dollars at the selling rate of USD/EUR, or 0.811 8. This means that the bank sells 1 United States dollar and receives 0.811 8 euros from the customer. So the customer sells 1 euro and gets 1/0.881 8 United States dollar, and then the customer sells the dollar to the bank and gets the Swiss franc, so the bank buys the dollar and sells the Swiss franc. For clients, a dollar sold would yield 1.624 0 Swiss francs ,and 1/0.811 8 dollar sold would yield 2.003 5[= 1.624 8 × (1/0.811 0)].

②When United States dollar is the quoted currency in the exchange rate of the two currencies, the cross rate is still calculated through cross division.

Given: CAN/USD = 0.895 0 - 0.895 3, GBP/USD = 1.58 7 - 1.588 0.

Calculate the exchange rate of GBP/CAN.

In this case, at the position of the base currency, the exchange rate for this given base currency in the cross calculation is still the denominator.

In this example, the intermediate currency United States dollar is the quoted currency at the given two exchange rates. In the calculation of cross rate GBP/CAN, GBP is the base currency, and CAN is the quoted currency. It can still be analyzed from the customer's perspective. The buying rate of GBP/CAN, from the perspective of the customer, is obtained from following steps: firstly one British pound is sold for buying United States dollars and then at the buying rates of GBP/USD 1.587 0, 1.772 6[= 1.587 0 × (1/0.895 3)] Canadian dollars are exchanged, which is the buying rate of GBP/CAN.

With the same way of calculation, the selling rate of GBP/CAN is 1.774 3[= 1.588 0 × (1/0.895 0)].

That is, the buying price of GBP/CAN is 1.587 0/0.895 3 = 1.722 6, and its selling price is 1.588 0/0.895 0 = 1.774 3.

Therefore, the exchange rate of GBP/CAN is 1.772 6 - 1.774 3.

③United States dollar is the base currency in the exchange rate of one currency and the quoted currency in another. The cross rate is calculated by vertical multiplication (same side multiplication), that is, the bid price and the asking price of two exchange rates are respectively multiplied.

For example: known GBP/USD = 1.587 0 - 1.588 0 ,USD/EUR = 0.811 0 - 0.812 0.

Calculate the cross rate of GBP/EUR.

Train of thought: The bank quotes a bid price of GBP/EUR, meaning the bank's client sells 1 pound and buys a number of euros. Therefore, the customer must first sell 1 pound to the bank for US $1.587 0 (at the bank's GBP/USD bid price); then sells the US $1.587 0 (at the bank's bid price of USD/EUR) for 1.587 0 × 0.811 0 euros, which is the bid price of GBP/EUR quoted by the bank. When banks offer GBP/EUR for sale, a similar line of thinking can be considered.

In conclusion: The bid price of GBP/EUR is 1.587 0 ×0.811 0 = 1.287 1 and the asking price is 1.588 0 ×0.812 0 = 1.289 5, so the exchange rate of GBP/EUR is 1.287 1 – 1.289 5.

Obviously, the calculation of the cross rate involves the costs of two transactions. Whether by multiplication or division, each time the intermediary currency is offset, the transaction cost will be added again, and the price difference between the bid price and the asking price will increase again. This method can also be used to check the results.

Banks do not indicate which is the base rate and which is the cross rate when they announce their exchange rates with other currencies. If a customer asks the bank for the rate of exchange between non-dollar currencies, the bank will usually quote the cross rate directly. Although cross rates are becoming more and more common and accepted by professional traders, they are still not the main form of trading. For banks, cross rates are still taken as two trades against the dollar.

【Case for analysis】

In case 2.2, Li Lin's calculation result is correct. He achieved it based on two basic exchange rates, 1.00 USD = 1.142 6 CHF and 1.00 USD = 6.836 0 CNY. That is: cross rates of exchange is first obtained through 1.00 CHF = (6.836 0/1.142 6) CNY, and then the cost of foreign exchange is calculated in (6.836 0/1.142 6) ×100 = 5.982 8 million RMB.

Task 2.3 Calculation and application of spot rate and forward rate

【Case for demonstration】

Case 2.3 On October 15, 2009, Li Lin found that the exchange rate of United States dollar to Swiss franc in the New York foreign exchange market was 1 United States dollar = 1.014 1 – 1.015 9 Swiss franc, and the three-month forward rate rose 0.003 5 – 0.003 0.

【Question】

How can Li Lin determine the three-month forward rate?

【Relevant knowledge】

(1) Spot rate

Spot rate refers to the rate of spot foreign exchange transactions, namely, the exchange rate used by both parties for delivery on the spot date, which is normally one or two business days after the trade date. Here, delivery refers to the giving and receiving behavior of the seller and the buyer performing the transaction contract and clearing money and goods. Spot rate is spot exchange rate, which is the basis of making forward exchange rate. Spot rates are determined by the supply and demand of currency at the time of spot delivery. Generally speaking, the exchange rate quoted on the foreign exchange market refers to the spot rate except that the forward rate is specifically indicated.

(2) Forward rate

Forward rate refers to the exchange rate at which foreign exchange buyers and sellers sign a foreign exchange trading contract in advance and go through delivery formalities at the agreed time. Forward foreign exchange business refers to the business of buying or selling foreign exchange by appointment. Usually, the buyer and the seller need to sign a contract specifying the currency, quantity, exchange rate, and delivery date of the transaction.

Forward foreign exchange trading is a kind of pre-arranged transaction, which is introduced to avoid foreign exchange risks because foreign exchange buyers have different time for requiring foreign exchange funds. Therefore, forward rate is a kind of open exchange rate. The time of open delivery generally lasts from 1 month to 1 year, and the most common deadlines are 1, 3 and 6 months. Different delivery date leads to different forward rate.

(3) The calculation of forward exchange rate

Forward rate is based on spot rate and represented by "premium", "discount" and "parity" of spot exchange rate. If the forward rate is higher than the spot rate, the price difference is called premium. If the forward rate is lower than the spot rate, the difference is called discount. If the forward rate is equal to the spot rate, we call it par.

In different pricing methods, the foreign exchange rate and the bid price move differently, so the forward rate is also calculated differently. In direct quotation, the fluctuation of foreign exchange rate is in the same direction as that of the bid price of local currency. The calculation formula of forward rate is as follows:

Forward rate = spot rate + premium (− discount)

In indirect quotation, the rise and fall of foreign exchange rate are in the opposite direction with the increase and decrease of the bid price of local currency, and the calculation formula of forward rate is as follows:

Forward rate = spot rate − premium (+ discount)

The rule for judging whether it is premium or discount is: in direct quotation, the front number is smaller (greater) than the rear number, which is called premium (discount); while in indirect quotation, the figure in front is greater (smaller) than and the figure behind, which is called premium (discount). Therefore, the calculation of forward rate can be further simplified as follows: given two figures of the forward rate, if the former is smaller than the latter, do addition, if the former is bigger than the latter, do subtraction.

Note: the forward rate is not the spot rate in the future. It may be higher, lower or equal to the future spot rate. In the real exchange rate, if the former figure is smaller than the latter, no matter which bidding method is adopted, that is, no matter which comes first, the bid price or the selling rate, in the final result, the forward rate always features small front figure and big rear figure.

(4) Classification of exchange rates

There are many ways to classify exchange rates. The exchange rates mentioned above are the exchange rates that we usually encounter. From the perspective of foreign exchange trading by banks, exchange rates can be divided into buying rate and selling rate. In terms of setting exchange rate, exchange rates can be divided into benchmark rate and cross rate. From the delivery term of foreign exchange transations, the exchange rates can be divided into spot rate and forward rate. In addition, there are some other types of exchange rates, which can be listed as below.

①In terms of exchange rate system, exchange rates can be divided into fixed rate and floating rate.

Fixed rate refers to the exchange rate, which is basically fixed and fluctuates little between one currency and another. In gold standard system, the fixed rate was determined by the amount of gold in two countries' coins. Its fluctuation is limited by the level of the exchange rate that caused gold to be imported and exported, and the range of fluctuation indicated the cost of transporting gold between two countries. Under the Bretton woods monetary system from the World War Ⅱ to the early 1970s, the international monetary fund (IMF) member countries set the gold content and exchange rate against United States dollar. Fluctuations in the exchange rate were strictly limited within one percent above or below the official rate. Due to its small range of fluctuation, this exchange rate is also called the fixed rate.

Floating rate comes from the situation where the monetary authorities of a country do not stipulate the official exchange rate of its currency against other currencies, nor do they have any upper or lower limits of exchange rate fluctuations. With the floating rate, the domestic currency is subject to the supply and demand of the foreign exchange market and fluctuates freely. When the supply of foreign currency exceeds the demand, the foreign currency depreciates, the domestic currency appreciates, and the foreign exchange rate falls. On the contrary, the foreign exchange rate rises. Local monetary authorities should intervene appropriately in the foreign exchange market to prevent the exchange rate from fluctuating too much, so as to maintain the stability and development of their domestic economies.

②In terms of payment advice in foreign exchange transactions, exchange rates can be divided into telegraphic transfer rate, mail transfer rate and bill exchange rate.

T/T Rate is the rate at which a bank notifies its foreign branches or correspondent banks to pay the drawee after it has sold foreign exchanges by using the telegraph as the means of transmission. Telegraphic transfer is one of the most rapid means of international money transfer. Banks cannot use customer funds, so the telegraphic transfer rate is the highest. It is the benchmark exchange rate in the foreign exchange market. Generally speaking, exchange rates published by foreign exchange market are telegraphic transfer rates.

M/T Rate is a method of remittance by which the bank notifies the bank at the place of payment to transfer the funds to the payee after the bank sells the foreign exchange. The M/T rate is lower than the T/T rate because of the longer time required for a postal transaction and the availability of customer funds during the postal transaction period.

D/D Rate means that when a bank sells foreign exchange, it issues a draft payable by its foreign branch or correspondent bank to the remitter, who brings it with him or sends it abroad for withdrawal. D/D rates are generally lower than T/T rates because there is an interval between the selling of foreign exchange and the payment of foreign exchange, during which the bank can take up the customer's funds.

③In terms of the business hours of foreign exchange banks, exchange rates can be divided into opening rate and closing rate.

Opening rate is the exchange rate used by foreign exchange banks when they just start a business, conduct foreign exchange trading on a business day.

Closing rate is the rate at which a foreign exchange bank trades at the end of its foreign exchange transactions on a business day.

With the development of modern science and technology and the modernization of foreign exchange trading equipment, foreign exchange markets around the world have become integrated. The opening exchange rate of a foreign exchange market is often affected by the closing exchange rate of the foreign exchange market in the previous time zone due to the time difference among major cities and the mutual influence of the exchange rates of major foreign exchange markets. The opening and closing rates are only a few hours apart, but in present days featuring volatile exchange rates, there often exist large discrepancies.

④In addition, people often talk about other exchange rates listed as following.

Bank Notes Rate is also known as the buying and selling price of banknotes, referring to the exchange rate used by a bank to buy or sell foreign currency notes. Theoretically speaking, the buying and selling price of cash should be the same as the buying and selling price of foreign exchange forms such as foreign currency payment vouchers and foreign currency credit vouchers. But in reality, because almost all countries prohibited free circulation of foreign currencies at home, transporting purchased foreign currencies to issuing countries or the regions permitting free circulation needs a certain amount of freight and insurance, which need to be borne by customers. Therefore, the exchange rate at which banks receive foreign currency notes is slightly lower than the buying rate in other forms of foreign exchange; however the exchange rate at which banks sell foreign currency notes is the same as the foreign exchange selling rate.

The Official Rate is the exchange rate set and announced by a country's foreign exchange management agency. In countries with strict foreign exchange control, all foreign exchange transactions are under the unified management of the exchange management agencies. Foreign exchange cannot be bought and sold freely. Foreign exchange market rate does not exist, and all transactions must be conducted at the official rate.

The Black Market Rate is the rate at which foreign exchange is bought and sold in the black market for foreign exchange. In countries under strict foreign exchange control, all foreign exchange transactions are conducted at the official exchange rate. Some holders of foreign currency sell their foreign exchange at a higher rate than the official exchange rate on the black market, which allows them to exchange more domestic currencies and thus become foreign exchange suppliers to the black market. While those who cannot obtain or obtain insufficient foreign exchanges at the official exchange rate buy foreign exchanges from the black market at a price higher than the official exchange rate, thus becoming the demanders of foreign exchange in the black market.

Nominal Rate, also known as the market exchange rate, is in contrast with the real exchange rate and refers to the amount of one currency that can be exchanged for another. Nominal exchange rates are usually set against a specific currency, such as United States dollar or Special Drawing Rights, which are taken as the standards. Exchange rates are usually subject to the changing values of United States dollars and Special Drawing Rights. But nominal rate cannot reflect the actual value of two currencies. It indicates the foreign exchange transaction price that changes with the supply and demand of foreign exchange in the foreign exchange market.

Real Exchange Rate is the legal exchange rate, which is set according to the parity of coins or the parity of gold. In gold standard system, countries set the amount of gold of each coin unit. The comparison of the gold content of two currencies is called mint par. This is the exchange rate of the real value of two currencies in the gold standard system, the real exchange rate with the gold standard. In the circulation system of paper currency, paper currency is the value symbol of gold. In the beginning, the gold content of paper currency was stipulated. The comparison of the gold content of such paper currency is called gold parity, which serves as the foundation for determining the exchange rate. Later, because legally prescribed gold content of the paper currency and the actual amount of gold represented in the note became separated from each other, thus the exchange rate of paper currency is determined by the comparison of its real value. In short, the basis for determining the exchange rate in both the gold standard system and the paper currency circulation system is the comparison of the real value of the currency. The real exchange rate does not fluctuate according to the supply and demand of the foreign exchange market. It is not the exchange rate of actual foreign exchange trading in the market, but the basis of foreign exchange trading. In the foreign exchange market, the actual exchange rate for buying and selling foreign exchange is always deviates from the real exchange rate.

(5) RMB exchange rate system

RMB is China's standard currency and its only legal currency in circulation. The current RMB exchange rate is characterized as follows.

①The RMB exchange rate system is a single managed floating exchange rate system. Following the exchange rate requirements by the International Monetary Fund and the World Trade Organization for member countries. China adopts a single exchange rate system. Published by the People's Bank of China daily, the RMB market exchange rate is applicable to all transactions between foreign currencies and RMB and includes both foreign exchange receipts and payments between Chinese-funded enterprises and foreign-funded enterprises, as well as capital flows between residents and non-residents. The RMB market exchange rate published by the People's Bank of China on a daily basis is floating. In addition, the foreign exchange rates listed for trading by designated foreign exchange banks may freely float within the 2.5% range specified by the People's Bank of China.

Therefore, RMB exchange rate is a floating exchange rate. At the same time, it is also a managed floating exchange rate, which is mainly reflected in: when the market exchange rate fluctuates greatly, the central bank can intervene in the foreign exchange market through foreign exchange trading to keep it stable.

②The RMB exchange rate is based on market supply and demand. The benchmark exchange rate published by the People's Bank of China on a daily basis is the weighted average price of United States dollar, Japanese yen, euro and Hong Kong dollar generated by the transactions in the inter-bank foreign exchange market in the previous trading day. The benchmark exchange rate is determined by the market and based on market supply and demand, which is an important part of China's exchange rate system reform since 1994.

③RMB exchange rate adopts direct quotation method, while foreign exchange trading adopts a double quotation method. The direct quotation is expressed in RMB converted into the corresponding amount in the foreign currency with 1 unit or 100 units as the standard. The quoted prices published by foreign exchange banks are divided into buying rate of exchanges, selling rate of exchange and purchasing price for cash. The price of selling foreign cash is consistent with the price of selling spot exchange.

【Case for analysis】

In case 2. 3, because United States dollar-Swiss franc quotation in New York foreign exchange market is an indirect quotation. When the forward rate is a premium, the list price should change in the opposite direction. That is forward rate = spot rate-premium. So, the three-month forward rate is calculated as follows:

$$\begin{array}{rr} & 1.014\,1\text{–}1.015\,9 \\ - & 0.003\,5\text{–}0.003\,0 \\ \hline & 1.010\,6\text{–}1.012\,9 \end{array}$$

The three-month forward rate is: 1United States dollar = 1.010 6 – 1.012 9 Swiss franc.

Task 3 Analyze the factors influencing exchange rate fluctuations

【Objects】

(1) Master various factors affecting exchange rate fluctuations;

(2) Learn to analyze the impact of exchange rate fluctuations on the economy;

(3) Through this task, students are inspired to not only look at the present but also consider the future when doing international trade business, and both be able to conduct micro-operation and observe and analyze the problems with a broader view.

【Tasks】

(1) Expand, analyze and summarize the factors affecting exchange rate changes through major international political and economic events;

(2) Summarize the impact of exchange rate fluctuations on the economy through case study.

【Requirements】

(1) Correctly analyze various factors affecting exchange rate changes;

(2) Can preliminary analyze the extent to which an industry or a product is affected and propose countermeasures to it according to the changing exchange rate.

【Case for demonstration】

(1) Case 3.1 Miss Wang is a sales manager of a foreign company. In the past two years, the RMB exchange rate has been hitting new highs, and the exchange rate of RMB against United States dollar is getting higher and higher. For Miss Wang, who likes traveling abroad, the benefits are growing. The appreciation of RMB means that RMB becomes more valuable in foreign countries, which directly reduces the cost of overseas travel and makes Miss Wang's outbound travel plan more affordable and feasible.

"Miss Wang told the reporter that RMB accelerated its appreciation last year, therefore she chose several places where the currency was settled in US dollar as her tourist destinations, in which way the same kind of goods in yuan cost much less than it used to be." In addition, because Hong Kong dollar is currently pegged to United States dollar, RMB is increasing "more expensive" than Hong Kong dollar as a result of the continuous high exchange rate of RMB against United States dollar. Therefore Hong Kong also becomes one of Miss Wang's major travel destinations.

Miss Wang said she was keen on shopping in Hong Kong, and the appreciation of RMB was a good piece of news for people like her and had attracted many mainland tourists to the city. "I went to Hong Kong mainly to buy cosmetics, perfume, etc. After the appreciation of RMB, the money saved can be seen immediately after comparison. For example, for the same goods worth HK $ 1 000, it used to cost 1 040 yuan to buy, but now it only costs 833 yuan, which is equivalent to making 167 yuan for yourself. One trip to Hong Kong, and you can save approximately a thousand yuan on shopping. It is a real bargain to buy things in Hong Kong, and I can buy more goods with low prices, which makes me very happy." In addition, as the yuan continues to appreciate, tickets to some local attractions are becoming cheaper. Take the tickets to Disneyland as an example, Miss Wang saw on a website that the booking price for a single ticket was listed at just over 290 yuan, lower than previous 310 yuan.

It is well-known that as an important duty-free zone in the world, Hong Kong has always been the first choice of consumption for mainland tourists due to its unique geographical location and cultural environment integrating China and the west. RMB is more expensive than Hong Kong dollar, which undoubtedly reduces the cost for mainland tourists to visit Hong Kong and enables them to enjoy cheaper Hong Kong tours, thus attracting more tourists to Hong Kong.

"When the yuan appreciates, we Chinese will buy foreign goods at lower prices. In my opinion, the exchange rate represents the external value of a country's currency. The appreciation of RMB means that the same amount of RMB can be exchanged for more foreign currencies, consequently, we can buy more, which is a good news for me because I often go abroad and love buying foreign goods. Now when I travel abroad to buy things, I feel more confident than before."

(2) Case 3.2 In November 2010, Deng Hua'ning, the Newsweek reporter for *Outlook*, obtained a joint report on quantitative analysis of export enterprises from Jiangsu Academy of Social Sciences and the Department of Commerce. The report shows that against the backdrop of the rising real exchange rate of RMB and the ever increasing exchange rate of RMB against United States dollar, RMB appreciation has a large negative impact on electromechanical, textile and garment enterprises.

From July 2005 to November 2010, the real appreciation of RMB against United States dollar has reached 24.85%, which has had a superimposed effect on enterprises, and the capacity of export enterprises adapting themselves to the risks is gradually weakening.

Such is the fact. Since the exchange rate reform, the export growth of Jiangsu electromechanical industry, textile and garment industry has been decreasing year by year. Among them, the export growth rate of the electromechanical industry decreased from 43.1% in 2005 to 12.2% in the first half of 2008. In the same period, the export growth of textile and garment industry decreased from 24.8% to 11%. The survey from 100 textile, garment and electromechanical enterprises in Jiangsu province (50 textile and garment enterprises and 50 electromechanical enterprises) shows that the impact of RMB appreciation on these enterprises is obvious.

On the one hand, enterprises' ability to deal with exchange rate risks has been weakened with each passing year. From 2005 to 2008, the difference between the export cost per United States dollar of these 100 enterprises and the exchange rate of RMB against United States dollar in the same period of time dropped year by year, revealing the superposition effect with RMB appreciation. The ability of enterprises to deal with exchange rate risks was continuously weakened. The declining profit margin of export product sales from the textile clothing industries and the electromechanical industries reflected decreasing capability of enterprises to cope with the stronger RMB.

On the other hand, there exists a long-term stable relationship between RMB real exchange rate and the export of electromechanical, textile, and garment products. Statistics show that for every 1 percentage point appreciation of the real exchange rate, mechanical and electrical exports in Jiangsu will decrease by about 0.63 percentage points, and textile and garment exports will decrease by about 1.47 percentage points. For every 1 percentage point increase in the real exchange rate volatility of RMB, mechanical and electrical exports in Jiangsu will decline by 0.02 percentage points, and textile and garment exports will decline by 0.04 percentage points.

Generally speaking, if the nominal exchange rate of United States dollar against RMB stays at 1: 6.5 for a long time, textile and garment export enterprises in Jiangsu will be greatly impacted. Firstly, the growth rate of Jiangsu textile and garment export may drop to zero. Secondly, the profit of textile and garment export enterprises will drop sharply, and many enterprises will go bankrupt, which will further affect the employment and social stability. Therefore, without relevant supporting policies, the excessively rapid appreciation of RMB in the future will bring greater downside risks to the export of the textile and garment industry.

【Questions】

What impact will the appreciation of RMB have on China's economy?

【Relevant knowledge】

(1) Main factors affecting exchange rate movements

All foreign exchange transactions involve the exchange of one currency for another. At any given time, the real exchange rate will be determined largely by the supply and demand of the corresponding currency. Demand for one currency means the supply of another. Similarly, supply of one currency also means demand for another. The following factors affect the supply and demand of currency and thus the exchange rate (figure 1.11).

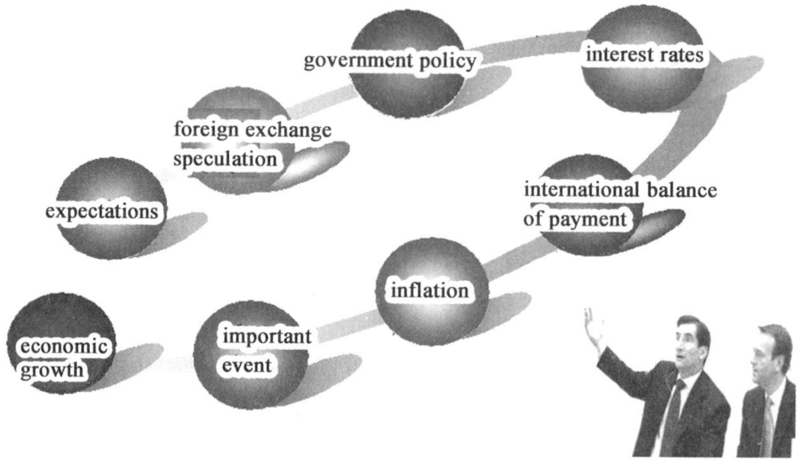

Figure 1.11 Main factors influencing exchange rate fluctuations

①International payments

The balance of payments position of a country will lead to the fluctuation of its currency exchange rate. The balance of payments is the sum of all the external economic and financial relations of a country's residents. A country's balance of payments reflects its economic status in the world and also affects the operation of its macro and micro economy. The impact of balance of payments is ultimately the impact of supply and demand for foreign exchange on exchange rates.

Income from foreign exchange is generated by an economic transaction (such as exports) or a capital transaction (such as foreign investment in the domestic country). Unless foreign currency is converted into the domestic currency, foreign exchange usually cannot be freely traded in the domestic market. Therefore the supply of foreign exchange in the foreign exchange market develops. Foreign exchange expenditures are incurred as a result of an economic transaction (such as imports) or a capital transaction (investing abroad). The need for foreign exchange arises in the foreign exchange market because it is necessary to convert domestic currency into foreign currency to meet the economic needs of each country.

These transactions, combined together and recorded in the balance of payments statistics, constitute a country's foreign exchange balance of payments. If foreign exchange income exceeds expenditure, the supply of foreign exchange will increase; while if foreign exchange expenditure is greater than income, the demand for foreign exchange will increase. When the supply of foreign exchange increases, if the demand remains the same, the price of foreign exchange will decrease, and the value of local currency will rise accordingly. When the demand for foreign exchange increases, if the supply remains the same, the price of foreign exchange will rise directly and the value of local currency will fall correspondingly.

②Economic growth rate

The economic growth of a country is the fundamental factor that determines its exchange rate. When a country's economic development speeds up, its production and operation status and fiscal revenue will be improved. Consequently, the employment rate will increase, and the price enjoys its stability. The value represented by the currency of the country will be high, and the currency of the country will appreciate. Otherwise, the currency of that country will depreciate. However, after the economic growth rate increases, the national income will also rise, which may boost the demand for imported goods and services. As a result, the demand for foreign exchange will get expanded and the exchange rate of the domestic currency will fall. Further analysis is needed as to whether increased demand for imported goods and services will lead to a decline in the exchange rate of the domestic currency:

Firstly, for export-oriented countries, economic growth is driven by the increase of export trade, which means that the increase of export trade outweighs that of import trade, making the exchange rate rise instead of causing it to fall.

Secondly, if both domestic and foreign investors are optimistic about the country's economic growth, they are likely to increase their investments in the country. Consequently, the deficit of the current account is offset with a surplus in the capital account. At this point, the exchange rate may not fall but rise.

③Changing interest rates

When one country's main interest rate rises or falls relative to another's, low-interest currencies are to be sold and high-interest currencies are to be bought in pursuit of higher returns. As demand for currencies with relatively high interest rates increases, the currency will appreciate against other currencies.

Let's say there are two countries, A and B, neither of which has exchange controls, and money can flow freely between them. Interest rates were raised by 1% as part of the country's monetary policy. At the same time, the interest rate in country B stays the same. There is a huge amount of short-term hot money in the market, which moves from country to country in search of the best interest rates. When country A's dominant interest rate rises, other things being equal, huge amounts of short-term hot money will flow into country A in pursuit of higher interest rates. When hot money leaves country B, huge amounts of currency of country B will be sold for country A's currency. So the demand for country A's currency goes up, and the result is that A currency strengthens against B currency. This is the case between the two countries. In fact, it is also applicable to the global market today. Over the years, the free flow of capital and the elimination of foreign exchange controls have been the general trend. This trend has facilitated the free flow of short-term international hot money, sometimes called "hot money". It should be noted that investors will only move money to regions or countries with high interest rates if they believe that exchange rate movements will not offset the returns from high interest rates.

④Differences in the rate of inflation

Inflation means a weaker currency, higher prices and lower purchasing power. On the contrary, deflation indicates rising purchasing power. Therefore, domestic and foreign inflation rates are the main factors affecting the trend of exchange rate fluctuations.

First of all, the inflation rate of a country can affect its import and export, thus affecting the current account of the external balance of the country or region.

For example, if a country has inflation and the domestic cost of its export commodities and services increases. It will inevitably raise the international price of its commodities and services, thus weakening the international competitiveness of its commodities and services and affecting export trade and foreign exchange income. At the same time, the relatively cheap prices of imported goods stimulate the increase of the quantity of imported goods and the demand for foreign exchange, which is not conducive to the current account situation of the country.

For example, before inflation, suppose an import and export company of our country buys color TV sets in China at the price of 800 yuan per set and exports them to an overseas country at the price of 100 dollars (suppose the current excharge rate between USD and CNY is 100:827). After the transaction, the company will make a profit of 27 yuan (excluding other costs) on sales of $100 per unit, which is equivalent to 827 yuan. If inflation occurs, the price of color TV set purchased in China rises from 800 yuan/each to 900 yuan/each, but the export price is still 100 dollars for each set. Consequently, the enterprise will lose 73 yuan. To keep the profit of RMB 27 in each set, the company has to increase the export price above $100, which will affect the product competitiveness in the international market.

Secondly, inflation occurs in a country, the country's real interest rate (nominal interest rate minus inflation rate) is bound to drop. If the inflation rate of a country is higher than that of other countries for a long time, it will cause capital outflow, which will affect the capital account of its external balance.

⑤Major international economic, political and military events

Major international political, economic and military contingencies can also have an impact on exchange rates. If global tension rises, it will lead to instability in the foreign exchange market, which will lead to abnormal inflows and outflows of some currencies, and the final possible result will be large fluctuations in exchange rates. The stability of political situation is related to the stability of currency. Generally speaking, the more stable a country's political situation is, the more stable its currency is.

⑥Government intervention

The direct form of government intervention in the exchange rate is to change the supply and demand relationship of foreign exchange by buying and selling foreign exchange through the central bank in the foreign exchange market, thus affecting the foreign exchange rate or local exchange rate. Generally speaking, the purpose of the government to adopt the exchange rate policy is to stabilize the exchange rate, avoid the exchange rate fluctuation which will increase the risk in international trade and financial activities and curb foreign exchange speculation. It could also aim to make the exchange rate conducive to the country's economic development or to help achieve a strategic goal of the government. In addition, governments can influence the trend of foreign exchange rate in the foreign exchange market by adjusting domestic monetary and fiscal policies, influence the psychology of foreign exchange market traders through official comments, and intervene foreign exchange market directly or indirectly through joint efforts with other countries.

⑦Psychological expectation

Psychological expectation refers to people's expectation of the appreciation and depreciation of a certain currency. Such expectations have a great impact on exchange rate movements. If people expect a currency to depreciate in the near future, they will sell it so much that it will fall in value. Conversely, if people expect a currency to appreciate in the near future, they will rush to buy it, causing its exchange rate to rise.

⑧ Speculative behavior

Speculation by major market players is also an important factor affecting exchange rate movements. In the foreign exchange market, the proportion of transactions directly related to international trade is relatively small. Most trading is essentially based on speculation, which will lead to the movement of different currencies and in turn have an impact on exchange rates. When people conclude that the exchange rate of a certain currency will rise after an analysis on the factors affecting the exchange rate movements, they rush to buy it and cause the rise of the currency to become a reality. On the contrary, when people expect a currency to fall, there will be in a rush to sell it, causing the exchange rate to fall.

In short, the factors affecting exchange rate movements are very complicated. In addition to the above mentioned ones, other factors such as foreign trade policy, foreign exchange control, natural disasters, economic structure, price of various financial assets, economic cycle, information transmission, political situation and ideology can also influence exchange rate. All these factors interweave with each other, interact with each other and offset against each other, forming a complex system that affects the supply and demand relationship in the foreign exchange market. Exchange rate movements are the result of the interaction of various factors in the system.

(2) The impact of exchange rate on the economy

The impact of exchange rate on the economy is shown in figure 1.12.

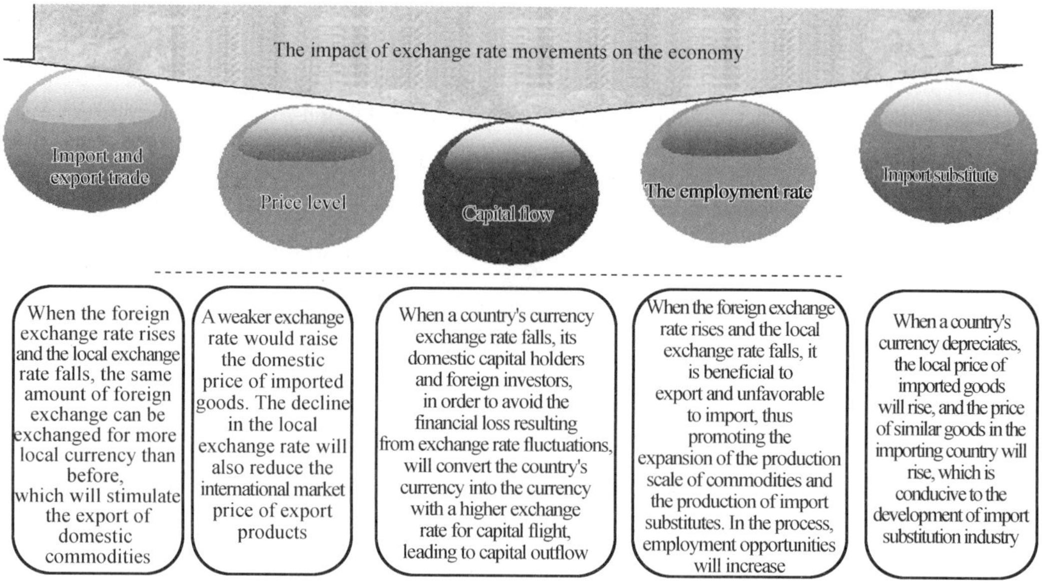

Figure 1.12 The impact of exchange rate on the economy

Exchange rates are affected by many factors. In turn, exchange rate movements will have a greater impact on the economy, affecting the development of both domestic economy and international economy. Especially in the process of today's world economic integration, this influence will grow even greater. Therefore, all countries in the world regard exchange rate as an important economic lever to adjust the development pattern of their own economy and even the economy in the world. The impact of exchange rate fluctuations on the economy is mainly exhibited in the following aspects:

①The impact on import and export trade

Exchange rate fluctuation will directly affect domestic foreign trade. When the foreign exchange rate rises, the local exchange rate falls. The same amount of foreign currency can be exchanged for more local currency, which will stimulate the export of domestic goods. At the same time, local currency can only be exchanged for less foreign exchange, so it can only buy fewer foreign goods, and the country's imports will fall.

②The effect on prices

A country's falling exchange rate also has a big impact on its prices.

On the one hand, a weaker exchange rate would raise the domestic price of imported goods.

For example, suppose an enterprise in China imports a certain kind of commodity priced at \$100 /t in the international market. The market exchange rate at that time is USD 1 = RMB 8.27. If the exchange rate remains unchanged, the enterprise can buy a ton of this product with RMB 827. However, when the local currency exchange rate falls from USD 1 = RMB 8.27 to USD 1 = RMB 8.50, it will cost RMB 850 to import a ton of the same commodity at the same price in the international market. This raises the cost of imports and forces the domestic price of the commodity to rise.

It is worth noting that if the quantity of imported goods is not effectively under control, or imported goods account for a large proportion of the total amount of goods, the increase in the price of imported goods will exert great pressure on promoting the overall price level. This pressure is not only reflected in the rising prices of imported manufactured goods, but also in the growing costs of products with imported products as intermediate products or raw materials, and even in the increasing price of domestic products related to imports. Therefore, the devaluation of a country's currency must be followed by measures to restrict imports and control prices in order to maintain the stability of domestic prices.

On the other hand, a fall in the domestic exchange rate also lowers the international market price of its exports.

For example, suppose an export enterprise in China sells a certain kind of product priced at \$100 in the international market with exchange rate of RMB 8.27 against United States dollar. If the market exchange rate becomes RMB 8.50 against United States dollar and the international market price remains unchanged, the enterprise will increase its income by 23 yuan for exporting one unit of the product. The international market price of the product will be lower than \$100 if the income remains the same, which is conducive to reducing the international market price of export commodities.

The appreciation of the local currency brings the opposite effects. It will make the domestic price of import and export commodities (the price in local currency) fall, the export is restricted, and the import expands correspondingly.

③The impact on capital flows

Firstly, the impact on short-term capital flows. The changes of various exchange rates in the foreign exchange market have a great impact on short-term capital flows. When the exchange rate of a country falls, domestic fund holders and foreign investors, to avoid losses from exchange rate fluctuations, will convert the currency of the country into the currency with a higher exchange rate for capital flight, resulting in capital outflow. At the same time, foreign investors would transfer the funds out of the country because the value of assets valued in that country's currency falls, which will not only shrink the scale of domestic investment, affect the development of the national economy, but also worsen the country's balance of payments. The appreciation of a country's currency has the opposite effect on short-term capital flows.

Secondly, the impact on long-term capital flows. The devaluation of a country's currency will be particularly beneficial for foreign companies to invest in the country. Because foreign investors can invest in production with lower prices after the country's currency falls. On the contrary, the appreciation of a country's currency will stimulate them to invest abroad.

④The effect on employment rate

When the foreign exchange rate rises and the local exchange rate falls, it is good for export and bad for import. Thus, the expansion of the production scale of commodities and the production of imported substitutes will be promoted, and employment opportunities will increase in the process. In addition, if a country's currency depreciates, foreign investors can obtain the same means of production material with less money. If depreciation happens in an overpopulated developing country, this country will create a larger market for foreign investors, thus further develop its advantages in the production of labor-intensive products, improving its employment rate.

⑤The impact on import substitution industry

When a country's currency depreciates, the price of imported goods in local currency will rise, and the price of similar goods from the importing country will rise, which is conducive to the development of import substitution industry. For a developing country, if the price of imported agricultural products increases, domestic prices of similar agricultural products will rise, which has very dramatic significance for the supply of agricultural raw materials, the improvement of agricultural labor productivity and narrowing the income gap between urban and rural areas.

⑥The impact on the world economy

Fluctuating exchange rate of a country will not only affect its domestic economy, but also have various effects on the economy of other countries. The extent of its impact depends on the country's economic development, exchange controls, market conditions, and so on.

Generally speaking, the economy of developing countries develops on a smaller scale and their currencies are not taken as a means of payment and valuation in international economy, so exchange rates in these countries can only influence the economy of their trading partners. That is to say, depreciation in a country's currency will result in the trade surplus, while its partners may suffer from trade deficit. Nevertheless, for developed countries, the impact of their exchange rates on other countries' economies is quite large in both scope and extent. Because, firstly, the currency of developed countries can generally serve as the means of valuation and payment in international economic transactions, hence the fluctuations of its currency exchange rate will affect the economy of all countries. Fluctuant exchange rate of United States dollar has a particularly big impact on the world economy. United States dollar dominates current international trade and financial activities and some developing countries try their best to maintain a fixed exchange rate against United States dollar. If the exchange rate of United States dollar rises, the exchange rate of developing countries maintaining a fixed exchange rate with United States dollar will rise against other countries, which may exert a negative impact on their trade balance. Secondly, the depreciating currencies of developed countries will generate huge trade surpluses, which also means that other countries that trade with them will have corresponding huge trade deficits, thus significantly affecting the balance of payments of other countries. Thirdly, currencies from developed countries tend to function as the reserve currencies in international reserves, and fluctuations of their exchange rates will affect the value of reserve assets of other countries. Fourthly, the currencies of developed countries often act as instruments of international credit, and their exchange rate fluctuations will affect the debt burden of other countries.

【Case for analysis】

Stronger yuan would affect China's economy in both positive and negative ways.

(1) The positive impact of RMB appreciation on Chinese economy

①Prices of foreign products will fall, which will help increase China's imports of high-quality consumer goods and production equipment from abroad and improve living standards and industrial manufacturing.

② Manufacturers relying on imported raw materials can lower their purchasing cost. Processing export accounts for a large proportion in China's foreign trade, and the import content of processed export products is relatively high. After RMB appreciates, the price of imported raw materials will be correspondingly reduced, which will reduce the cost of manufacturers relying on imported raw materials.

③Domestic enterprises have stronger abilities to invest abroad. At present, China pays more attention on export and the introduction of foreign capitals, but with further integration with the international market, Chinese companies will continue to expand overseas investment to expand sales channels. The appreciation of the RMB is helpful to improve the ability of Chinese enterprises to invest in foreign markets and promotes them to "go out", which can not only reduce the cost for manufactures using imported raw materials but also promote further acceleration of the internationalization of Chinese enterprises.

④Profits of foreign-invested enterprises in China will increase a lot.

⑤It is favorable for people to study abroad. Stronger yuan will be beneficial for Chinese citizens to study abroad, and more families will be able to send their children overseas to study at their own expense.

⑥It will help relieve the pressure of repaying capital and interest of foreign debts. The amount of local currency required to repay the capital and interest of the external debt will be correspondingly reduced, which will alleviate the external debt burden to some extent.

⑦ The appreciation of RMB can serve as a foundation for RMB to enter into the world. The appreciation of RMB will bring confidence to the people of the world, and the RMB will become an international currency naturally.

⑧ It promotes China's gross domestic product(GDP) status. According to the 2011 *World Economic Beige Book* released by the Chinese Academy of Social Sciences on December 26, 2010, China surpassed Britain, France and Germany and became the third largest shareholder of the IMF, what's more, China's GDP surpassed Japan in 2010 and became the second largest economy in the world. This increases the attractiveness of China's currency and facilitates China's economic position in the world economy.

⑨ It increases national tax revenue.

⑩ Chinese people's international purchasing power has been increased.

(2)The negative impact of RMB appreciation on Chinese economy

The appreciation of RMB will affect the stable development of China's foreign trade, attracting foreign capital, domestic employment, price level and financial reform, and affect the comprehensive competitiveness of many industries in China. The detailed analysis is displayed as follows.

①It causes great harm to China's foreign trade exports.

In the past ten years, China's export has not only maintained rapid growth, but also become an important factor driving China's rapid economic growth. It is of great significance to maintain the rapid growth of export in the future. On the one hand, a stronger yuan would increase the cost of production and labor for exporters. If the international market price remains unchanged, the decline of export profit will seriously affect the enthusiasm of exporters. On the other hand, if the exporter raises the price in order to maintain a certain profit, it will weaken the international competitiveness of the export products, which is not conducive to the continuous expansion of the export and the promotion of the product's share in the international market. Especially at present, China mainly exports manufacturing products that can easily be replaced. Once the export is blocked, the manufacturing industry is easily transferred abroad, thus losing the advantage of low labor cost that China has as a developing country. Since the products of labor-intensive enterprises are of low quality and added value, the appreciation of RMB will harm the price competitiveness of a large number of labor-intensive export products in the international market. At the same time, new protectionism is on the rise in international trade, some developed countries set up all kinds of non-tariff barriers such as environmental standards, quality standards, technical and health standards to restrict imports and abuse anti-dumping measures to protect their domestic market. China's labor-intensive exports are vulnerable to the limitation of anti-dumping measures, which renders the export situation more serious.

②Appreciating RMB will lead to the declining attraction on foreign capital and decrease direct investment from foreigners to China. Firstly, the appreciation of RMB will not only directly increase the cost of foreign investment in China to build factories and purchase equipment, but also increase the labor cost of foreign investment in China, which will further affect China to attract foreign investments. Secondly, the operation of foreign enterprises in China has gradually entered a mature development period. The requirement for foreign profit remittance is also increasing year by year. The appreciation of RMB will increase the foreign exchange earnings of their profits and may increase the scale of capital outflow, thus exerting pressure on the balance of international payments. This will affect the scale of profit reinvestment of foreign-invested enterprises and the process of industrial localization, which is not conducive to the sustainable development and upgrading of China's processing trade industry.

③A stronger yuan would reduce Chinese companies' profit margins and increase employment pressure.

The impact of RMB appreciation on the export industry and foreign direct investment will eventually be reflected in employment, which is bound to have a certain impact on the improvement of the current employment environment. In addition, the rise of RMB exchange rate will lead to the rise of the price of non-traded goods (such as land, labor and other factors of production) in China, thus weakening domestic demand and bringing serious negative impacts on the employment market.

④The fiscal deficit will increase due to the appreciation of RMB exchange rate and affect the stability of monetary policy.

Due to the appreciation of the RMB, in order to maintain the basic stability of the RMB exchange rate, the central bank must purchase a large amount of foreign exchange in the foreign exchange market, thus increasing the base currency in the form of funds outstanding for foreign exchange. And issued currency would flow into the main institutions and individuals holding foreign exchanges. Their investment intention and direction may be deviated from economic development's demand for capital utilization, which may cause those without investment intention or without intention to invest in production to gain a lot of money, while some private investors who have projects and investment intentions lack financial support. Therefore, although the money supply continues to grow, the difference in supply structure leads to the inefficient use of funds, which affects the impact of monetary policy.

⑤It affects the balance of international payments and the stability of financial markets.

Under the influence of the market expectation of RMB appreciation, international arbitrage speculative capital will enter China through various channels and form new pressure on RMB appreciation. This speculative capital is unlikely to be invested in industry, but flows into the highly active financial security market featuring easy conversion into cash. In this case, a large amount of short-term capital flows into the security market through a variety of channels to pursue profits, which will become a potential source of financial market turmoil and easily trigger monetary and financial crisis, affecting the sustainable and healthy development of China's economy.

Extracurricular exercise

(1) Analyze the main factors affecting exchange rate fluctuation with examples.

(2) Analyze the impact of exchange rate fluctuations on macroeconomics and microeconomics with examples.

(3) Group discussion on "the impact of the financial crisis on the import and export trade of a certain industry or a product in China and corresponding measures". Write a paper of 2 000 ~ 3 000 words, upload it through course website in the form of a word document, and submit the paper discussion records and examination records of the group.

Task 4 Import and export quotation

【Objectives】

(1) Be clear about the principles of quotation for import and export trade;

(2) Can correctly apply the buying price and the selling price in the import and export quotation;

(3) Master the skills of import and export trade quotation.

【Tasks】

(1) Understand the principles of import and export quotation;

(2) Make import and export quotations by using buying and selling prices;

(3) Apply import and export trade quotation skills.

【Requirements】

(1) Be clear about the principles of quotation for import and export trade;

(2) Correct application of buying and selling prices in import and export quotation;

(3) Master the skills of import and export trade quotation, and be able to quote prices based on commodity characteristics, customer conditions, settlement methods and payment period, etc.

【Lead-in case】

RMB settlement pilot program in foreign trade and its hard currency status recognized.

An executive meeting of the state council recently decided to launch RMB settlement pilot programs in goods trade among Guangdong, the Yangtze River Delta region and Hong Kong and Macao and among Guangxi, Yunnan and Association of Southeast Asian Nations(ASEAN). This means that imports and exports in these regions can be settled directly in RMB, which is officially recognized as a "hard currency" in these regions.

(1) It is conducive to reducing export risks

Previously, according to the relevant regulations of China's foreign exchange management, enterprises can only use foreign currency for foreign trade settlement, that is, overseas enterprises use United States dollars to pay domestic enterprises. Domestic enterprises must go to the bank for foreign exchange settlement after receiving United States dollars and convert the received United States dollars into RMB. Even if foreign enterprises hold RMB, they cannot directly pay it to domestic enterprises.

However, the continuous depreciation of United States dollar has caused troubles to domestic export enterprises: if there are no risk hedging measures, payment loss may happen due to the depreciation of United States dollar from the signing of a contract to the actual account, what's more, the current trend of depreciating United States dollar has no end in sight. Zhao Xijun, deputy director of the institute of finance and fiscal studies at the People's University of China, pointed out that in response to the financial crisis, the United States issued a large number of dollars, which will inevitably cause further depreciation of United States dollar in the future after being released from financial institutions.

Li Xiangyang, deputy director of the institute of world economics and politics at the Chinese Academy of Social Sciences, pointed out that using RMB as the settlement currency in international trade can avoid exchange rate risks caused by fluctuations of foreign currencies. The autonomy of the yuan's stable value is in China's hands, and companies do not have to worry about exchange rate fluctuations.

(2) It will accelerate the internationalization of RMB

Li Xiangyang said the use of RMB as the settlement currency is an official recognition. In fact, Chinese yuan has been circulating in Vietnam, Thailand and other Southeast Asian nations. Previously, the head of the Ministry of Commerce once said that with the development of economic and trade cooperation between China and the ASEAN, RMB had become the transaction currency in some regions. The People's Bank of China also acknowledged that RMB had become the main currency for border trade settlement in neighboring countries such as Russia, Mongolia, Vietnam, Myanmar and Nepal. The State Administration of Foreign Exchange has estimated that more than 30 billion yuan is circulating abroad.

Since the outbreak of the Southeast Asian financial crisis in the 1990s, the call for RMB internationalization has been growing. Li Xiangyang believes that the internationalization of RMB is a medium-term and long-term goal, and promoting RMB as a trade settlement currency is the only way to internationalization.

Although Chinese yuan is not a fully convertible currency in the international market, the Chinese government has significantly accelerated the pace of its internationalization recently. Earlier this month, China and Russia held talks on promoting trade in their own currencies. In the middle of this month, the People's Bank of China and Bank of Korea signed a bilateral currency swap agreement, through which the two countries can provide short-term liquidity support of up to RMB 180 billion to each other.

(3) RMB settlement can significantly reduce exchange rate risks

The State Council issued seven policies to stabilize foreign trade, and experts said that "almost all available policies have been used".

①Policy interpretation

The executive meeting of the State Council confirmed the policy measures to ease the difficulties of export enterprises and maintain the steady growth of foreign trade, including steadily promoting the transformation and upgrading of processing trade, improving import and export financial services and expanding the import of domestic products in demand. The biggest focus is to conduct RMB settlement trials for goods trade among Guangdong, the Yangtze River Delta region and Hong Kong and Macao, and among Guangxi, Yunnan and the ASEAN. Our reporter interviewed relevant experts for the first time, undertaking a detailed interpretation of the policies and measures introduced.

②Offer gift packages to exporters at the end of the year

The seven policies are not blind stimulus to exports, but targeted regulations. "Yesterday, Zhang Yansheng, director of the Foreign Economic Research Institute of the National Development and Reform Commission, pointed out in an interview with our reporter that policy has played a great role in accelerating the transformation of trade growth mode, trade restructuring and strengthening trade and investment interaction."

China's exports fell 2.2 percent in November compared with a year earlier, the first negative growth since June 2001, according to the General Administration of Customs. Imports also plunged 17.9 percent on year-on-year basis, the first negative growth since February 2005.

Lan Qingxin, assistant dean of the School of International Economics at the University of

International Business and Economics, told reporters: "unilateral policies are no longer very effective, and the government has to put together a series of measures to deal with the impact of the financial crisis on domestic exports."

Seven policies to stabilize exports are a big gift package given by the government to export enterprises at the end of the year. The person in charge of a foreign trade enterprise in Dongguan, Guangdong province, told reporters excitedly after hearing the news: "These policies issued by the government are real solutions to the current plight of export enterprises."

Reporters noted that the seven policies cover all aspects of promoting import and export. In Lan's view, almost every available policy has been used. These policies not only reflect the government's efforts to save the market, but also to a certain extent directly stimulate the position of China's export enterprises in the international arena and stimulate the growth of China's export.

③Products should be imported after a careful selection

Experts believe that these policies not only aim at stabilizing exports, but also imports. Zhang Hanya, vice President of the China Investment Association, told reporters that the measures sent a signal that foreign trade policies should focus on imports. "The import problem now becomes more acute, according to the goal proposed by the state that both import and export need protection, import policies are urgently needed, the most important focus of the policies and measures is to protect imports."

Imports plunged 17.9 percent in November compared with a year earlier, the first negative growth since February 2005, according to the General Administration of Customs. The trade surplus for November was $40.09 billion, hitting new height in the past 4 months.

For imported products, it is also necessary to make a selection, and we cannot carry out the "fetch principle". According to Zhang's analysis, China needs to import products that are conducive to industrial upgradings, such as advanced technologies, key equipment, components, important energy and raw materials mentioned in the measures.

④The RMB internationalization strategy gets started

The press noted that the meeting also pointed out that RMB settlement trials were carried out for goods trade among Guangdong, the Yangtze river delta region and Hong Kong and Macao, and among Guangxi, Yunnan and the ASEAN.

"The RMB settlement pilot is very important." Zhang Yansheng told reporters, "one of the biggest lessons of the financial crisis for our country is that the risk of foreign exchange is too big." Settlement in RMB can greatly reduce the risk of export enterprises.

Hu Zhihao, a professor at the Institute of Finance and Banking under the Chinese Academy of Social Sciences, said that encouraging the widespread use of RMB in trade and investment, and allowing foreign companies to use RMB directly when conducting trade with Chinese companies, could greatly promote the restructuring of Chinese enterprises. It could also be seen as part of a broader strategy to internationalize the RMB.

Experts also said that these measures would extend the monetary function of the RMB outside China, which will help maintain the stability of the bilateral exchange rate and maintain regional financial security when the destructive force of the financial crisis continues to deepen.

Wu Xiaoqiu, director of the Institute of Finance and Securities at the People's University of China, told the media that the outbreak of the financial crisis fundamentally reflects the problems in the unipolar monetary system, and a new monetary system featuring stable structure and mutual restraint among United States dollar, euro and RMB must be established.

⑤The dominant position of United States dollar remains to be unshakable

However, in Mr Hu's view, "the measures proposed by the State Council are still a very preliminary step in the strategy of RMB internationalization." In fact, the volume of traded goods and RMB settlement between China and the ASEAN are very small. Although the United States was hit hard by the financial crisis, United States dollar's status as the international settlement currency remains unshakable. However, when China's domestic financial market is still in the primary stage waiting to be improved, the full internationalization of RMB is not only difficult to achieve, but also unfavorable to China's economy.

Even if the trial of RMB international trade settlement starts, there are still three problems to be solved. Lian Ping, the chief economist of the Bank of Communications, pointed out that firstly, a certain number of foreign trade enterprises should be willing to accept international trade settlement in RMB. Secondly, pilot banks carry out relevant technical and process transformation; at the same time, the domestic foreign exchange system and regulatory system also need to be carefully adjusted. "This is a long-term process, and it is appropriate to steadily push forward the 'periphery' of the RMB." Zhuang Jian, an economist with the Asian Development Bank.

Task 4.1 The principles of quotation in import and export trade

In the process of negotiation on import and export trade, the most important point is the negotiation on price. The setting of import and export commodity price, the choice of payment currency and the determination of actual payment time of a country are all directly related to its foreign trade balance, hence directly affect the final result of its international balance of payments. Therefore, on the basis of mastering the principles of import and export trade quotation, we need to make full use of the skills of import and export trade quotation to improve our abilities of foreign quotation and speed up the transaction, so as to improve the success rate of the transaction and further improve the economic benefits of enterprises. In real practice, what aspects should be paid attention to?

【Case for analysis】

(1) Case 4.1 After graduating from a fashion institute, Zhang Shan entered into a foreign trade enterprise in the year 2008, when the US subprime mortgage crisis triggered the global financial crisis. Zhang Shan really valued this hard-won work, so he worked very hard. He looked for steel import enterprises, but the effect is not ideal. Finally, a business made an enquiry to him, Zhang Shan made a quotation with the export price of his company in 2006, but the final negotiations failed, why?

(2) Case 4.2 In October 2008, an import and export enterprise in Jiangsu received an inquiry from a customer in North America. In order to facilitate the business, the company immediately made a quotation at a low price. But the negotiations failed, why?

(3) Case 4.3 Default under D/A, an import and export group corporation in China's coastal area has been in cooperation with company B of Australia for more than 3 years, and the two sides have always maintained a good trade relationship. At the beginning of their cooperation, the order quantity of company B was not large, but was stable with duly payments. Later, with the mutual understanding and familiarity between the two parties, our import and export company provided company B with favorable payment terms, from the initial L/C (Letter of credit) at sight, D/P (documents against payment) at sight, D/A (documents against acceptance) 60 days to D/A 90 days, and the bilateral trade volume increased from sixty, seventy thousand dollars per year to seven, eight hundred thousand dollars.

In September 1999, company B placed another order with the import and export company with the total value of United States dollar 250 000 CIF Melbourne. However, without conducting a strict credit audit on the customer, our import and export company agreed to grant D/A 180 days credit terms. In November 1999, all the goods were shipped as scheduled, and the import and export company delivered relevant documents to the bank in time.

In May 2000, when the drafts are due for acceptance, company B asked for the delay of the payment on the grounds that the market was bad and most of the goods had not been sold. After that, our company kept sending faxes and E-mails to company B, demanding it to pay for the goods or return the goods. Company B apologized for the delay of the payment and promised to pay as soon as possible.

In November 2000, company B could only pay US $30 000 to the import and export company for its financial difficulties. Our company agreed and demanded immediate remittance. Even so, company B continued to default on payments on the excuse that its treasurer was sick or its chief executive was on vacation.

In January 2001, the general manager of company B, Mr. K resigned. Before that, all the transactions between our company and company B were concluded through Mr. K. Since then, company B had no replies to all the letters of the import and export company. By March 2001, our company lost contact with it.

In May 2001, the Oriental International Factoring Center accepted the case and knew through investigation that company B filed for bankruptcy in March 2001. The Oriental International Factoring Center tried its best to minimize the company's losses by applying for creditor's rights for the company in time.

However, according to the initial report of the local clearing committee, the Oriental International Factoring Center learned that company B's total debt is three times its total assets, what's more, more than 90% of its assets have been mortgaged to banks. It was evident that our import and export corporation would suffer a huge loss from the bad debt.

Case 4.4 In August 2007, a company of China planned to import a batch of goods from the

United States. After the agreement, D/P three-month forward payment was adopted and the payment could be made in both United States dollar and euro. During the negotiation, according to relevant data, the inflation of the United States increased sharply compared with the previous quarter, and the balance of payments deficit also increased year on year, which caused panic in the foreign exchange market. At the same time, inflation and the balance of payments across the European Union remained unchanged. Question: what currency should our company choose as the currency of account? Why?

【Questions for discussion】

(1) How to choose different ways of quotation for different kinds of goods?

(2) How to choose the appropriate way of quotation based on different commodities in trade?

(3) How to choose the appropriate way of quotation according to different means of settlements?

(4) How to choose the appropriate quotation according to currencies and actual payment period involved in the quotation?

【Relevant knowledge】

(1) How to choose different ways of quotation according to different kinds of goods.

As exporters, when choosing export products, they should choose the products with their own comparative advantages. In addition, they can also consider consumable goods for export, i. e. , the goods with short lifespan, large demand and large potential export volume; moreover, the time for sales and transport also needs to be considered to adjust the quotation. Generally speaking, if the goods to be sold are in high season with its demand exceeding its supply, its price can be appropriately higher. Nevertheless, if goods to be sold is in the off-season with its supply exceeding its demand, its price should be appropriately reduced. Exporters should not only consider the market price at not only the time of quotation, but also the market price at the time of delivery. In addition, delivery time and transportation cost will also affect the export quotation.

(2) How to choose the appropriate way of quotation according to different commodities in trade.

In foreign trade, different quotation methods should be chosen according to the strength and character of different importers. In addition, when trade with old customers, we will also pay attention to develop new customers at any time to expand international economic exchanges.

(3) How to choose the appropriate way of quotations according to different means of settlements.

In international trade, there are three main methods of settlement: remittance, collection and letter of credit.

①Settlement by remittance

Also called remitting to pay, remittance falls into the category of commercial credit, namely, the drawee actively gives money to the payee through banks or other means. Remittance, based on whether capitals transfer in the same direction as the settlement tools flow, can be divided into favorable remittance and reverse remittance. The mode of remittance settlement can be divided into M/T, T/T and D/D. In international trade, remittance settlement is mainly used for advance payment, cash delivery and credit sale.

②Settlement by collection

Collection is a method of payment in which the exporter presents the draft and entrusts the bank to collect payment from the importer. Collection methods include D/A and D/P. Since collection settlement is a kind of commercial credit, the bank has "three irresponsibilities": that is, it is not responsible for examining the authenticity of documents; not responsible for the buyer's payment; not responsible for the real situation of the goods. Therefore, if the importer does not fulfill his obligations of receiving and paying goods according to the contract, the exporter will face the risk of unsafe and untimely collection of foreign exchange. The method of settlement by collection is seldom used in foreign trade. It is generally used in exporting slow-selling goods to the country with good credit and loose payment control. To adopt the method of collection settlement, it is necessary to do a detailed investigation in the preliminary stage.

③Settlement by letter of credit

A letter of credit is a written promise by the bank to the seller under the instruction of the buyer to pay against the stipulated documents within a certain period of time. Letter of credit is a conditional bank payment commitment, which belongs to bank credit. As long as all documents provided by the seller are in full compliance with the letter of credit, the issuing bank shall assume the primary responsibility for payment. This mode of settlement not only guarantees the export can receive the foreign exchange safely and timely, but also guarantees the import can receive all the correct documents on time, which is beneficial to both sides of the transaction.

In foreign trade, letter of credit is the most widely used method of settlement.

(4) How to choose an appropriate quotation according to the currency and time for payment.

Generally, import and export contracts are valued and paid by convertible, internationally acceptable or mutually agreed means of payment. In foreign trade, there are three major currencies to choose from in quotation: domestic currency, the currency of the other country, the currency of a third country. Theoretically speaking, it is more favorable to use hard currency for export transactions, while it is more reasonable to use soft currency for import contracts. For us, if we pay in RMB, there will be no exchange rate risk losses. Sometimes, in order to effectively avoid the risk of exchange rate fluctuations, in addition to the currency of payment, the currency of account is adopted for hedging.

According to the common international practice, if the exchange rate of two currencies is calculated according to the exchange rate at the time of payment, the payment for goods can be recovered in the amount of the currency of account.

①If price is made by the hard currency while payment is made by the soft currency, the conversion rate between the two currencies will be in the seller's favor at the date of payment and in the buyer's favor at the date of signing.

②If the "soft currency" is used at pricing while the "hard coin" is used for payment, the conversion rate between the two currencies will be in favor of the buyer at the date of payment and the seller at the date of signing.

The way that is usually safer, and easier for buyers and sellers to reach an agreement is to use a basket of currencies and to pay with the agreed currency. The basket of currencies is composed of a number of selected currencies, and its exchange rate is calculated by the weighted average of the exchange rates of these selected currencies, therefore it is relatively stable.

[Extracurricular exercise]

An import and export company in our country exports a batch of goods. Both the currency of pricing and the currency of payment are United States dollars. According to the exchange rate at that time, the goods are priced at 1 million United States dollars after the local currency is converted into United States dollars with one month collection period. It is estimated that United States dollar will depreciate after a month. Question: should this import and export company maintain its quoted price of 1 million United States dollars, why?

Task 4.2 The application of buying and selling price in the quotation of import and export trade

Foreign exchange transactions involve conversion of different currencies. While in foreign trade payment and settlement, different currencies should be delivered in different ways in different periods. The final ratio between two currencies varies in different forms of foreign exchange business. Mastering the methods and general rules of exchange rate conversion is the most basic requirement in international finance and international trade practice.

When making a quotation, exporters not only need to accurately calculate the proportional relationship between currency and local currency, but also often encounter the situation that the importer requires to change the currency of settlement, so exporters often face the problems of exchange rate conversion. When using the buying price and selling price of exchange rate to carry out the converted quotation, he must know whether the quotation method of the exchange rate adopted by the market is direct or indirect, and at the same time, whether the converted currency is domestic or foreign. Since there is usually a difference of 1‰ to 3‰ between the buying price and the selling price of the exchange rate, if the importer or exporter fails to calculate correctly in the conversion of the commodity price, in the quotation and in the fulfillment of the payment, he or she may suffer losses. Therefore, in the import and export trade quotation, we must focus on how to use buying and selling prices reasonably.

[Case for demonstration]

Case 4.5 Hong Kong Renhe Trading Company wanted to export 10 machines at the original price of HK $100 000 each. The foreign importer demanded the price to be quoted in United States dollar. At the time, the buying rate of United States dollar against the Hong Kong dollar on the Hong Kong Foreign Exchange Market was 7.797 and the selling rate was 7.816. How much United States dollars should the Hong Kong exporter quote for their exports? If you don't quote in this way, how many United States dollars will you lose?

Case 4.6 Hong Kong Renhe Trading Company planned to export 100 lathes at the original price of US $8 000 each set. Its foreign importer requested the quotation to be made in the Hong Kong dollar. At that time, the exchange rate of the Hong Kong Foreign Exchange Market was presented as follows: the buying price of United States dollar against the Hong Kong dollar was 7.720 2, and the selling price was 7.735 5. After careful calculation, the company's salesman quoted 6 176 160 Hong Kong dollars (800 000 ×7.720 2). Is his quotation reasonable? If not, how much should he quote?

Case 4.7 China Hengde Machinery Import and Export Corporation planned to export 10 machines at the original price of 50 000 Swiss francs each. At that time, the exchange rate in the Zurich Foreign Exchange Market was listed as follows the buying price of one United States dollar against Swiss francs was 4.430 0, and the selling price was 4.440 0. How much should China Hengde Machinery Import and Export Corporation quote for its exports in United States dollar?

【Questions for discussion】

(1) When converting local currencies into foreign currencies for export commodities, shall we adopt the buying price or the selling price?

(2) When converting foreign currencies into local currencies for export commodities, shall we adopt the buying price or the selling price?

(3) How can we convert one foreign currency into another?

【Relevant knowledge】

(1) For export commodities, the buying price shall be adopted when local currencies are converted into foreign currencies.

If the exporter needs to quote in foreign currency instead of local currency, the buying price shall be used. Because the exporter changed from receiving the local currency to receiving the foreign currency, after receiving the foreign currency, the exporter needs to sell the collected foreign currency to the bank to get the local currency. That is to say, the exporter sells foreign currency for local currency. And the bank pays local currency for foreign currency, so the buying price should be used when the bank buys foreign currency.

(2) For export commodities, the selling price shall be adopted when foreign currency is converted into domestic currency.

If the exporter previously quotes in foreign currency but now wants to quote in local currency, the selling price shall be used. Because, instead of receiving foreign currency, the exporter now receives domestic currency. The exporter needs to calculate how much local currency should be quoted to receive the amount of foreign currency previously wanted. So when receiving payment for goods, the exporter needs to sell the local currency to the bank for foreign currency, that is to say, the exporter buys foreign currency, while the bank sells foreign currency and receives domestic currency, thus the selling price should be applied.

(3) The conversion of one foreign currency into another foreign currency shall be conducted according to the exchange rate quoted on the international market.

When two foreign currencies are to be converted into each other, the currency of the country where the market's quotation is adopted shall be taken as the local currency, no matter whether the market price is marked directly or indirectly and where the buying rate or the selling prate is placed. For export commodities, when the local currency is to be converted into the foreign currency, the buying price is applied, when the foreign currency is to be converted into the local currency, the selling price is applied.

【Tasks】

(1) According to the above principle of "buying rate shall be applied to the conversion of local currency into foreign currency for export commodities", case 4.5 is calculated as follows:

①United States dollar price of the export goods is \$100 000 ÷ 7.797 0 = US \$12 825.45

Therefore, the Hong Kong exporter should quote a total of US \$12 825.45 for its exports.

②If the exporter uses the selling price instead of the buying price in its quotation, the calculation can be done as follows:

$1:7.816\ 0 = X:100\ 000$

$X = 100\ 000 \div 7.816\ 0 = 12\ 794.27$ United States dollar

Therefore, if the exporter uses the selling price instead of the buying price, the offer is quoted at US \$12 794.27, a loss of US \$31.18 (12 825.45 − 12 794.27) compared with using the buying price.

(2) According to the above principle of "selling price shall be applied in the conversion of foreign currency into domestic currency for export commodities", case 4.6 is analyzed as follows:

We know from the case: the foreign importer requests the quotation to be changed from United States dollar to the Hong Kong dollar, that is, the foreign currency is to be changed to the local currency, so the selling price should be applied in the conversion. However, the salesman uses the buying price to convert the quotation, which is unreasonable. The correct way of calculating quotation should be as follows:

Let the quoted price of export commodities be Hong Kong dollars X:

$1:7.735\ 5 = 800\ 000:X$

$X = 800\ 000 \times 7.735\ 5 = 6\ 188\ 400$

Therefore, the Import and Export Company should quote HK \$6 188 400 for its export lathes.

(3) According to the above principle of "converting one foreign currency into another foreign currency at the exchange rate quoted in the international market", the calculation of case 4.7 is as follows:

Since the quotation on the Zurich Foreign Exchange Market (with direct quotation method) is adopted, the Swiss franc should be regarded as the local currency. From the case, we know that the foreign tradesman asks the quotation to be changed from Swiss francs to United States dollars, that is, the domestic currency is to be changed into foreign currency. Therefore, the buying rate shall be applied. And the calculation can be done as follows:

Assuming that the export commodities shall be quoted at United States dollar of X:

$1:4.430\ 0 = X:50\ 000$

$X = 50\ 000 \div 4.430\ 0 = 11\ 286.68$

Therefore, China Hengde Machinery Import and Export Corporation should quote the US

$11 286.68 for its export machinery.

Task 4.3 Quotation skills in import and export trading

Task 4.3.1 Quotation techniques in payment at sight

[Case for demonstration]

Case 4.8 Kunshan Fulex Fashion Co., Ltd. exported a batch of garments at the original quotation of 1 200 000 Swiss francs with payment at sight. But the foreign merchant requested the quotation to be made in United States dollar. It is known that the exchange rate of a Swiss bank at that time was: spot exchange rate: 1 United States dollar = 1.603 0 - 1.604 0 Swiss francs. Please make a quotation on the basis of the discussion.

[Questions for discussion]

(1) How many United States dollars should we offer, provided that the importer is willing to pay at sight?

(2) How many United States dollars will be lost if our salesman does not understand the rules of conversion?

[Relevant knowledge]

The so-called payment at sight refers to the way of payment within a relatively short period of time after the transaction of import and export commodities. At present, except for a few countries such as the United Kingdom and the United States, most countries or regions in the foreign exchange market adopt the direct quotation method or United States dollar quotation method to announce the spot exchange rate, instead of adopting the indirect quotation method which takes the local currency as the standard in its conversion into a certain amount of foreign currencies. In addition, many foreign exchange markets mainly announce the exchange rates of developed countries in relation to their domestic currencies. The exchange rates of other countries' currencies against their local currencies are not known, which requires the exchange rate to be cross-calculated. Therefore, understanding and mastering the conversion between direct quotation method and indirect quotation method is the basis of spot exchange rate conversion and import and export quotation.

(1) The quotation techniques in spot payment in export

In international trade, when exporting commodities, exporters always quote prices in a given currency from the perspective of export quotation or change currencies in quotation at the request of importers. Therefore, they have to face complicated exchange rate conversion problems among different currencies in their quotations.

If both parties agree that the importer shall pay at sight, the exporter shall pay attention to three points when making an export offer:

First, the offer should be based on the basic principles of export quotation;

Second, focus on the reasonable application of foreign exchange buying price and selling price;

Third, pay attention to the conversion skills among different currencies and problems concerning hard currency and soft currency.

Under spot payment, currency conversion can be classified into the following categories.

①Given: foreign currency/local currency, calculate: local currency/foreign currency.

The conversion from foreign currency/local currency to local currency/foreign currency refers to the conversion from direct quotation method to indirect quotation method. Foreign currency/local currency means how much local currency a foreign currency is equal to. Local currency/foreign currency indicates how much foreign currency is equal to one unit of local currency. The conversion of foreign currency/local currency into local currency/foreign currency is the conversion of the amount of local currency against one unit of foreign currency into the amount of foreign currency against one unit of local currency. In foreign trade, exporters may be required to quote the price of their exports in foreign currency as well as in local currency. Therefore, the conversion from direct quotation method to indirect quotation method is necessary.

Solution: 1 ÷ the specific number of local currency.

Case 4.9 Assume that in the Hong Kong Foreign Exchange Market, the exchange rate is quoted by direct quotation method. One day the exchange rate of United States dollar against the Hong Kong dollar was USD 1 = HKD 7.7950. The unit price of Hong Kong export commodities is HK $10 in local currency. How much can the Hong Kong merchant quote if the importer requests the quotation in United States dollars instead?

Analysis: exchange rate conversion comes before the quotation.

Step 1: exchange rate conversion. Convert the exchange rate, taking a unit of foreign currency as the standard into the exchange rate, taking a unit of local currency as the standard. That is, convert the exchange rate, taking a unit of United States dollar as the standard into the exchange rate taking a unit of Hong Kong dollar as the standard.

Convert USD 1 = HKD 7.795 0 to HKD 1 = USD 1 / 7.795 0, i.e., HKD 1 = USD 0.128 3.

Step 2: export quotation. Convert local currency into foreign currency, namely, convert Hong Kong dollar quotation into United States dollar quotation.

Based on the converted exchange rate of local currency against foreign currency, the price of an export commodity is HK $10 in local currency, which is 0.128 3 × 10 = US $1.283 0 when converted into United States dollar, therefore the export commodity is quoted as US $1.283 0.

②Given: the buying price (selling price) of foreign currency/local currency, calculate: the buying price (selling price) of local currency/foreign currency.

The conversion and quotation of the buying rate and the selling rate from foreign currency/local currency to domestic currency/foreign currency refer to the conversion and quotation of the buying rates and selling rates from direct quotation method to indirect quotation method. That is to convert the buying price and selling price of a foreign currency against the domestic currency into the selling price and buying price of domestic currency against the foreign currency, i.e., the buying rate (selling rate) of the local currency against the foreign currency is based on the buying rate (selling rate) of the foreign currency against the local currency.

Solution: 1 divided by the original selling price of foreign currency/local currency is the buying price of local currency/foreign currency; 1 divided by the original buying price of foreign currency/local currency equals to the selling price of local currency/foreign currency.

For example, one day, the price of Bank of China is 1USD = 6.814 6/6.842 0 CNY. Please calculate CNY/USD.

Analysis: translocate 6.814 6 and 6.842 0 above the denominator.

CNY/USD = (1/6.842 0)/(1/6.814 6) = 0.146 2/0.146 7

③ Given: quoted foreign currency/local currency, calculate: local currency/unquoted foreign currency.

The way to find the exchange rate of the local currency against an unquoted currency is as follows:

A List the mid-point exchange rate for the domestic currency against a quoted major reserve currency, such as the pound or United States dollar.

B Calculate the intermediate exchange rates between this convertible currency against unquoted foreign currencies in major international financial markets such as the London financial market and the New York financial market.

C Use the intermediate exchange rates in A and B to calculate the exchange rate of the domestic currency against the unquoted foreign currency. Divide B by A, that is, B/A = the exchange rate of local currency/unquoted foreign currency; divide A by B, that is, A/B = the exchange rate of unquoted foreign currency/local currency. Calculation can be done through the above two intermediate exchange rates.

Case 4.10 An exporter in the Hong Kong market has received a request from a Danish importer to quote him in two currencies: the Hong Kong dollar and Danish krone. The Hong Kong foreign exchange market does not list the exchange rate of the Hong Kong dollar against the Danish krone. The intermediate exchange rate of the Hong Kong dollar against a listed major reserve currency (the British pound) is known: 1 British pound = 12.30 HK dollars; on the latest day in London foreign exchange market the intermediate exchange rate of British pound against Danish krona is 1 British pound = 10.9560 Danish krone.

How should the exporter quote?

Follow the above procedure.

Analysis:

A—first list the intermediate exchange rate of the Hong Kong dollar against one quoted major reserve currency (such as British pound);

B—Check the midpoint exchange rate of 1 pound against DKR in London foreign exchange market on that day or the latest day, 1 pound = 10.956 0 Danish krone;

C—The ratio of HKD/ DKR is B/A, i.e., 10.956 0/12.30 = 0.890 7, i.e., 1 HKD = 0.8907 DKR.

The rate of DKR/HKD is A/B, i.e., 12.3/10.956 0 = 1.122 7, i.e., 1 DKR = 1.122 7

HKD.

Based on the above calculation method, the Hong Kong exporter is able to convert the cost of his exports from Hong Kong dollar into Danish kroner and offer prices to Danish importers.

④Conversion between different currencies.

The external quotation of an export commodity involves many countries and many currencies. According to United States dollar quotation method and non-United States dollar quotation method in the international foreign exchange market, there are three methods of converting exchange rates between different foreign currencies for three situations.

a. Find the exchange rate between quoted currencies under the condition that the base currencies are the same but the quoted currencies are different.

Cross-divide the bid price and the selling rate of the two base rates. Make the buying rate which comes from the division of the small number by the large number smaller than the selling rate which comes from the division of the large number by the small number, so that the former quoted number is smaller than the latter quoted number in the newly calculated two exchange rates.

Case 4.11 A bank in the international foreign exchange market quoted the exchange rates of United States dollar against Hong Kong dollar and United States dollar against the Japanese yen as follows:

1 United States dollar = 7.791 0/7.798 0 HK dollar(US $/HK $ = 7.791 0/7.798 0)

1 United States dollar = 100.00/100.10 Japanese yen (United States dollar/Japanese yen = 100.00/100.10)

Find: the buying rate and the selling rate of the Hong Kong dollar against the Japanese yen.

Analysis:

Bank buying rate of HK dollar against Japanese yen = the buying rate of United States dollar against Japanese yen/the selling rate of United States dollar against HK dollar = 100.00/7.798 0 = 12.823 8

the selling rate of HK dollar against Japanese yen = the selling rate of United States dollar against Japanese yen /the buying rate of the United States dollar against HK dollar = 100.10/7.791 0 = 12.848 2

therefore, the cross-exchange rate of Hong Kong dollar against the Japanese yen, namely, the buying rate and selling rate of Hong Kong dollar against the Japanese yen, is 12.823 8/12.848 2

The bank's buying rate of Hong Kong dollar against the Japanese yen means that banks buy Hong Kong dollar and sell Japanese yen at the same time. The bank's selling rate of Hong Kong dollar against Japanese yen means that banks sell Hong Kong dollar and buy Japanese yen at the same time.

b. With different base currencies but same quoted currencies, please find the exchange rate between these base currencies.

The buying price and the selling price of the two basic exchange rates are cross-divided respectively, so that the buying rate obtained by dividing the small number by the large number is less than the selling rate obtained by dividing the large number by the small number, so that the former quoted price of the two newly calculated exchange rates is less than the latter quoted price.

Case 4.12 The exchange rates of Australian dollar and New Zealand dollar against United States dollar quoted by a bank in the international foreign exchange market are:

1 Australian dollar = 0.731 0/0.733 0 United States dollar (Australian dollar/United States dollar 0.731 0/0.733 0)

1 New Zealand dollar = 0.602 0/0.608 0 United States dollar (New Zealand dollar/United States dollar 0.605 0/0.608 0)

Calculate: The buying rate and the selling rate of Australian dollar against New Zealand dollar.

Analysis: the buying rate of Australian dollar/New Zealand dollar = the buying rate of Australian dollar against United States dollar/the selling rate of New Zealand dollar against United States dollar = 0.731 0/0.608 0 = 1.202 3

the selling rate for Australian dollar to New Zealand dollar = the selling rate for Australian dollar to United States dollar/the buying rate for New Zealand dollar to United States dollar = 0.733 0/ 0.602 0 = 1.217 6

therefore, the buying rate and the selling rate of Australian dollar against New Zealand dollar is 1.202 3/1.217 6.

c. Find the exchange rate between a base currency and another quoted currency under United States dollar quotation system and non-United States dollar quotation system.

Multiply one buying rate and another buying rate, one selling rate and another selling rate of the two basic exchange rates, and make the buying rate obtained from the small number multiplied by another small number is smaller than the selling rate obtained from the large number multiplied by another large number, so that the former quoted price of the two newly calculated exchange rates is smaller than the latter quoted price.

Case 4.13 In the international foreign exchange market, a bank quoted the exchange rates of United States dollar against Swiss francs in USD quotation and Great Britain Pound against United States dollar in non-United States dollar quotation as follows:

1 United States dollar = 1.482 0/1.485 0 Swiss francs (United States dollar/Swiss francs = 1.482 0/1.485 0)

1 Great Britain Pound = 1.540 0/1.542 0 United States dollar (Great Britain Pound/United States dollar = 1.540 0/1.542 0)

Please find the buying rate and the selling rates of 1 pound against Swiss francs.

Analysis: the buying rate of Great Britain Pound/Swiss franc = the buying rate of Great Britain Pound/United States dollar × the buying rate of United States dollar against Swiss franc = 1.482 0 × 1.540 0 = 2.282 3

the selling rate for sterling against Swiss francs = the selling rate for sterling against United States dollar × the selling rate for United States dollar against Swiss francs = 1.485 0 × 1.542 0 = 2.289 9 therefore, the buying rate and the selling rate of Great Britain Pound against Swiss franc are 2.282 3/2.289 9.

(2) The techniques of accepting prompt payment quotation in import business

In the import business, there are two situations when considering the acceptable quotation level for the foreign quotation requiring immediate payment:

①Convert the import quotations in different currencies of the same commodity into the quotations in local currency for comparison, and then select the acceptable quotation.

For the imported goods, because foreign quotations are in different currencies which have different values, they can not be directly compared. Instead, they can be converted into the local currency before comparison.

Case 4.14 Suppose a Chinese enterprise plans to import watches. The unit price of each watch is quoted in two currencies with CHF 100 and USD 66 respectively. Suppose the spot exchange rates of Swiss franc and United States dollar against RMB published by China on the day of trading are:

CHF 1 = CNY 2.978 1 – 2.993 5

USD 1 = CNY 4.710 3 – 4.733 9

Which quotation should the importer choose?

To determine which quotation is more cost-effective for import, the importer can apply the spot exchange rate in conversion. If the two quotations are converted into RMB, the result can be seen directly through comparison. According to the principle, the selling price should be applied in the quotation conversion of foreign currency into domestic currency.

The Swiss franc quotation can be converted into: $100 \times 2.993\,5 = 299.35$ RMB

United States dollar quotation can be converted into: $66 \times 4.733\,9 = 312.44$ RMB

From the comparison of these two results, it can be visibly seen that the RMB cost quoted by Swiss francs is lower than that quoted by United States dollars. If other factors are not taken into account, Chinese importers are more willing to accept the quotation by Swiss francs.

②Convert the import quotations of the same commodity in different currencies into the quotations in the same currency according to the spot exchange rate table in the international foreign exchange market, compare them and then choose the acceptable quotation.

As in the above case, the results can be seen directly after comparing the two quotations in dollars or Swiss francs.

Firstly, calculate the cross exchange rate between United States dollar and Swiss franc. According to the cross exchange rate cross-calculation principle, we can get:

USD 1 = CHF 4.710 3/2.9935 – 4.733 9/2.978 1 = CHF 1.574 4 – 1.589 6

The original quotation is 100 Swiss francs. If the quotation is in United States dollar, it should be 100/1.5744 = 63.52 United States dollars. therefore the Swiss franc quotation is more acceptable.

【Tasks】

(1) If the importer is willing to pay at sight, we refer to the foreign exchange quotation of a

Swiss bank at that time, so the Swiss franc is regarded as the local currency, and in the conversion of local currency into foreign currency, buying price of the bank should be adopted, therefore we should quote United States dollar price: 1 200 000/1.603 0 = 748 596.38 United States dollars.

(2) If the importer fails to follow conversion rules, he will lose:

1 200 000/1.603 0 − 1 200 000/1.604 0 = 748 596.38 − 748 129.68 = 466.7 United States dollar.

Task 4.3.2 Quotation techniques with forward payment

【Case for demonstration】

Case 4.15 Changzhou Diesel Engine Factory in our country plans to export a batch of diesel engines with the original quotation of 1 500 000 Swiss francs at the spot payment. Now the foreign trader demands United States dollars quotation, and the payment should be made 6 months after the shipment. It is known that the exchange rate of a Swiss bank at that time is:

Spot rate: 1 United States dollar = 1.603 0 − 1.604 0 Swiss francs, 6-month forward premium: 0.150 0 − 0.120 0.

Q: How much should we quote in United States dollars?

【Questions for discussion】

How to conduct foreign exchange conversion and quotation under forward payment?

【Relevant knowledge】

The so-called forward payment refers to a payment method stipulated in the contract to settle the claims and debts in a certain period after the transaction of import and export commodities. Since the formation of international buyer's market, a large number of import and export trade has adopted the way of deferred payment. It takes a long time from the conclusion of contract to the actual payment. What's more, the floating exchange rate system is widely adopted by countries all over the world. Therefore deferred payment brings exchange rate risks to both importers and exporters. When making quotations for export commodities with the forward payment, we should take into account the change both in the quote currency and in the payment currency to avoid risks and reduce losses caused by the change of exchange rate.

(1) Quotation skills of forward payment in the export business

Generally speaking, if an export commodity is quoted in hard currency and the other party demands forward payment, the exporter may quote at the original price. On the contrary, if the export price is quoted in soft currency and the other party demands forward payment, the export price can be added with a discount rate for a certain period on the basis of the original price, that is, the foreign price can be appropriately raised so as to ensure that the export income will not suffer losses.

①Direct forward exchange rate is used as the criterion of forward payment quotation.

In this way, we can judge the premium and discount of the forward exchange rate through the specific figures of the forward exchange rate and then choose the appropriate quotation according to the basic principles of quotation.

②In the exchange rate table, the forward discount (point) number can be used as the quotation criterion for the forward collection.

In the forward exchange rate table, premium currency is the currency of appreciation and discount currency is the currency of depreciation. In the export trade, for the forward payment of the importer, when the exporter makes a foreign quotation, if the quoted currency is at a premium, the quotation should be made at the original price. In the case that the quoted currency is at a discount, the forward discount points of soft currency shall be used as the standard for the markup amount of the goods in the deferred collection quotation of exporters to reduce the loss after discount.

Case 4.16 Our company exports machine tools to the United States at the original price of 2 000 United States dollars per unit under a three-month payment. At the request of the importer, we are now quoting Swiss francs whose forward rate will be at a discount three months later. The spot rate for United States dollars/Swiss francs in the New York foreign exchange market on the trading day is USD 1 = CHF 1.603 0 – 1.604 0. And the 3-month forward discount points are 135 ~ 140. How should the exporter quote?

Analysis: In the New York foreign exchange market, United States dollar is the local currency, while the Swiss franc is the foreign currency. From the forward point arrangement rising from 135 to 140, we can predict the Swiss franc forward exchange rate will fall. Therefore, when the export goods are quoted in Swiss francs, the forward discount points of Swiss francs should be added to the price.

The unit price of export commodities is calculated as:

Forward rate: USD 1 = CHF(1.603 0 + 0.013 5) – (1.604 0 + 0.014 0) = CHF 1.616 5 – 1.618 0

Since the quoted market is in New York where United States dollar is the local currency, we should follow the principle of "buying price adopted in converting local currency into foreign currency". And the price in the New York market is quoted in indirect quotation method, so the quoted price is 2 000 × 1.618 0 = 3 236 Swiss francs.

③The annual rate of discount in the exchange rate table can also be used as the quotation criterion for deferred collection.

Using the discount rate of soft currency in the exchange rate table as the criterion for commodity markup in the deferred collection quotation of exporters, our purpose is to analyze the markup range of export commodities receiving payment in soft currency. In practice, the discount currency in the forward exchange rate table is the currency with a depreciation trend, while the annual discount rate for the currency is the annual rate of depreciation of the discount currency (to premium currency). If the original quotation of the export commodities is in hard currency (i.e., premium currency), while the foreign trader requires the quotation in soft currency (i.e., discount currency), the exporter shall add the discount rate of a certain period to the converted price when converting the premium currency amount into the discount currency amount according to the spot exchange rate for the loss of the currency discount.

The annualized rate of currency discount (premium) figure is calculated as follows:

Annual premium (discount) rate = (forward rate-spot rate)/spot rate × (12 /month) × 100%

Case 4. 17 Great Wall food company exports frozen pork at the original price of 1 150 pounds per ton under a 6-months payment. At the customer's request, the quotation is changed to Danish kroner. The spot rate of Great Britain Pound against Danish kroner in the London foreign exchange market is GBP 1 = DKR 9.454 5 – 9.457, 6 months forward points 14.12 – 15.86, the annual rate = 3.17%.

Q: How much should the company quote in Danish kroner?

Analysis: calculation procedures and methods

a. Convert the pound price of a ton of frozen pork into Danish krone price. According to the exchange rate table of the London foreign exchange market, pound is the domestic currency, and Danish krone is the foreign currency. According to the buying price principle, the Danish krone price per ton of frozen pork should be 10 876.125 (1 150 × 9.457 5).

b. Since the business is to be paid in six months when Danish krone against Great Britain Pound is at a discount with an annual rate of 3.17%. If the annual rate is converted to a six-month rate, the discount should be at 3.17% × 6/12.

c. Add the discount rate of Danish krone against Great Britain Pound (that is, 3.17% × 6/12) to the price of goods to offset the loss of DKR value declining within 6 months. Therefore, DKR should be quoted as GBP instead, and the receivables after 6 months are: 1 150 × 9.457 5 × (1 + 3.17% × 6/12) = 11 048.511 DKR.

(2) The technique of accepting forward payment quotation in import business

In the import business, if it takes several months from the transaction to the payment, the forward exchange rate is the basis for determining the markup range of accepting soft currency (discount currency) for foreign quotations of one soft currency and one hard currency. The basic principle is that the markup range of the forward quotation cannot exceed the forward exchange rate of corresponding currencies, otherwise, it is acceptable to receive the hard currency quotation.

Case 4. 18 Nanjing Dawn Company imports mechanical parts from Switzerland, and the payment will be made 3 months later. The relevant exchange rates in Zurich Foreign Exchange Market are:

	the spot rate	3 months forward rate	
1United States dollar	2.000 0	1.980 0	Swiss franc

If the price is quoted as follows: 80 United States dollars per unit, 145 Swiss francs per unit.

Question: which offer is acceptable to us?

Analysis: We convert United States dollar quotation into the Swiss franc price based on the three months forward and then compare it with the original Swiss franc quotation or convert the Swiss franc quotation into United States dollar price based on the three month forward, and then compare it with the original United States dollar quotation.

a. Convert Swiss franc quotation in United States dollars quotation based on three months forward.

145 ÷ 1.980 0 = 73.23 (United States dollar) < 80 United States dollar

Therefore, it is more appropriate to accept the original quotation in Swiss francs.

b. Convert United States dollar quotation into Swiss franc quotation on a three months forward basis.

80 × 1.980 0 = 158.4 (Swiss francs) > 145 Swiss francs

Therefore, it is more appropriate to accept the original quotation in Swiss francs.

Both calculations show that it is more appropriate for us to accept the quotation in Swiss francs.

【Tasks】

(1) Calculate forward rate

Under the direct quotation method, the exchange rate moves in the same direction as the quotation number. Therefore, the forward exchange rate is calculated by subtraction when it is at a discount.

1 United States dollar = (1.603 0 − 0.150 0) × 1.453 0 − (1.604 0 − 0.120 0) × 1.484 0 Swiss francs = 1.453 0 − 1.484 0 Swiss francs

(2) Calculate quotation level according to the forward exchange rate

Since the forward dollar is at a discount, the loss of discount should be added to the currency quotation so as not to cause any loss to the quotation. Supposing we should quote United States dollars at X.

1∶ 1.4530 = X∶ 1 500 000

Therefore: X = 1 500 000 ÷ 1.453 0 = 1 032 346.87 United States dollar

Therefore, for three months forward payment, we should quote US $1 032 346.87.

【Extracurricular exercise】

(1) A businessman from Hong Kong is exporting 100 sets of products A at the original price of 3 000 United States dollar per set. Now the foreign importer wants to change the price to HongKong dollar. At that time, the exchange rate between United States dollar and Hong Kong dollar in the Hong Kong Foreign Exchange Market is the buying rate: 1∶ 7.789 0 and the selling rate: 1∶ 7.791 0. Questions: ①How much money should Hong Kong exporters quote in Hong Kong dollars for their exports? ②How many Hong Kong dollars will he lose if he doesn't quote this way?

(2) The base price for the export goods of our Hong Kong Renhe Commercial Co., Ltd. is 100 000 Hong Kong dollar. How can we make the quotation, if the customer requests us to quote in United States dollars? Suppose the exchange rate between United States dollar and Hong Kong dollar in the Hong Kong Foreign Exchange Market on that trading day is USD 1 = HKD 7.032 5 − 7.042 5.

(3) Suppose Hengde Trading Co. , Ltd. in our country imports watches at the unit price of CHF 100 and USD 66. Which quotation is more favorable for my importer? Suppose the spot exchange rates of Swiss franc and United States dollar against RMB in the Foreign Exchange Market of our country on the trading day are CHF 1 = CNY 2.978 4 – 2.993 3 and USD 1 = CNY 4.710 3 – 4.733 9 respectively.

Module 2 Foreign exchange exposure prevention and transfer ability

Task 5 Identify and analyze foreign exchange exposure

【Objects】

Be able to identify different types of foreign exchange exposure;

Be able to make a preliminary analysis on the components of foreign exchange exposure.

【Tasks】

Understand the concept of foreign exchange exposure;

Identify the main types of foreign exchange exposure;

Analyze the components of foreign exchange exposure.

【Requirements】

Correctly identify the types of foreign exchange exposure;

Be able to make a preliminary analysis on the components of foreign exchange exposure.

【Lead-in】

International speculators have driven down the Thai baht

In mid-May 1997, international currency speculators dumped Thai baht, causing its exchange rate against United States dollar to hit the lowest point in ten years. The Central Bank of Thailand had to intervene with billions of United States dollars to stabilize the baht temporarily, but at a high cost: foreign exchange reserves fell sharply by US $4 billion in May alone, what's more, interest rates soared, which brought heavy burden to businesses and resulted in rising prices, in addition, the stock market plunged. In order to stimulate exports and revive the economy, as well as curb the Thai baht speculation, on July 2, the Thai government decided to abandon its 13-year pegging to United States dollar and announced the Thai baht to float, consequently, the Thai baht depreciated by 18% that day with its depreciation rate once exceeding 100%. The speculative manipulation of international financial speculators is the direct cause of the sharp depreciation of the Thai baht, but the financial crisis in Thailand has its deep economic and social roots.

Its foundation of economic growth does not fit into its domestic economic structure. For more than a decade, Thailand's rapid economic growth has been mainly driven by exports, but its exports are relatively unitary, mainly focusing on electronic products, with its industrial structure very similar to that of other Southeast Asian nations. This economic structure makes Thai economy vulnerable to foreign competition from the international market. Affected by the world's weak demand for electronics in 1996, combined with the rising cost of export products caused by climbing domestic labor costs, export growth fell to 3% from 22.5% in 1995. Current-account deficit kept widening, amounting to $16 billion in 1996, accounting for more than 8% of the GDP. All these severely shook the foundation of the Thai baht stability, allowing international currency speculators to raise the devil.

Opening up the domestic market to foreign capitals does not suit the currency exchange rate system. In 1992, the Thai government lifted controls on the capital market and opened its domestic market to foreign investments, while maintaining the original policy of pegging Thai baht to United States dollar. In order to maintain the stability of Thai baht against United States dollar, Thailand has a long-term policy of high-interest rates, which attracted a lot of foreign capitals, but at the same time weakened the government's macro-control ability by adjusting the interest rate. Although Thailand's economy has slowed in recent years, to keep Thai baht stable the government has been unable to cut interest rates to stimulate economic growth. Since the interest rate of Thai baht is higher than that of United States dollar and its exchange rate is pegged to United States dollar, foreign investors who invest in Thai baht assets can not only get a higher interest rate but also do not have to bear the exchange rate risk. After the opening of the capital market in Thailand, a large number of foreign capitals entered the Thai market to earn interest rate spreads, and a considerable part of these foreign capitals is short-term hot money, which will quickly withdraw when there is any disturbance, which sets the stage for turmoil in Thailand's financial markets.

While introducing a large number of foreign investments, the Thai government failed to offer effective guidance to them. Due to the pegged exchange rate of Thai baht against United States dollar and high-interest rate policy, a large amount of foreign capitals flowed into Thailand, causing Thailand's external debt to jump from US $20 billion in 1992 to US $90 billion. Lacking timely guidance from the government, a large number of foreign capitals poured into the real estate market at the very beginning and attracted capitals from Thailand banks to the real estate market (accounts for about 30% of the total amount of bank loans). Constantly real estate companies constantly borrowed a lot of foreign debts against their houses, bringing about ever-rising prices in Thailand real estate market. Thus, instead of promoting the effective growth of the national economy, the inflow of foreign capitals increased the bubble elements in economic growth. Due to the change of basic economic conditions, the real estate price dropped sharply and the real estate developers became insolvent, which caused a sharp increase in the bad debts of banks (it is estimated that the total bad debts of Thai banks exceeded 20 billion dollars in 1997), which reduced the ability of the banking industry to resist financial risks.

At the beginning of the 1970s, major developed countries in the world abandoned the fixed exchange rate system and adopted the floating exchange rate system. Due to unstable exchange rate movements, foreign exchange risks are becoming increasingly serious. Especially in the late 1990s, the outbreak of the Asian financial crisis caused many Southeast Asian nations' currencies to depreciate sharply and these countries suffered huge losses. This puts important issues as preventing foreign exchange exposure and strengthening foreign exchange exposure management in front of the governments and every foreign exchange trader.

Task 5.1 Concepts and types of foreign exchange exposure

【Case for demonstration】

Case 5.1 Our import and export company planned to introduce large-scale projects from Japan in 2006. The total price and expenses were to be settled in yen in a total amount of 3 billion according to the requirements from the Japanese side. When the deal was signed in June, the exchange rate was 250 yen to 1 United States dollar. The total amount of 3 billion Japanese yen was almost worth 12 million United States dollars. Since then, the yen had been appreciated and by mid-April 2007, when the down payment was due, the yen had appreciated to 200 yen against 1 United States dollar. And the total amount of payment was worth 15 million United States dollars. We suffered a loss of US $3 million due to exchange rate fluctuations.

Case 5.2 In January, a Chinese financial institution issued bonds in Tokyo, Japan. The bonds are denominated in Japanese yen and issued in a total amount of 10 billion yen, with an annual interest rate of 8.7%, the maturity period of 12 years and the total repayment amount of 20.4 billion yen. According the foreign exchange management system and other conditions at that time, the financial institution needs to buy yen in dollars when it is due to clear yen. When issuing Japanese yen bonds, the exchange rate of United States dollar against Japanese yen was 1: 222.22, while the exchange rate of United States dollar against Japanese yen fell to 1: 109.89 when it's time to pay off. The yen rose as high as 102% against the dollar, which makes the Chinese financial institution suffer 102% (in dollars) in economic losses.

Case 5.3 A Japanese bank bought US $1 million and sold US $900 000 of it, and the rest amount was US $100 000. If the closing price on that day was 150 yen per dollar, the bank would get 15 million yen back from selling 100 000 dollars. If the dollar fell to 110 yen per dollar on the foreign exchange market the next day, the bank would only recover 11 million yen with a loss of 4 million yen.

【Questions for discussion】

What is foreign exchange exposure?

What are the characteristics of foreign exchange exposure?

What are the types of foreign exchange exposure?

【Relevant knowledge】

(1) The concept of foreign exchange exposure

Foreign exchange exposure refers to the possibility of an increase or decrease of the value of assets or liabilities expressed in foreign currencies caused by the unexpected change of foreign exchange rate in the foreign economic, trade and financial activities by an organization, economic entity or individuals within a certain period of time. The change could be a loss or an additional benefit. Foreign exchange exposure, in a broad sense, refers to the risk that has both the possibility of loss and the possibility of profit. In a narrow sense, it only refers to the risk that may bring losses to economic entities. Foreign exchange exposure in a broad sense will be discussed here.

Most foreign exchange risks have two sides. A loss on one side is a gain on the other side, but in foreign exchange options trading, they can also be one-sided.

(2) Characteristics of foreign exchange exposure

It can be seen from the concept that foreign exchange exposure has the following characteristics:

①It results from unexpected exchange rate movements. If the exchange rate fluctuations are predicted, they will be taken into account and handled by the decision-makers in advance. Therefore, they do not bring about foreign exchange risks. Only unexpected changes in the exchange rate will generate foreign exchange risk.

②It occurs when money is exchanged. It is generally believed that foreign exchange risks arise from the exchange between different currencies. As long as there is an exchange between currencies, foreign exchange risks will inevitably occur. When assets and liabilities denominated in foreign currency are converted into local currency, foreign exchange risks will occur due to exchange rate fluctuations.

③It results in changes in the enterprise anticipated cash flow. Indeed, some expected future cash flows in local currencies may also be exposed to foreign exchange risks. For example, a company sells products in domestic markets, and meanwhile competes with an American company. In this case, if the exchange rate of United States dollar changes, the changing exchange rate will naturally affect the present value of the expected future cash flows of the two companies through their changing production cost and sales price, consequently increasing or reducing the company's competitiveness with the company from the United States.

④It may bring both losses and benefits.

(3) Classification of foreign exchange risk

Economic entities engaged in international economic activities and the institutions in charge of the state's foreign exchange reserves usually receive and pay a large amount of foreign currencies, hold bonds and debts in foreign currencies internationally and express the value of their assets and liabilities in foreign currencies. Due to the different currencies used by different countries and the frequent changes of exchange rates between countries, foreign exchange risks may occur in the process of international economic exchanges. According to the source of risk and the ultimate degree of its influence, foreign exchange risk is divided into transaction risk, economic risk and accounting risk. The risk in business activities is trading risk, the risk in the results of business activities is accounting risk, and the risk in the expected operating income is economic risk.

①Transaction risk

Transaction risk, also known as settlement risk, refers to the risk resulting from the changing value of receivable assets and that in the local currency of payable debts due to exchange rate fluctuations in the international economic activities of an economic entity or individuals denominated in foreign currency for trade and non-trade transactions. Transaction risk refers to the risk of currency delivery of outstanding creditor's rights and debts after exchange rate fluctuations, which is the most common and one of the major foreign exchange risks encountered by international enterprises. It is mainly manifested the following three aspects of import and export trade, international lending and foreign exchange trading.

a. Transaction risk in import and export business

In the import and export trade of goods or services, it takes at least one month from the signing of the contract to the settlement of the payment for goods or services, sometimes half a year or even one year. In this process, fluctuating exchange rate will lead to the change of the local currency value of accounts receivable and accounts payable. And importers will face the risk of rising exchange rate of payment and exporters will face the risk of falling exchange rate of receipt. For the importer, if the trade contract is settled in foreign currency, and the foreign exchange rate in settlement is higher (lower) than it when the contract is signed, the importer will pay more (less) domestic currency, and consequently suffer a loss (gain benefits). For the exporter, if the trade contract is settled in foreign currency, and the foreign exchange rate at the time of settlement is higher (lower) than it is at the time of signing. The exporter will receive more (less) domestic currency and will benefit (suffer). In all, in international trade, the risk of foreign exchange settlement has existed since the beginning of commodity and service transactions until the final completion of trade settlement. Import and export enterprises are mainly faced with this kind of risk.

b. Trading risk in international indebtedness

In international credit activities denominated in foreign currency, during the period from the occurrence of claims and debts to the repayment of claims and debts, the creditor's income decreases and the debtor's payment increases due to the fluctuation of foreign exchange rate. And this risk constitutes the repayment risk of external claims and debts. That is to say, in the debtor-creditor relationship of a foreign currency, creditors are exposed to the risk of depreciation of exchange receipts at maturity, and debtors are exposed to the risk of appreciation of the currency they are due to repay. At the time of repayment of foreign currency claims and debts, if the foreign exchange rate rises, the creditor will receive more local currency and the debtor will pay more local currency, thus the debtor's liabilities increase. If the foreign exchange rate falls, creditors will receive less local currency and debtors will pay less local currency, creditors' assets decrease. In case 5.2, the financial institution of China issues yen bonds in the international financial market, which is a kind of financing behavior, so the institute is a debtor. When paying off, the exchange rate of yen against United States dollar rises, the financial institution has to pay more United States dollars and therefore suffer economic losses.

c. Trading risk in foreign exchange trading

In foreign exchange trading, the exchange rate will change from the signing date to the delivery date. The party of the forward foreign exchange contract to be delivered may need to exchange more or less currencies for another currency after the expiration of the contract, thus foreign exchange risk occurs and it constitutes the buying and selling risk of foreign exchange. For those enterprises buying foreign exchange, they risk paying more of their own currency when it comes due; while for those enterprises selling foreign exchange, they face the risk of foreign exchange appreciation and local currency depreciation. Therefore, foreign exchange banks are exposed to the risk of exchange rate fluctuations in the process of intermediary foreign exchange trading. When the bank holds a long position in foreign exchange, that is, the bank buys more foreign exchanges than it sells. If the foreign exchange rate rises (decreases), the local currency value of the foreign exchange assets held by the bank will increase (decrease). When a bank holds a short position in foreign exchange, it sells more foreign exchanges than it buys. If the foreign exchange rate rises (decreases), the local currency value of the foreign exchange liabilities held by the bank increases (decreases). When banks close their foreign exchange positions, they run the risk of receiving less or paying more in their own currency. Main performances of trading risks is shown in table 5.1.

Table 5.1 Main performances of trading risks

<table>
<tr><th></th><th>Trading party</th><th>Money of account appreciates</th><th>Money of account depreciates</th></tr>
<tr><td>Importer</td><td rowspan="3">Payer</td><td rowspan="4">Loss
(increased exchange cost)</td><td rowspan="4">Gain
(decreased exchange cost)</td></tr>
<tr><td>Non-trade payer</td></tr>
<tr><td>Debtor</td></tr>
<tr><td>Short position</td><td>Banks need to buy this foreign exchange</td></tr>
<tr><td>Exporter</td><td rowspan="3">Payee</td><td rowspan="4">Gain
(decreased exchange cost)</td><td rowspan="4">Loss
(increased exchange cost)</td></tr>
<tr><td>Non-trade receiver</td></tr>
<tr><td>Creditors</td></tr>
<tr><td>Long position</td><td>Banks need to sell this foreign exchange</td></tr>
</table>

②Accounting risk

Accounting risk, also known as assessment risk, transfer risk, charging risk, translation risk, conversion risk, book risk, refers to the economic entity's possible book losses or gains resulting from exchange rate fluctuations when certain assets, liabilities, revenues and expenses in foreign currencies in the balance sheet are converted into relevant items expressed in domestic currency in the enterprise accounting activities according to the provisions of the accounting system.

Suppose a multinational corporation in Hong Kong has a branch in country M. The balance sheet of the branch on December 31, 2008 is shown in table 5.2.

Table 5.2 The balance sheet of the branch in country M on December 31, 2008

Monetary unit: country M dollar(MD)

Asset	Amount	Liabilities and owner's equity	Amount
Cash	40 000		
Accounts receivable	60 000	Liabilities	100 000
Plant and equipment	120 000	Equities	160 000
Inventory	40 000		
Total	260 000	Total	260 000

When preparing consolidated financial reports, a multinational company in Hong Kong needs to convert their balance sheets into the sheets denominated in Hong Kong dollars at a specific exchange rate. Assuming that the current exchange rate is HKD 1 = MD 2.000 0, the converted balance sheet is shown in table 5.3.

Table 5.3 Balance sheet of a branch company in country M on December 31, 2008

Monetary unit: Hong Kong dollar

Assets	Amount	Liabilities and owners' equity	Amount
Cash	20 000		
Accounts receivable	30 000	Liabilities	50 000
Plant and equipment	60 000	Equities	80 000
Inventory	20 000		
Total	130 000	Total	130 000

If on March 1, 2009, the exchange rate becomes HKD 1 = MD 1.250 0, then the converted balance sheet is shown in table 5.4.

Table 5.4 Balance sheet of a branch company in country M on March 1, 2009

Monetary unit: Hong Kong dollar

Assets	Amount	Liabilities and owners' equity	Amount
Cash	32 000		
Accounts receivable	48 000	Liabilities	80 000
Plant and equipment	96 000	Equities	128 000
Inventory	32 000		
Total	208 000	Total	208 000

Accounting risk is a kind of accounting behavior, which occurs after business activities and mostly happens between the parent company of a multinational company and its subsidiaries. It measures the damage from the parent company's point of view. The resulting losses are not real losses at the time of actual delivery, but only losses on paper. Generally speaking, after a company is registered in a country, according to the principle of sovereignty, accounting statements must use the currency of the registered country as the accounting currency (that is, the reporting currency used by economic entities in the preparation of financial statements). In the process of accounting treatment and balance sheet preparation, enterprises cannot prepare in multiple currencies at the same time, but can only use their own currencies. They shall convert various assets and liabilities denominated in foreign currencies into those in their own currencies at certain exchange rates so as to collect and prepare comprehensive financial statements. Accounting risk does not involve cash flow or wealth transfer, and does not necessarily represent the change of the actual economic situation of the enterprise, because the actual foreign exchange transaction does not occur in the conversion process. However, once the exchange rate between the functional currency (that is, the money used by economic entities in their daily business activities) and the accounting currency changes, even if the amount of foreign currency assets and liabilities of enterprises has not changed, but in accounting, the number of bookkeeping currency will change correspondingly, thus causing the company to have book loss or gain. This paper loss can affect the results of the company's business report to shareholders and the public, which may lead to the fluctuation of the stock price of the enterprise, thus affecting enterprise operation and management, enterprise benefits evaluation and taxation.

For example, a multinational diesel engine company has a subsidiary in the United States. On June 1, 2007, the subsidiary purchased a batch of parts and components in the United States with the payment for goods of United States dollar 200 000 by check. All goods were put into storage and the exchange rate of United States dollar against RMB that day was 1: 7.27. By the accounting date (Dec. 31), the exchange rate was 6.9 yuan to 1 dollar. The RMB conversion loss of this batch of parts and components on the book was 74 000 yuan, namely $(7.27-6.9)\times$ 200 000 yuan.

③Economic risk

Economic risk, also known as business risk, refers to the potential risk that international enterprises' earnings measured in local currency will decrease in a certain period of time in the future due to unexpected fluctuations in foreign exchange rates.

Economic risk can be understood in two aspects. On the one hand, economic risk is targeted at unexpected changes in the exchange rate. The expected impact of exchange rate fluctuations on business operations can be taken into account by enterprises in advance in business decisions such as product pricing, so as to avoid economic risks. However, unexpected exchange rate fluctuations can affect the earnings of enterprises by affecting their production costs, sales prices, sales quantities and other aspects, bringing a great negative impact on the production and operation of enterprises. Enterprises can only take countermeasures after the event. On the other hand, economic risk is aimed at the expected future earnings of the enterprise. Economic risk is the overall forecast of the enterprise's future cash flow changes, focuses on the impact on the enterprise as a whole.

Economic risk centers on the analysis of business operation results, which is to predict, plan and conduct economic analysis by taking enterprises as the whole, involving all aspects of capital, marketing, procurement and production. Whether economic risks can be avoided largely depends on the company's ability to predict future exchange rate fluctuations, which is dynamic and subjective to a certain extent. The accuracy of economic risk prediction directly affects the strategic decisions of overseas enterprises in financing, sales, business objectives and production. Therefore, for enterprises, the loss caused by economic risk is much more important and serious than it is caused by accounting risk or trading risk. Differences between three exchange rate risks is shown in table 5.5.

Table 5.5 Differences between three exchange rate risks

Points of different	Economic risk	Trading risk	Accounting risk
Time of occurrence	Predict future earnings	In the process of business operation	In the results of business operation
Authenticity of gains and losses caused	Potential	Real	On the book
Perspectives to measure gains and losses	The whole enterprise	Single transaction	Parent company
Time to measure risks	Long term	One time	One time
Form of gains and losses	Dynamic and subjectivity	Objectivity	Objectivity

Task 5.2 Components of foreign exchange exposure and their correlations

【Relevant knowledge】

(1) Components of foreign exchange exposure

Foreign exchange risk generally consists of three factors: local currency, foreign currency and time. Receivables, borrowing and lending of monetary capitals and other foreign currency receipts and payments in business activities all need to be converted with the local currency, which is a common indicator to measure the economic effect of an enterprise. Time is an important factor from the final payment of the principal and interest on the loan, the closing of the transaction to the final receipt/payment of accounts. The exchange rate of foreign currency against local currency may change within a certain period of time, thus generating foreign exchange risks. If an enterprise does not use foreign currency in a foreign transaction but uses its local currency to conduct the receipt and payment, the transaction will not involve the conversion of foreign currency into domestic currency, so there is no risk resulting from the exchange rate fluctuation and therefore foreign exchange risk does not exist.

(2) The relationship among components of foreign exchange exposure

The time structure of a foreign currency account receivable and payable has a direct impact on the magnitude of foreign exchange risks. The longer the period, the more likely it is that exchange rates will fluctuate during that period and the larger foreign exchange risks. On the contrary, the shorter the period, the less likely it is that exchange rates will fluctuate and foreign exchange risks will be relatively smaller.

Foreign exchange risk is composed of time risk and value risk. The longer the time structure is, the greater the foreign exchange risk is. For example, shortening the time period of collecting or paying a foreign currency debt and changing the time structure can help to reduce foreign exchange risks, but the exchange rate fluctuation risk in the conversion of domestic currency against foreign currency still exists, so the value risk cannot be eliminated. Assuming an enterprise has a foreign exchange income after 60 days, both time risk and value risk exist there. Now the enterprise wants to transfer the time risk from the future to the present, it can borrow a foreign exchange loan with its amount equal to the future foreign exchange income and set the repayment date for the loan at 60 days, namely, use the foreign exchange income after 60 days to repay this foreign exchange loan. In this way, the time risk is eliminated, but the value risk affected by exchange rate fluctuations still exists. The loan in foreign currency can be sold for local currency and then invested in local currency, so as to obtain investment profits to offset the value risk. Therefore, to completely eliminate foreign exchange risk, we should eliminate both time risk and value risk.

To understand foreign exchange risk, we should pay attention to the following two aspects:

①The fact that one party does not have foreign exchange risk does not mean that the other party does not have foreign exchange risk either. When charging in local currency, domestic enterprises can get rid of foreign exchange risks, while foreign enterprises are still exposed to foreign exchange risks.

②Not all foreign exchange funds will have to bear losses from foreign exchange risks. In fact, losses are borne only by exposure to exchange rate movements. The more the position, the bigger the risk; and the less the position, the smaller the risk. Foreign exchange position refers to the balance position of all sorts of foreign currency accounts held by economic entities, namely the stock of its foreign currency assets or liabilities. The difference between foreign exchange assets and liabilities is the part of assets or liabilities exposed to foreign exchange risk, called an insured position

【Extracurricular exercise】

(1) British ABC Company imports a batch of medical equipment from Germany priced at 1 million United States dollars with payment due in 6 months. The market exchange rate at the time of signing is: GBP 1 = USD 1.8010. Calculated at this exchange rate, the British importer shall pay GBP 555 200 (1 000 000 ÷ 1.801 0 = 555 247). However, three months later, when ABC Company in the UK handled the payment, the dollar appreciates and the exchange rate becomes GBP = USD 1.702 0.

①Is there any foreign exchange risk in this transaction? If there is, it exists on which side?

②What kind of foreign exchange risk does this case belong to?

③How much should ABC pay in GBP?

④How much is the loss for the party at risk?

(2) A Chinese financial institution raised a sum of 10 billion yen in Japan to extend a 10-year fixed interest loan in United States dollars to a domestic enterprise at a rate of 7%. At that time, the dollar was traded at USD 1 = JPY 200, and the financial institution sold 10 billion yen for 50 million dollars. But ten years later the dollar was traded at USD 1 = JPY 150, the institution should repay 10 billion yen.

①What kind of foreign exchange risk can this case be classified into?

②How many United States dollars does the financial institution need to repay the 10 billion yen loan?

③What is the amount of risk the financial institution takes in the process of fund-raising?

(3) Our Dawn Trading Limited Company imports a batch of equipment from Germany at the price of 5 million euros with deferred payment for 3 months. When the contract is signed, the exchange rate between euro and RMB is 1 euro = 7.950 0 RMB yuan. When the payment is made three months later, the exchange rate between euro and RMB becomes 1 euro = 8.020 0 RMB yuan. Question:

①Is there any foreign exchange risk existing in this transaction? If there is, which side suffers losses?

②What kind of foreign exchange risk does this case belong to?

③How much RMB should our Dawn Trading Limited Company pay?

④What is the amount of loss for the party at risk?

(4) Dawn Trading Limited Company in our country signs a batch of commodity export contracts with the foreign trader with the amount of 1 million dollars. At the time of shipment, we receive a sight draft for $1 million from a foreign merchant. The exporter sells the sight draft to the bank at the current exchange rate (USD 1 = CNY 8.250 0) and receives RMB 8.250 0 million. If the payment is collected by collection at the time of shipment, it will take 2 months. If the exchange rate is USD 1 = CNY 8.235 6 upon the receipt of payment.

Question: What is the time risk and value risk that Dawn Trading Limited Company faces respectively?

Task 6 Precautions against foreign exchange exposure

【Objective】

Understand the meaning and strategy of foreign exchange risk management.

Be able to carry out preliminary foreign exchange risk prevention.

【Tasks】

Take precautions against foreign exchange risks.

【Requirements】

Be able to carry out preliminary foreign exchange risk prevention.

【Lead-in】

RMB against United States dollar falls below 7, and garment, toy and shoe companies are facing a slowdown in exports.

Yesterday, China Import and Export Fair was on its third day. According to previous experience, it should be at the beginning of the peak period of purchasing. However, a visit to the Liuhua Road Exhibition Hall revealed that the bustling and jostling scenes at the Canton fair failed to appear again. Some exhibitors had nothing to do, so they played computer games with their laptops. One exhibitor sighed, "Bleak! Customers today are even fewer than that on the first day of the exhibition in previous years."

(1) Textile and garment enterprises are facing the pressure of "three rates and two prices"

In the first two months of this year, China's textile and garment exports increased by only 5.7%, and Guangdong, the leading textile and garment export province, reported negative growth for the first time. Gloomy mood pervaded the whole industry. Hardly did they rejoice for the 50% surge of exports in March, RMB in early April plunged into the "6" era, which once again worried textile and garment foreign trade enterprises.

Mr Li Guoqiang said the biggest difficulties facing apparel and textile companies were the "three rates and two prices": exchange rates, interest rates, export rebate rates, raw material prices and labor prices.

In order to alleviate the pressure from RMB appreciation, enterprises generally solved the problem by signing short-term contracts and locking forward exchange rates. Some enterprises tried to shorten the performance period of the contract.

Replacing United States dollar with the euro or some other currency was also a popular solution. But Shantou Textile Import and Export Company's manager Xie believed that the euro also has the risk.

By comparison, raising prices was perhaps one of the most straightforward approaches. Li Keguo privately told the reporter, the quotation for their products on this Canton Fair increased 15%. Through a lot of hard bargaining, the transaction was generally concluded with an approximately 7% increase in the price. And the cost is, trade volumes were down 30% compared with the same period last year.

But the reporter noted that many enterprises were very cautious about their price increase with it ranging mostly between 3% and 5%.

Gao Zhiyan said, "The old customers are easier to accept price increase, so our strategy now is to maintain our old customers and try to avoid customer losses. But it will take some time for customers to realize that the price increase in Chinese manufacturing industry is irreversible."

Ms Wu of Hangzhou also expressed that, she would rather receive less orders now than run business at a loss: "Buyers are selecting manufacturers. In fact, manufacturers are also selecting quality customers."

(2) Shoe manufacturing companies in Guangdong are encountering "anti-dumping"

At this year's Canton Fair, footwear, a traditional export commodity of Guangdong province, also suffered coldness. One executive in charge of a leather shoes company in Dongguan told reporters that they tried to use non-United States dollar currencies when negotiating with buyers. If the buyer insisted on United States dollar settlement, the price based on September delivery would be increased by about 7%, and the price of goods delivered at the end of the year will be increased by about 10%.

(3) Price increase was stuck in a dilemma

Different from raising rice directly, singing agreements to maintain value was a preferred practice adopted by many shoe manufacturers. Since long-term contracts were signed between them and the buyers, and the delivery time was basically after the autumn, they tried their best to seek the understanding from the buyers when negotiating, and made an agreement on the maintenance clause in the contract. According to its stipulation, a forward settlement should be carried out at the current exchange rate, so as to lock the risk.

Under the influence of various factors such as the appreciation of RMB, many shoemakers have to increase prices of products to relieve their operation pressure. There is no denying that many small and medium-sized shoe manufacturers are still weak in their bargaining power, and they face such a deadlock: either suffering shrinking profits and even economic losses if prices are not raised or facing the risk of losing customers if prices remain unchanged.

(4) Exports to the EU increased in the first quarter but with declining unit prices

According to the statistics of Guangzhou customs, in the first quarter of this year, Guangdong exported 750 million pairs of shoes, down 20.1% compared with the same period last year. The exports were worth US \$2.32 billion, claiming an increase of 5.4%. Among them, 120 million pairs of shoes were exported to the European Union, growing by 34.4% with a total value of 370 million United States dollars, indicating an increase of 22.8%. But the average price (hereinafter referred to as the average price) was 3.1 United States dollars per pair, down by 8.7%.

While the overall export of Guangdong shoes dropped sharply, its export to the EU increased sharply, but the unit price continued to fall. "This could easily trigger a new anti-dumping case from the EU against our exports," one industry professional said in a worried voice.

Customs statistics show that the average unit price of exports by private enterprises and privately owned businesses is much lower than the average price of whole exports. In the first quarter, the average export price for private firms was just US \$1.68 a pair, less than 60% of the total average price. While the average export price of individual businesses is US \$0.35 / pair, less than one-fifth of the total average price. Compared with the same period last year, the average export prices of private enterprises and individual businesses fell by 15% and 48%

respectively.

Relevant people pointed out that shoes produced by the above mentioned two kinds of enterprises were of low grade with low added. They accounted for 55% of the total exported shoes, but their value only made up 28.9% of the total. Lacking competitiveness in international arena, our products had to join the competition by relying on low prices. Besides further squeezing profit margins, heavy discounts may also trigger an anti-dumping case by the European Union.

Task 6.1 the Concept and Strategy of Foreign Exchange Exposure Management

【Relevant knowledge】

(1) Foreign exchange risk management

The so-called foreign exchange risk management refers to that foreign exchange holders prevent, avoid or eliminate the risks in foreign exchange business operations by identifying, measuring and controlling risks, so as to reduce or avoid possible economic losses. The fluctuation in foreign exchange market makes it possible for international enterprises to encounter risk losses, which affects the production and business operation of enterprises, so it is necessary to put these risks under management and control.

In the management of foreign exchange risks, we should follow the principles of prevention by classification and risk minimization, namely we should correctly identify foreign exchange risks from companies and banks and take different precautions against different types of risks, while at the same time try to reduce foreign exchange risk positions as much as possible, and minimize risks by taking advantage of the forward exchange rate, futures options, offset arbitrage and other methods.

(2) Strategies for foreign exchange risk management

Based on different circumstances, foreign exchange risk management involves mainly three strategies listed below.

①Complete offset strategy

Completely offset strategy, namely the bank or enterprise the foreign conducts short selling on foreign exchange so as to eliminate foreign exchange exposure forehead in order to achieve the goal of avoiding risks. This strategy is mainly applicable to the situations of weak power, insufficient foreign experience, slow reaction to market information and big exchange rate fluctuations.

②Partial offset strategy

Partial offset strategy, that is, according to the forecast on the exchange rate, banks or enterprises take different measures for different risk related projects so as to eliminate only part of the amount of exposure and keep part of the amount of exposure for profit to seek profit opportunities (of course, it also entails the risk of possible losses). This is an active strategy for managing foreign exchange risks.

③No offset strategy

Completely no offset strategy, namely to expose foreign exchange exposure to foreign exchange risk without any offset. This strategy is suitable for the situation featuring slight fluctuating exchange rate and small volume of foreign exchange business, therefore it is a negative way to handle foreign exchange risks.

Task 6.2 Foreign exchange exposure prevention

Foreign exchange risk is a systematic risk with great uncertainty. In order to achieve the best efficiency of risk management at the minimum cost in our international business activities, we should have foreign exchange risk awareness and establish the foreign exchange risk management mechanism so as to make relevant scientific predictions and analyses, and design and select the feasible plans to prevent and reduce losses.

The prevention of foreign exchange risks refers to taking some corresponding measures to measure and control the possible foreign exchange risks in the future before their actual occurrences, so as to prevent, avoid or eliminate the risks and losses in foreign exchange business operations. At present, the most frequently used measures to prevent foreign exchange risks are listed as the following.

Task 6.2.1 Valuation in local currency

【Case for demonstration】

Case 6.1 Jiangsu Chengguang Foreign Trade Co., Ltd. has concluded a deal with an American merchant. The contract stipulated that we shall export 500 metric tons of a certain commodity at United States dollar 450 per metric ton. The exchange rate at the time of signing the contract was USD 1 = CNY 8.282 0, and the export RMB income shall be RMB 1 863 450 yuan ($450 \times 500 \times 8.2820 = 1863450$). However, according to the contract the goods shall be paid 2 months after shipment, so the settlement shall be conducted at the exchange rate quoted by the bank at the time of settlement, and the exchange rate after 2 months was changed into: USD 1 = CNY 8.275 0. Try to analyze the foreign exchange risks for both exporters and importers during the transaction.

【Questions for discussion】

What kind of currency is used by the importer? Is there any foreign exchange risk?

【Relevant knowledge】

When local currency is chosen for settlement and liquidation, there will be no exchange transactions between domestic and foreign currencies or between different foreign currencies. Therefore, no matter how the exchange rate changes, it is always the other party that bears risks. So by using the domestic currency pricing method we can completely avoid foreign exchange risks. Therefore, both importers and exporters strive to use their own currencies.

At present, the export of major developed countries is mostly priced at their local currencies, such as the United States, the United Kingdom, etc., and the settlement of Japanese enterprises' import and export in yen is also on the rise day by day. But not every country can do so in its own currency. This method is mainly applicable to countries where currencies can be freely converted.

Of course, in fact, settlement in local currency is to transfer the exchange rate risk from one party to the other party, which is generally unwilling to accept it. And this brings some difficulties to the trade negotiation. Therefore, only concessions on price or time limit to compensate for the risk of the other party can help complete the transaction.

Since the yuan is not yet a freely convertible currency, it has limited range of usage in international trade. Many import and export enterprises in our country have to use other foreign exchanges in foreign trade and technology and equipment import. When pricing at foreign exchange, we should pay attention to the principles of "consistency in borrowing, use and return" and "same currency in import and export", so as to reduce currency exchange risks.

【Tasks】

In case 6.1, for the American importer, the price is quoted in his local currency, so no matter how the exchange rate changes, for the import of this consignment he only needs to pay US $225 000 (450 × 500 = 22 500), without conversion between the foreign currency and the local currency, so no foreign exchange risk exists.

But for the exporter, due to the fluctuation of exchange rates, his final income after conversion into local currency becomes different, and foreign exchange risk does exist. In the above case, the exchange rate after two months is: USD 1 = CNY 8.275 0. At this time, the actual payment received for the export of the above goods is 1 861 875 yuan (450 × 500 × 8.275 0 = 1 861 875), which is 1 575 yuan less than the expected income when the contract is signed (1 863 450 − 1 861 875 = 1 575).

Task 6.2.2 Choice of invoicing currency

【Case for demonstration】

Case 6.2 An exporter from the US exports a consignment of goods to Japan, priced at 1 500 000 Japanese yen, which should be recovered in 10 000 United States dollars at maturity under the spot exchange rate of 1 dollar against 150 yen. However, when the payment is due, the exchange rate becomes USD 1 = JPY 125, and the US exporter can recover 12 000 dollars (1 500 000 ÷ 125 = 12 000), which is 2 000 dollars more than it when the contract is previously signed.

Case 6.3 Suppose in 2007, a German company imports 10 thousand pounds of goods under the spot exchange rate of 1GBP against 1.25 euros, but when the actual payment is made three months later, the exchange rate is GBP 1 = EUR 1.15. At this time, the company only needs to pay 11 500 euros for 10 000 pounds, saving 1 000 euros.

【Questions for discussion】

(1) The US exporter prices his consignment at Japanese yen, why can he get more dollars when the payment is due?

(2) The German import company prices the consignment in euros. Why can it pay fewer euros on the mature date?

【Relevant knowledge】

(1) The concept of choice of invoicing currency

The Choice of Invoicing Currency is a way of management aimed at reducing foreign exchange risks through the choice or collocation of contract currencies. Choosing the right pricing and settlement currencies is the most common and basic method for enterprises to avoid foreign exchange risks. In the international financial market, there exist not only local currency and foreign currency, but also hard currency and soft currency. In import and export trade, there are three pricing methods: ①in the importer's own currency; ②in the exporter's own currency; ③in the currency of the "third country". It is an important way to prevent foreign exchange risks for enterprises to choose an appropriate currency in the process of trading when they can't win over their local currency pricing.

(2) The application of the choice of invoicing currency

①Hard currency for export, and soft currency for import

In the international balance of payments, hard currency refers to the currency with stable exchange rate and appreciation trend. Soft currency refers to the currency with large exchange rate fluctuation and depreciation trend. To be specific, in international trade, enterprises should try their best to use hard currency for the settlement of export, and choose soft currency for import payment of foreign exchange and debts, that is, "accept hard and pay soft". In this way, when the time comes to settle the contract, exporters or creditors will receive more local currency due to the appreciation of the foreign currency, while importers or debtors will pay less local currency due to the depreciation of the foreign currency. At the same time, the chosen currency should be consistent with the foreign currency of the enterprise's current income and payment, so that exchange losses on foreign currency receivables will be offset by the exchange gains on accounts payable. In practice, however, currency selection is not a matter of wishful thinking, because both parties want to choose their own favorable currencies, thus passing on the exchange rate risk to the other party. Therefore, disputes or even deadlocks often arise between the two sides in their choice of currencies. And the principle of "receive hard, pay soft" is a flexible way to break these deadlocks and conducive to facilitate a deal. For example, we can adjust commodity prices, including the risk of exchange rate fluctuations in commodity prices, and at the same time, we can adapt the strategy of half-hard currency and half-soft currency, so that both buyers and sellers do not suffer from any loss, and can enjoy equality and mutual benefit together.

②Choose a convertible currency

In the international financial market, convertible currencies can be converted into any other kind of currencies without limitation. In international trade settlement, consignments are generally priced in foreign currencies such as United States dollar, euro, Japanese yen, British pound and other currencies. On the one hand, it enables enterprises to quickly convert into favorable currencies before unfavorable exchange rate fluctuations, thus helping them to transfer foreign exchange risks. On the other hand, these currencies feature good market liquidity and are convenient for settlement, allocation and application.

③Mix the soft and hard currencies

Under the floating exchange rate system, the exchange rate fluctuates frequently, and "soft" and "hard" currencies are relative, and temporary. This period of time it is a hard currency, but after a period of time, it may become a soft currency. In import and export trade, it is generally difficult for one of the two parties to bear all the exchange rate risks alone, when the payment is requested to be in a certain currency. A combination of hard and soft currencies, on the one hand, can make the exchange rate risks reasonably shared between the two parties and facilitate the transaction, and on the other hand, can help reduce foreign exchange risks because the effect of the rise of one currency can be offset to some extent by the fall of the exchange rate of another currency. At present, some import and export contracts with large amounts of money are priced in four currencies, two hard and two soft, which can offset the sharp rise and the sharp fall risk of different currencies. This prevents buyers and sellers from suffering heavy losses due to sudden changes in exchange rates when using the unitary currency. When combining hard and soft currencies, we should indicate the pricing currency, pricing time and the exchange rate of hard and soft currencies in the contract. Since most of China's import and export trade and foreign loans are priced in United States dollars, the stability of United States dollar exchange rate is directly related to the interests of Chinese enterprises. Meanwhile, EU countries have become important partners of China in foreign trade. The full circulation of euro in 2002 further affected the exchange rate of euro and the exchange rate between euro and RMB. Therefore, China's import and export enterprises should pay special attention to the trend of the exchange rate between United States dollar and RMB and between euro and RMB.

Task 6.2.3 Foreign exchange transaction act

【Relevant knowledge】

Ways to avoid foreign exchange risks are mainly as follows.

(1) Spot contract

Spot contract refers to the management method that a company with foreign exchange claims or debts signs spot contracts with foreign exchange banks to avoid foreign exchange risks. Spot transaction to prevent foreign exchange risks needs to realize the reverse flow of funds. If the enterprise has export proceeds to collect in the near future, it should sell corresponding foreign exchange positions in the hand; if the enterprise has import payment in the near future, it should buy corresponding spot foreign exchange. When using spot contracts to eliminate foreign exchange risks, we should make sure that the date of payment for goods and the date of settlement for foreign exchange transactions must be the same. Since spot foreign exchange transactions only fix the exchange rate on the third day in advance, their hedging effect is very limited.

Case 6.4 Company A in the United States will pay 10 000 pounds for imports within two days. The company can immediately purchase pounds at the spot exchange rate of GBP 1 = USD

1. 520 0/10. Two days later the company pays the bank in dollars, the bank pays the company in pounds, and the company pays the exporter in pounds.

A company purchased GBP 10 000 for USD 5 210, realizing the reverse flow of foreign exchange funds and eliminating the exchange rate risk within two days.

(2) Foreign currency futures

The future contract refers to the management method of reducing or eliminating foreign exchange risks through trading foreign exchange futures by companies with foreign exchange claims or debts. This is the method of buying (selling) futures contracts with the same amount in the futures exchange as in the spot market at a specific time in the future, but traded in the opposite direction, in order to compensate for the actual price risk caused by price changes in the spot market at a certain time in the future by selling (buying) futures contracts.

In order to prevent the losses caused by less payment resulted from the future depreciation of the settlement currency, the exporter may sell the futures contract first upon signing the contract, and then buy the futures contract for hedging the risks. The gains (losses) from "selling first, buying later" in the futures market can offset the losses (gains) in the spot market. In order to prevent the losses caused by overpayment result from the future appreciation of the pricing and settlement currency, the importer should buy the futures contract in the futures market and sell the futures contract when the contract is due for hedging when singing foreign trade contract. If the settlement currency appreciates (depreciates) in the future, the gains (losses) by "buying first, selling later" in the futures market can offset the losses (gains) from buying settlement currency in the spot market. In this way, both importers and exporters can reduce foreign exchange risks.

The choice of foreign exchange futures also depends on the reliability of exchange rate prediction and credit risk. However, futures have a unique margin system, which neither limits risks nor returns. That is to say, in case of non-performance, a security deposit shall be paid. Therefore this hedging tool can meet the needs of "moderate" or "conservative" risk management strategies.

Case 6. 5 A company from the United States exports goods to Britain for one million pounds. The American exporter can sell six-month sterling futures on the foreign exchange futures market to protect themselves against the fall in the pound six months later. If the spot rate in the foreign exchange market at that time falls, so will the price of the pound in the futures market. In this way, the American company can buy back the sterling futures contract at a lower price, offsetting the loss in export value with the profits on the futures (the difference between selling the sterling futures at a higher price and buying the sterling futures at a lower price).

(3) Foreign exchange option

Option contract refers to the management method that companies with foreign exchange claims or debts trade foreign exchange options through the foreign exchange options market to reduce or eliminate foreign exchange risks. In other words, by signing contracts in the foreign exchange options market, one can obtain the right to buy or sell a certain amount of foreign exchange within a certain period of time at an agreed price and pay a certain amount of option premium.

Exporters buy put options to avoid depreciation of receivables. If the market exchange rate falls below the agreed rate of the option contract upon recovery, the exporter chooses to fulfill the contract and sell the foreign currency received at the higher agreed rate. If the market rate rises above the agreed rate plus the option premium (ignoring the commission), instead of fulfilling the contract the exporter sells export proceeds at a higher market price. Importers buy call options to avoid losses from the appreciation of the accounts payable. If the market exchange rate is higher than the agreed rate of the option contract when the contract is due for payment, they can choose to perform the contract and buy the foreign currency required for payment at the lower agreed rate. If the market rate falls below the agreed rate minus the option premium (ignoring the commission), they can choose not to perform the contract and buy the foreign currency required for payment at the lower market rate.

From the perspective of avoiding foreign exchange risks, foreign exchange options are the extension of foreign exchange forward contracts and foreign exchange futures. But the foreign exchange forward contract is unchangeable. Even if the exchange rate moves in a favorable direction before the expiration of the contract, the contract must be fulfilled upon agreement, so that relevant trading parties have to lose the exchange gains that could have been obtained. After signing a currency futures contract, although they could cancel the original contract by a reverse transaction before its expiration when the exchange rate moves toward the favorable direction so as to continue to enjoy the following benefits. But security deposits must be paid for the futures contract, and profits and losses must be calculated according to the settlement price on a daily basis with additional margins if necessary, otherwise, futures contracts that have been made will be auctioned off. Options, on the other hand, provide relevant parties with free choices. The buyer may give up his fulfillment of the contract, so as to obtain unlimited benefits from the fluctuating market. Instead of clearing options on a daily basis, you only need to pay the premium, which is called option premium or insurance premium, which is paid by the buyer to the seller when the contract is made so as to obtain the option to fulfill the contract. Therefore, this hedging tool can be applied to "aggressive" style strategies for risk management. In case 6.5, if the US exporter uses foreign exchange option contracts, he can buy a 1 million pound put option at the agreed exchange rate of 1 pound = $1.50 after paying a certain amount of premiums. On the expiration date of the contract, if the exchange rate of Great Britain Pound falls below US $1.50, the enterprise can fulfill the contract; but if the exchange rate of Great Britain Pound rises above US $1.55, the enterprise can abandon the contract and sell sterling directly in the foreign exchange market. The cost paid by the enterprise is the option fee.

(4) Currency swap

Currency swap refers to method with which both parties agree to exchange different currencies with the same duration and the same interest in accordance with the agreed terms in a certain period of time in the future and are responsible for foreign exchange transactions for borrowing principal and interest payable by the other party and exchange the principal again when the transaction is due. In currency swap transactions, because the exchange rate is predetermined, traders do not have to bear the risk of exchange rate fluctuation and thus it plays the role of hedging against risks. Generally speaking, the notional principals of the currencies exchanged between two parties should be equal to each other at the spot rate at the beginning of swapping. Currency swaps are suitable for debit and credit occasions where both parties have the same identity (i. e., both are borrowers or lenders). The swap is based on the current spot exchange rate, or on a predetermined forward rate with the amount of exchange rate agreed upon by both parties and comparatively long time period. Therefore, it is much simpler to avoid long-term foreign exchange risks than futures and forward contracts. In addition, it features low cost and flexibility in enterprise financing. Therefore, it is widely adopted among enterprises.

Case 6.6 Suppose both company A and company B want to borrow a sum of money. Company A plans to borrow pounds while company B wants to borrow dollars. Their borrowing costs in dollars and pounds are listed respectively as follows:

	United States dollar	Great Britain Pound
company A	5%	8%
company B	7%	6%

How can these two companies use swap transactions to prevent foreign exchange risks?

Obviously, company A has an advantage in borrowing dollars, while company B has an advantage in borrowing pounds. After negotiation, company A and company B make a currency swap transaction: A borrows United States dollar 1.5 million at the interest rate of 5%, B borrows Great Britain Pound 1 million at the interest rate of 6% (assuming the exchange rate at that time is GBP 1 = USD 1). Then they swap their currencies (the term is 5 years, interest swap happens every half year and principal swap happens at the end of the term). Through the swap, each side saves 2% in the cost of borrowing. Since the nominal principal at both the beginning and the end of the term remains the same, the exchange rate risk is avoided.

(5) Swap transaction

The swap transaction method refers to the management method that enterprises sign sale or purchase contracts for forward foreign exchanges to avoid foreign exchange risks while signing spot foreign exchange purchase or sale contracts. It requires importers and exporters to simultaneously conduct two foreign exchange transactions with the same amount and different delivery periods in opposite directions, so as to eliminate time risk and value risk. It is a typical hedging method in international credit business.

Case 6.7 A company in China will receive a payment of 1 million United States dollars one month later, and will spend another 1 million United States dollars two months later. Then the company can sign a swap contract with the foreign exchange bank to sell 1 million United States dollars with one month term and buy 1 million United States dollars with two-month term later. Suppose: the forward exchange rate of 1 month is: \$1 = ¥7.365 0/70; The forward exchange rate for the 2-month period is: \$1 = ¥7.267 0/70. The company can obtain the swap income while preventing risks at the same time.

Task 6.2.4 Matching and pairing

【Case for demonstration】

Case 6.8 When a company has a payment of US $100 000 which is due in three months, it should try to export goods of the same amount of United States dollars, so that an equal amount of United States dollars receivable after three months can offset United States dollars payable after three months, thus eliminating foreign exchange risks.

【Questions for discussion】

What method should the company choose to prevent foreign exchange risks?

【Relevant knowledge】

(1) Matching

The so-called Matching method refers to a management method in which a company eliminates or mitigates exchange rate risks by bringing foreign currency receipts and payments to balance when arranging foreign businesses. A way to do this is to create a foreign exchange flow in the same currency at risk, with the same amount, the same duration but in the opposite direction. In this way, foreign exchange funds come in and out, evening up foreign exchange positions, thus avoiding foreign exchange risks.

The Matching approach has a highly limited scope for application, because it's very difficult for an international company to achieve a "Perfect Matching" of currencies receivable and payable on a per-transaction basis, meanwhile, this method heavily relies on the close co-operation among the purchasing, sales and finance departments.

In practice, foreign exchange risks can also be reduced or avoided if the currencies received and paid in foreign transactions are the same, as well as those borrowed, used, received and returned. This method can be used in trades with a large sum of money and one-off foreign exchange risks.

(2) Pairing

The so-called pairing method means that when facing foreign exchange risks of a certain currency, the enterprise can create a reverse flow of another currency associated with this currency to eliminate its foreign exchange risks. The idea is that when a transaction occurs the enterprise hedges against exchange risks by taking advantage of the flow of funds in another currency in the opposite direction, but with the same amount of money and the same period of time. The two currencies as a pair are usually tied together by some institutions using a pegged exchange rate. When a currency with foreign exchange risks appreciates or depreciates against the local currency, the currency of the third country in the pair also appreciates or depreciates accordingly. Pairing method works when the exchange rate of the two currencies as a pair often indicates a highly positive correlation.

The difference between the matching method and the pairing method is that the former is based on the hedging of the same currency, while the latter is based on the hedging of two different currencies. The pairing method is more flexible and easier to use than the matching method, but it cannot eliminate all risks.

Task 6.2.5 Other methods to prevent foreign exchange exposure

【Relevant knowledge】

(1) Choose an appropriate settlement method

Based on the real situation, enterprises can choose appropriate ways of settlement to reduce foreign exchange risks. In order to receive foreign exchange safely and timely, the exporter shall carefully and flexibly choose an appropriate way of settlement according to the actual business conditions and the credit standing of the other party, and may prevent risks by means of sight L/C, usance L/C and collection. Generally speaking, L/C at sight is most consistent with the principle of safe and prompt receipt of exchange, followed by usance L/C, D/P, D/A and remittance. Payment by L/C is generally accepted in import business. Depending on the specific situation, the combination of letter of credit and collection method, letter of credit and remittance, remittance and bank guarantee can also be adopted.

(2) Barter trade

Barter trade is a method of management that eliminates foreign exchange risks by directly linking imports and exports in the form of goods exchanges, forming a commodity swap transaction. It is characterized by the fact that in the clearing process of a transaction, no actual payment of currency is involved, and the parties exchange commodities at a predetermined price, so that none of the parties in the transaction bears exchange rate risks. In this way, the currency of account and the currency of settlement are the same, so foreign exchange risks can be avoided. In the period of drastic fluctuations of exchange rates, barter trade can be used as a means for importers and exporters to prevent foreign exchange risks, but it is difficult to fully realize it. The goods to be sold by both sides should meet each other's needs in quality, quantity, time and other aspects.

(3) Price adjustment

The price adjustment method refers to the management method that importers and exporters allocate foreign exchange risks into the price through adjusting the prices of import and export commodities in the international trade negotiations, so as to reduce the foreign exchange risks caused by the use of foreign currency settlement. The price adjustment method cannot eliminate foreign exchange risks, but can only transfer foreign exchange risks. In the specific practice, exporters tend to adopt the method of hedging with markup, while importers tend to adopt the method of holding down prices.

①Hedging with markup

In the export, when exporters accept soft currencies, they can increase the price of export commodities to spread the exchange rate loss into the price of export commodities, so as to transfer the possible losses caused by the depreciation of soft currencies. According to international practice, the formula for calculating spot markup in international trade is:

Price of goods after markup = original price × (1 + expected depreciation rate of foreign currency)

The calculation formula of forwarding transaction hedging is:

The unit price of the commodity after markup = the original unit price × (1 + expected depreciation rate of foreign currency + interest rate) × the number of issues

②Hedging with markdown

In the import trade, after receiving the hard currency, the importer excludes the exchange rate loss from the price of the imported goods by lowering the price of the imported goods, so as to reduce the foreign exchange risks caused by the appreciation of the hard currency.

Unit price of goods after price reduction = original unit price × (1 - expected foreign currency appreciation rate)

The forward markdown can be calculated as follows:

The unit price of the commodity after price reduction = the original unit price × (1 - expected foreign currency appreciation rate + interest rate) × the number of issues

Task 7 Transfer of foreign exchange exposure

【Objective】

Master the method of transferring foreign exchange risks.

【Tasks】

Transfer of foreign exchange risks.

【Requirements】

Be able to shift the foreign exchange risks already formed preliminarily.

The transfer of foreign exchange risks means that after the occurrence of foreign exchange risks, some corresponding measures should be taken to measure and control the existing foreign exchange risks, so as to reduce or eliminate the risks and losses in foreign exchange businesses. At present, the common measures to shift foreign exchange risks are as follows.

Task 7.1 Forward contract

【Case for demonstration】

Case 7.1 SMITH company of the United States imports a consignment of goods from Japan at the price of 100 million Japanese yen, and the payment will be made in three months. With a spot rate of \$1 against 100 yen and a three-month forward rate of \$1 against 90 yen, the company decides to buy 100 million forward yen at \$1 111 111.11 to prevent a sharp appreciation of the yen. The company pays 111 111.11 yen more than it does when the contract is signed, which is the cost of forwarding trading. After three months, the company doesn't have to worry about rising costs, no matter what happens to the exchange rate.

Case 7.2 JOHN company of the United States exports goods to the United Kingdom. The two sides agree to price and settle the goods in pounds sterling. The consignment of goods is priced at 100,000 pounds. When the trade contract is signed, the exchange rate is 1 pound = 1.55 United States dollars, the payment amounts to $155 000. Worrying about the depreciation of Great Britain Pound six months later, the exporter sells 100 000 pounds to the bank at the forward exchange rate of 1 pound against $1.50, so as to receive $150 000 when the time is due. That's $5 000 less than when the contract is signed, which is what it costs the company to protect itself against foreign exchange risks by trading forwards.

【Questions for discussion】

1. How will American SMITH company transfer the risk of foreign exchange?
2. Is the approach of American JOHN company appropriate?

【Relevant knowledge】

The forward contract method of foreign exchange refers to the kind of management through which companies with foreign exchange claims or debts sign contracts with foreign exchange banks to buy and sell forward foreign exchange contracts to avoid foreign exchange risks. Through forward foreign exchange transactions, companies can determine the exchange rate and transaction amount in advance, which is the most direct and common means to prevent foreign exchange risks in the foreign exchange market, and therefore is widely used in many countries.

When the enterprise predicts that it will receive or pay a foreign currency payment at a certain date in the future, it will first sell or buy the currency in the forward foreign exchange market, fixing the unrealized exchange rate. Regardless of the changes in the exchange rate over the period of the contract, the enterprise can be certain that it will be able to receive or pay a certain amount of its domestic currency in the future. Forward exchange rates have been agreed upon at the time of signing and are not affected by changes in the exchange rate on the delivery date. Namely, through the forward foreign exchange contracts, enterprises transfer the time structure from the future to the present, and realize the write-offs of local and foreign currencies within the prescribed time limit, thus eliminating all foreign exchange risks.

The key to decide whether this hedging tool should be adopted is the prediction of future exchange rates. If the exchange rate prediction is wrong, the risk is locked but the gains are lost. Therefore, this hedging tool is often used in conservative style management strategies.

Task 7.2 Currency preservation

【Case for demonstration】

Case 7.3 Assume an export contract worth US $900 000, whose value is kept in Danish kroner, British pound and Singapore dollar. The weight they occupy is 1/3 each, and the exchange rates of United States dollar against them is set as: USD 1 = DKK 5, USD 1 = GBP 0.5, USD 1 = SGD 2. By the time of settlement, the exchange rates of the three currencies become USD 1 =

DKK 5.5, USD 1 = GBP 0.45, and USD 1 = SGD 1.8. In this way, the contract should be re-adjusted according to the exchange rate changes at that time, so as to achieve the purpose of maintaining value.

Case 7.4 Our export enterprise is scheduled to receive US $1 million in import and export payment three months later. To protect itself against a fall in the dollar three months later, the company added hedging clauses to its contracts with importers, setting United States dollar as the money of account, the yuan as the value of currency preservation, and fix the exchange rate between these two currencies as follows: USD 1 = CNY 8.275 0. The exchange rate fluctuation between USD and RMB is 1% (i. e., USD 1 = CNY 8.265 0). If the exchange rate changes beyond this range at the time of payment after 3 months, the original price shall be adjusted according to the agreed exchange rate.

【Questions for discussion】

How does the export contract achieve the goal of maintaining value?

【Relevant knowledge】

If when signing the import and export trade contract, due to the traditional business practices or other reasons, two parties choose the soft currency that may have a downward trend to price the goods, both parties can negotiate to conclude the appropriate value terms. The amount of its creditor's rights shall be preserved in a relatively stable currency or comprehensive monetary unit. The payment will be adjusted according to the exchange rate of the currency value against the currency of payment at that time when the payment is due to prevent the risk of exchange rate fluctuations. The ways frequently used to store value are listed below:

(1) Store value with integrated monetary units

Enterprises choose a comprehensive monetary unit to maintain the value of the contract. Since the integrated currency unit is composed of a certain proportion of hard currency and soft currency, the exchange rates of various currencies rise here and fall there. Therefore the overall average volatility will not be large, and exchange rate risks will be dispersed, thus effectively avoiding foreign exchange risks. When signing a trade, credit and investment agreement, if relevant parties determine to pay in a particular currency. Then in accordance with the prevailing market exchange rate, the currency will be converted into corresponding "basket of currencies" amount, which will be converted into the corresponding amount of currency of account in payment according to the exchange rate in the foreign exchange market again when the settlement is due. At present, special drawing Rights (SDRs) are widely used in the "basket of currencies". It is a basket of currencies with a weighted average value of major currencies such as United States dollar, pound, euro and yen. Its value is relatively stable and it is an ideal tool of preserving value.

(2) Gold proviso clause

When a contract with a long term and a large amount of money is concluded, the amount in the currency of payment shall be converted into gold according to the prevailing gold market price. When the actual payment date comes, if the gold market price rises, the amount in currency of payment shall increase correspondingly; otherwise, it decreases correspondingly. For example, if an exporter signs an export contract and with a payment of 1 million United States dollars. Suppose at that time, the gold content of US $1 is 1 gram of pure gold, then 1 million United States dollar will be converted into 1 million grams of gold. When the payment for goods is settled, the gold content of 1 United States dollar is 0.95 g, and 1 million grams of gold can be converted into 1.052 6 million United States dollars, so the importer should pay 1.052 6 million United States dollars. Gold hedging clause used to be a common way of hedging in international economic contracts. But because this clause is only used in the period of the fixed exchange rate, the currencies of various countries have been decoupled from gold, and the price of gold itself is not stable, so it is seldom used now.

(3) Exchange rate proviso clause

The contract stipulates that the price shall be quoted in hard currency and the payment shall be made in hard currency, specifying the exchange rate of the two currencies at that time. During the fulfillment of the contract, if the exchange rate of the payment currency falls, the amount in the contract shall be adjusted in equal proportion based on the exchange rate of the currency of payment on the payment date. In this way, the amount of the currency of price received will be the same as that when the contract is signed, and the loss of the falling currency of payment can be compensated. Depending on the specific business situation, you can choose one of the three types.

①Set the price in hard currency and make the payment in soft currency. The payment is made at the current exchange rate of the currency of price against the currency of payment, so as to ensure that the income does not decrease.

②Soft currency is used for both pricing and payment. However, the price of this currency against another hard currency is specified at the time of signing the contract. If it changes at the time of payment, the original price shall be adjusted according to the fluctuation of the rate of exchange.

③Determine an agreed exchange rate for the soft currency and the hard currency. If the exchange rate of these two currencies at the time of payment exceeds a certain range of agreed exchange rate, the original price shall be adjusted. This type is a flexible use of the first two types, and suitable for customers with frequent mutual exchanges, so as to promote and develop long-term economic cooperation between the two sides. If the depreciation rate of the soft currency against the hard currency is very low, for instance only 1.0% or 1.5%, the price will not be adjusted to show the other side concession and care; if the depreciation of soft currency exceeds 1.0%~1.5%, the original price will be adjusted.

Task 7.3 Leads & Lags

【Case for demonstration】

Case 7.5 A multinational company with a parent company in America, a subsidiary in

Britain and a subsidiary in Germany is forecasting a rise in the euro against the dollar and a fall in the pound against the dollar. In order to eliminate foreign exchange risks, how do transnational corporations use an early settlement of foreign exchange and delayed settlement of foreign exchange in their import and export businesses?

【Questions for discussion】

How will the company transfer foreign exchange risks?

【Relevant knowledge】

Early payment or delayed payment is also called leads and lags, which refers to the method where the economic entity changes the time for receipt and payment of foreign exchanges through early payment or delayed payment according to their own predictions on the currency exchange rate movement with the aim to reduce foreign exchange risks.

Generally speaking, in the export, if the exchange rate of the currency of price is expected to rise, the domestic currency depreciates, while the foreign currency appreciates, then the exporter can try to delay the export of goods, extend the term of the export draft or encourage the importer to postpone the payment. On the contrary, if the exchange rate of the quoted currency is expected to decline, it is necessary to sign export contracts with foreign businessmen as soon as possible and try to collect foreign exchanges in advance. In the import transaction, if the importer predicts that the exchange rate of the settlement currency will rise, the importer should try to buy the required goods in advance, or make the payment in advance so as to try to pay the foreign exchange in advance. On the contrary, if the exchange rate of the settlement currency is predicted to decline, the importer may postpone the purchase of goods from abroad or ask for deferred payment.

In the case of advance payment, debtors who pay for foreign exchanges usually get a certain amount of discount. The discount rate is usually negotiated by both the importer and the exporter. In this sense, an advance payment is equivalent to an investment, and receiving payment in advance is similar to a loan.

Task 7.4 BSI and LSI

【Relevant knowledge】

(1) BSI method

BSI (borrow-spot-invest) method, namely, borrowing-spot foreign exchange transaction—investment method, refers to the management method where the economic entity with foreign exchange receivables or payables avoids foreign exchange risks through the combination of borrowing, spot foreign exchange transaction and investment.

As a comprehensive way of hedging against risks, BSI can completely eliminate foreign exchange risks.

①For an enterprise with accounts receivable

In order to prevent exchange rate fluctuations, the company first borrows the same amount of foreign currency as the foreign currency receivable, and transfers the time structure of foreign exchange risks to the current exchange day, so as to eliminate time risks. At the same time, value risk is eliminated by selling borrowed foreign currency to the banks in spot transactions to convert it into local currency. There are costs associated with risk elimination, however, a part of the interest and other costs of borrowing can be offset by investment income which comes from the local currency deposited in the bank or put in investment. When the receivables are due, the foreign exchange received will be used to repay the bank loans.

②For an enterprise with accounts payable

In order to prevent foreign exchange risks, the company borrows the corresponding amount of local currency from the bank and purchases the foreign currency at the time of settlement from the bank, eliminating the value risk. Then it puts the purchased spot foreign currency into the international financial market for short-term investment with the term the same as that of foreign exchange accounts payable, which changes the time risk. When the payment term is due, the enterprise shall collect the foreign currency investment and make payment to the exporter. Income from foreign exchange investment can offset some expenses.

Although the above procedures for eliminating the exchange rate risks of accounts receivable and accounts payable all fall in three steps of borrowing, spot foreign exchange transaction and investment with the same result of making the income and the expenditure completely offset, the order of currency order different. The former features were borrowing foreign currency and investing in local currency while the latter is characterized by borrowing local currency and investing in foreign currency.

Case 7.6 A company in our country has an account receivable of $100 000 after 60 days. The company immediately borrows $100 000 for a 60-day period from a bank to protect itself against future losses on the dollar. After changing the time structure of the foreign exchange risk, the company converts the dollar into the local currency at the bank to eliminate the value risk. Suppose the spot exchange rate of the bank is USD 1 = CNY 7.360 0 – 7.377 0. The company shall convert United States dollar into RMB 736.0 (100 × 7.360 0) thousand yuan and then invest the money for a period of 60 days. After 60 days, it can repay the $100 000 which is due to the bank and use the gains from the investment to offset the interest on the loan.

(2) LSI method

LSI (lead-spot-invest), namely, early receive-payment and spot foreign exchange transaction and investment method, refers to the way of management where an economic entity with receivables or payables tries to avoid foreign exchange risks by combining payment in advance, spot foreign exchange transaction and investment after obtaining the consent of debtors or creditors.

LSI method is also a comprehensive hedging method, which can completely eliminate the foreign exchange risks. It can be practiced in two different situations.

①For an enterprise with foreign exchange accounts receivable

After obtaining the consent from the debtor, the company asks him to pay in advance with a certain amount of discount to eliminate the time risk. After the receipt of foreign currency receivables, the company immediately converts the foreign exchange collected into the local currency through spot transactions, thereby eliminating the value risk. In order to obtain certain benefits, the company reinvests the local currency converted back, and the resulted gains can fully or partially offset the discount loss caused by the exchange in advance.

Case 7.7 A Japanese company has an account receivable of \$100 000 from the American company after 90 days. In order to prevent exchange rate fluctuations, the company asks the American company to pay off the account within 2 days with a certain discount (the specific amount of discount is not considered at present) after being informed consent from the American company. The \$100 000 payment is immediately converted into the local currency through spot transactions and invested in the Japanese currency market. The time risk is eliminated by prepayment, and the value risk is eliminated by conversion into the local currency.

LSI and BSI are basically similar for the accounts receivable, but the difference is that with BSI borrowing money from the bank comes first, the borrowing interest becomes the cost, however, LSI requires the payer to pay the goods in advance by offering a certain discount which is the cost.

②For an enterprise with foreign exchange accounts payable

The company borrows the local currency from the bank, and then signs a spot contract with the bank to convert the local currency into the foreign currency. At last, the company pays the debt in advance with the foreign currency bought, and obtains a certain discount from the creditor, which can fully or partially cover the loss resulting from the interest of the loan.

The above procedures for eliminating the exchange rate risks of foreign exchange accounts receivable and accounts payable all fall into three steps. The foreign currency income and expenditure are completely offset with each other, and the cost paid can be fully or partially offset by the investment income. The difference between the two methods lies in that the former asks the payer to pay in advance, exchange foreign currency for local currency, and invest in local currency while the latter requires enterprises to borrow the local currency, exchange local currency for foreign currency, and pay in advance.

To sum up, among all the measures to prevent foreign exchange risks, some are adopted before risks occur, while others are adopted after risks already exist. Some risk prevention techniques can only eliminate the time risk, some can only eliminate the value risk, and some can eliminate both. Among them, the Matching method and the foreign exchange transaction method can be used independently for foreign exchange hedging, while the Leads & Lags, BSI method and LSI method must be combined with spot foreign exchange transactions to eliminate all foreign exchange risks to achieve the purpose of preserving the values of foreign exchanges.

【Extracurricular Exercise】

(1) A light industry company in China has exported a batch of goods to a customer in Singapore, whose original quotation was 10 000 pounds for prompt payment. Now the customer has asked us to quote in Singapore dollars and grants a one-month deferred payment. At that

time, the spot exchange rate at the Singapore foreign exchange market is GBP 1 = SGD 2.421 0 – 2.431 0, and the Singapore dollar exchange rate indicates a downward trend. How can our exporter eliminate foreign exchange risk?

(2) A Japanese businessman imported 10 000 metric tons of wheat from the United States at the price of 100 United States dollars per metric ton with 3 months forward payment. At that time, the 3-month forward rate at the Tokyo foreign exchange market is: USD 1 = JPY 115.50, with an expected payment of 115 500 000 yen (100 × 10 000 × 115.50 = 115 500 000). However, three months later, the exchange rate between United States dollar and Japanese yen becomes: USD 1 = JPY 120.00. Try to analyze the foreign exchange risks encountered by exporters and importers in their transaction process.

Module 3 International settlement operation and application ability

Task 8 Recognize, distinguise, issue and judge bills

【Learning objects】

(1) Understand various elements and functions of the bill;

(2) Make clear the parties to the bill and their behavioral relationship;

(3) Able to identify and distinguish various major bills;

(4) Can judge the validity of bills, etc.

【Tasks】

(1) Discuss basic knowledge about bills;

(2) Identify, issue and judge bills of exchange;

(3) Identify, issue and judge promissory notes;

(4) Identify, issue and judge checks.

【Requirements】

(1) Able to identify and judge major bills;

(2) Can correctly express the legal relationship between the parties concerned according to a certain business process.

International settlement is an economic activity to settle the creditor's rights and debts between countries by handling the receipt and payment of currencies through certain payment instruments and payment methods. Transactions of all kinds often happen between parties from two countries, whether between people, between organizations, between businesses or between governments, Commodity trading, service supply, international lending, capital allocation, international tourism, international grants, overseas remittance, inheritance, overseas study, income and expenditure, etc. , where debts and claims need to be settled and liquidated through the bank. Among them, the settlement of creditor's rights and debts caused by international trade is called the international trade settlement. The settlement caused by other factors such as economic, political and cultural exchanges is called the non-trade settlement. International trade settlement is the main component of international settlement. International settlement comes into being with the emergence of international trade. The main payment instrument used in traditional trade is goods (barter trade). As the trade developed, money was created, and gold and silver became instruments of payment. In the modern international trade settlement, a new payment instrument, bill, is adopted, and the bank is used as the intermediary for non-cash settlement, thus avoiding the direct transfer of money. International settlement instruments include bills of exchange, promissory notes and cheques, of which bills of exchange play the major part. International settlement instruments include bills of exchange, promissory notes and cheques, of which bills of exchange are mainly used. You will be able to master the usage of the three basic instruments, easily use them in the future work so as to achieve international payment and settlement.

Task 8.1 Discuss the Basic Knowledge of Bills

【Case for demonstration】

On March 5, 2008, Jiangsu Nam Kwong International Trading Corp. (hereinafter called Nam Kwong company,JNK) signed a sales contract with Hong Kong Nanhwa International Trading Co., Ltd. (hereinafter called Nanhwa company) to export a batch of fashion T-shirts to Nanhwa company with a total payment of 500 000 yuan. The delivery date was April 10, 2008. On March 15, the same year, Nanhwa company issued a forward Bank acceptance draft in favor of Nam Kwong company. The accepting bank was Bank of China (Jiangsu Branch), the bank of deposit of Nanhwa company, with a payment term of two months, which was handed over to Nam Kwong company on the same day. On March 20, Nam Kwong company presented the bill for acceptance, and on the same day it endorsed and transferred the bill to Nanjing Pharmaceutical Co., Ltd. Nanjing Pharmaceutical company presented the bill for payment to Bank of China (Jiangsu branch) on May 15 and obtained the bill payment. So far, Nam Kuong company and Nanhwa company have completed the settlement of the trade contract payment through the instrument of forwarding bank acceptance.

【Task for analysis】

In international settlement, bills are widely used. The reason why bills can replace cash for payment and settlement is that bills have unique properties and functions. Many parties sharing a very complex relationship with each other are involved in bills. The series of negotiable instruments by them are directly related to their own rights and interests. At the same time, the relevant laws and regulations on negotiable instruments are different in different countries. The task in this unit is divided into the following four sub-tasks:

Task 8.1.1 Clarify the concept, characteristics and functions of bills

Task 8.1.2 Know the parties to the bill

Task 8.1.3 Explain the basic terms relating to bills

Task 8.1.4 Understand the major laws on negotiable instruments

Task 8.1.1 Clarify the concept, characteristics and functions of bills

【Figtures for demonstration】

Figure 8.1 is the sample of two bills for you to understand the appearance of the bill.

Figure 8.1　Samples of international settlement instruments

【Questions for discussion】

Think about the following questions with the case study:

(1) What is a bill?

(2) What are the characteristics of a bill?

(3) What kind of role does a bill play in the settlements?

【Relevant knowledge】

(1) The concept of bills

Bills refer to negotiable securities that can be circulated and transferred with the purpose of paying a certain amount of money. It specifies a certain amount of money, which the drawer himself undertakes or instructs a drawee to pay unconditionally to the holder at a certain time.

With the rapid development of international trade, international settlement mainly uses non-cash settlement, that is, it does not directly use cash, but uses credit instruments that can replace cash as a means of circulation and payment to settle international creditor's rights and debts. The instruments of credit used to offset international claims and debts are called bills of exchange. In the broad sense, bills refer to all kinds of documents of title used in business, including property rights negotiable instruments and capital negotiable instruments, such as invoice, bill of lading, warehouse receipt, policy, etc. In the narrow sense, bills refer to the fund negotiable instrument issued and circulated in accordance with regulations, which is a credit instrument for the purpose of paying a certain amount of money. The bills we normally refer to negotiable instruments in the narrow sense, basically can be classified into bills of exchange, promissory notes and checks.

(2) Basic characteristics of bills

As the basis of bill service operation, the characteristics of bills refer to the common features shared by bills of exchange, promissory notes and checks as credit instruments to offset international claims and debts. As a non-cash settlement instrument, bills can replace money owing to the following characteristics:

①Right-setting

It means that the rights of the bill holders arise with the establishment of the bills and cannot be proved without them. The rights of bills emerge on the premises of their completion, the transfer of bill rights is valid on the premises of delivery, and bills must be presented before their exertion. The purpose of issuing bills is not to prove the existing rights, but to establish the rights.

②Non-causative nature

The validity of a bill is not affected by the reasons for the bill, and the rights and obligations on it are not valid for any reason. A bill is a security that does not need to be asked why. "Cause" here refers to the cause of the relationship between rights and obligations on the instrument. Of course, there are reasons for the emergence of bill rights. When the drawer issues the bill to the payee, there is usually a consideration relationship between them, that is, the drawer owes the payee debts, which may be the payment for goods or the previous arrears. The drawee pays for the instrument on behalf of the drawer because there is usually a financial relationship between them. These reasons are the basis of rights and obligations between parties to the bill. The non-causation of the bill is not to deny this relationship, but once the bill is established, the rights of the bill are separated from the causation relationship. The debtor-creditor relationship of the bill becomes independent and is no longer affected by the existence of the original basic relationship of the bill. As long as the negotiable instruments are recorded in a qualified and legal form, the assignee of the negotiable instruments shall acquire the rights to the negotiable instruments, and the payer shall pay unconditionally when due. This characteristic ensures the wide circulation of bills.

③Requisite in form

To make the bill legally effective, the form of negotiable instruments must conform to the provisions of the law and the necessary items to be recorded on the bill must be complete. For a bill, forms are requisite instead of causes. The negotiable instruments laws of various countries have stipulated detailed provisions on the forms and contents of negotiable instruments. The negotiable instruments are qualified and can be protected by laws only when their forms and contents are in line with the provisions of laws. Otherwise, the bill is defective, invalid, and will not be protected by laws. In addition to the forms and recording methods of the negotiable instruments, the forms of bill making, endorsement, presentation, acceptance, payment, guarantee and recourse shall all conform to the legal requirements. This feature can help to reduce bill disputes so as to ensure the smooth circulation of bills.

④Negotiability

Within a reasonable time limit prescribed by law, a negotiable instrument may be delivered or endorsed to transfer its rights to a subsequent party with simple but clear procedures. Negotiability is one of the basic characteristics of negotiable instruments. In general, bearer notes may be transferred on simple delivery, while a signed bill is negotiable only by endorsement. In the circulation of a bill, rights on a bill are effectively transferable only by endorsement or delivery without notifying the debtor. The assignee has full legal rights to obtain the instrument, and, if dishonored, has the right to institute proceedings against all parties in his own name. In addition, the rights of the holder who pays the consideration in good faith are protected by law, and are not affected by the defects of the rights of the prior party. This feature gives the assignee full rights to the instrument, which is of great significance to promote the wide application of negotiable instruments.

⑤Effect from meaning

The rights and obligations of a negotiable instrument shall be determined only by the meaning of the words contained therein. Both the creditor and the debtor shall be bound only by the meaning of the instrument and shall not be affected by any cause other than the words. The creditor of a negotiable instrument shall not claim his rights by anything other than the words, nor shall the debtor oppose the creditor by anything other than the words. The text and meaning of the words on the negotiable instruments provide a solution when the understanding of the parties concerned is inconsistent with the contents recorded on the negotiable instruments.

⑥Presentation

The creditor (holder) on the negotiable instrument must present the negotiable instrument to the drawee when requesting the debtor (drawee) to perform his or her obligations. If the holder fails to present the instrument, the drawee is not obliged to pay. Accordingly, *Negotiable Instruments Law* needs to stipulate the presentment deadline of negotiable instruments. If the deadline is exceeded, the liability of the payer is discharged.

⑦Resoursement

The holder of the negotiable instruments shall return the negotiable instruments received to the payer upon receipt of the payment. If the drawee is the principal debtor, the negotiable instrument relationship vanishes; if the drawee is the second debtor, he may have the right of recourse against his remote holder after payment. An instrument, once duly paid, is discharged and placed in the drawee's file. Therefore, bills cannot circulate indefinitely. Their circulation ends after the payment is due.

(3) Functions of bills

Widely used in every country, bills are used both as the payment instrument and the credit instrument, which are the two functions of cash. In addition, negotiable instruments can be used as the certificate of creditor's right, the accounting voucher and the object of taxation, but they are not legal cash. The role is mainly reflected in the following aspects:

①Exchange

As the traditional functions of bills, the exchange function and the settlement function refer to the use of bills instead of cash as a payment instrument to settle international claims and debts. From the earliest origin of bills, bills come into being to meet the need of "remit" and "exchange", which is of great social significance to us today. Settlement with cash is troublesome and risky. Through the transfer and exchange of bills, the transfer of funds and the settlement of creditor's rights and debts are realized, what's more, featuring safety, rapidity and convenience, bill settlement can avoid counting mistakes and save time. In modern social and economic life, the need of long-distance transfer of money makes the exchange function of bills still very important. Especially in modern international trade, the vast majority of international settlements are conducted by means of bills. Therefore, the role of bills is very prominent.

②Payment

As one of the basic functions of a bill, the payment function refers to the payment made in the transaction instead of cash through the legal circulation transfer procedure. Using bills instead of cash as a means of payment can not only avoid the insecurity of carrying large amounts of cash, but also avoid mistakes in counting notes and save time. With bills as the means of payment, not only unilateral payments, but also multilateral payments can be made, not just one-time payments, but also multiple payments may also be realized through transfer by endorsement. Taking bills as the main means of payment in commodity exchange activities not only meets the need of commodity economy development, but also exhibits the high stage development of commodity economy. In modern economy, bill payment occupies an increasingly large proportion in monetary payment.

③Credit

This is the core function of bills. A note is not a commodity. It is a written payment certificate built on the basis of credit, having no values itself. Its acceptance and circulation are based on the credit from bill relation. In the modern commodity transaction, the credit transaction is abundant. The seller usually cannot receive payment for the goods at the same time as they are delivered. If the buyer issues bills to the seller at this time, the creditor's rights can be clearly expressed with strong security, moreover, the settlement time is determined, the transfer procedure is simple, in addition, the discount system enables the holder to convert the bill into cash in advance. Both bills of exchange and promissory notes can serve as credit for a certain period of time, and cash can be obtained by transfer and discount, such as short-term credit or deferred payments in international transactions of goods. Before the bill is accepted by the creditor as a settlement instrument, the actual creditor's rights and debts have occurred, and the bill actually provides credit to the debtor on behalf of the creditor. The credit function has become one of the most important functions of bills.

④Financing

The financing function of bills is mainly realized through bill discount. In modern finance, bill discounting has become an important business. After this business emerged, the financing function of bills has become increasingly prominent. Operating bill discounting business, banks, in effect, provide capital to enterprises that need it. With the rise of direct financing, many large multinational enterprises choose bills as the credit carrier to raise funds. They obtain funds by issuing bills without any transaction background. At this time, bills have actually become a pure financing means.

【Task】

In the case study at the beginning of this section, in order to pay 500 000 yuan for the goods, Nanhwa company issued a bank acceptance draft to Nam Kwong company, which was transferred to the pharmaceutical company after endorsement. This draft is a kind of bill. After the draft is issued, Nam Kwong company obtains the relevant rights of the bill, which reflects bill's right to be paid. The reason for Nam Kwong company to draw the draft is that both parties have signed a contract for the sale of goods, but once the bill is effectively issued, it is separated from the contractual relationship of sales and purchase. Whether the contract is performed or effective, Nam Kwong company has the rights to the bill, which reflects the non-causation feature of the bill. Nam Kwong company presented the draft to Bank of China for acceptance, and the pharmaceutical company presented the payment to Bank of China, which reflects the presentation characteristic of the bill. Nam Kwong company transferred the bill to the pharmaceutical company by endorsement after acceptance, which reflects its negotiability. Nanhwa company used the bill of exchange instead of cash as the instrument to pay the contract, with the purpose of clearing the creditor's rights and debts with Nam Kwong company, which reflects the exchange (or settlement) function of the bill. In fact, on behalf of the pharmaceutical company, Nam Kwong company provides credit to the Nam Kwong company by transferring the endorsement of the draft to the pharmaceutical company, which reflects the credit function and financing function of the bill. Nam Kwong company gets the payment in advance by endorsing the draft to the pharmaceutical company. In fact, the pharmaceutical company provides credit to the Nam Kwong company, which reflects the credit function and financing function of the bill.

Task 8.1.2 Parties

【Pictures for presentation】

Figure 8.2 shows the schematic diagram of bill business, which clearly demonstrates the parties involved in bill business and their relations.

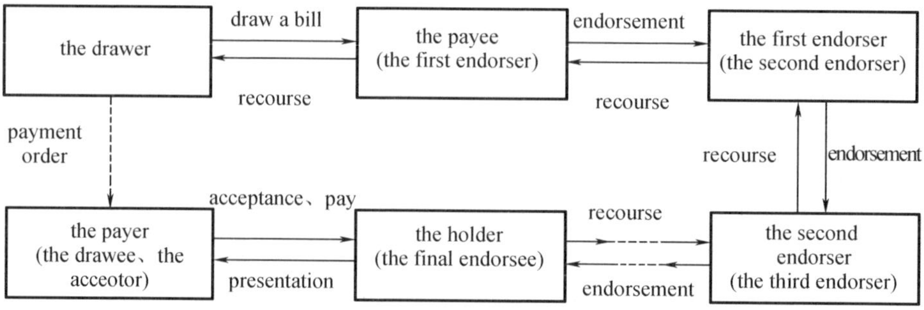

Figure 8.2 A diagram of bill business

【Questions for discussion】

Think about the following questions with the lead-in case study:

(1) What are the main parties involved in bill business?

(2) How are they related to each other?

Students can speak freely in their discussion and then under the guidance of teachers, students summarize the main parties to the bill and their relations.

【Relevant knowledge】

Parties to a negotiable instrument refer to participants involved in the negotiable instrument relationship, including immediate parties and remote parties. The immediate party, which is necessary to a bill, refers to the parties before the negotiable instruments enter into circulation. The drawer, the payer and the payee are the three basic parties in the negotiable instrument relationship. A bill cannot be established if there are no basic parties to it. In the circulation of bills, other parties (remote party) also emerge, such as endorser, endorsee, acceptor, guarantor and holder. Under certain circumstances, the same subject may have dual or multiple-party identities.

(1) The immediate parties to a bill

①Drawer

A drawer is a person who issues and signs an instrument and delivers it to the payee. At the time of the issue, the drawer must sign the bill. Legally speaking, once the negotiable instrument is issued, the drawer shall assume the guarantee liability of certain payment or acceptance made by drawee to the payee and the legitimate holder when the instrument is presented, until the instrument completes its mission and exits the circulation. In the event of recourse for the dishonor of an instrument, the drawer shall be liable for repaying the bill to the holder or to any endorser who is compelled to pay, provided that the necessary legal procedures have been formally taken for the refund. The drawer is the principal debtor of the instrument in the case of a sight draft or before the usance is accepted and becomes the secondary debtor after it is accepted.

②Payee

The payee is the person recorded on the bill to receive the payment and therefore is the principal creditor and beneficiary of the notes and the first holder of the notes. The payee shall have the right to demand acceptance and payment from the drawee, and shall have the right to demand payment from the drawer if payment is refused. The payee may transfer the instrument to another party. In the case of a bill to order, endorsement is required at the time of transfer. The payee becomes the first endorser of the instrument upon endorsement. Both the endorser and the drawee are liable for guaranteeing payment or acceptance of bills. When a negotiable instrument is dishonored and the holder has recourse against it, the payee shall be responsible for repaying the bill and then recover the money from the drawer.

③Payer

The payer, also known as the drawee, is the person who bears the obligation to pay, as specified on the instrument, that is, the person who receives the order to pay. The payer is not necessarily the debtor of the instrument and therefore is not necessarily liable for the payment. Payers shall have the right to decide whether to accept or reject the instrument at their own discretion. If the drawee does not accept the drawer's order, the payee or the holder shall not compel the drawee to pay or take the liability for the payment when due, so as to prevent the drawer from issuing a bill to another without cause. However, if a drawee has accepted a usance bill, thereby agreeing to the drawer's order to pay, thus becomes the principal debtor and is liable to pay when due. The drawee of a usance bill becomes the acceptor after accepting the bill. The payer shall collect the bill after the payment.

(2) The remote parties to a bill

①Endorser

An endorser is a person who transfers the instrument to others after receiving the instrument from the payee or the holder by signing the instrument in person (i. e. , endorsing). Every person legally holding an instrument may become an endorser. After the endorsement, the payee or the holder becomes the endorser, shifting from creditor to debtor, and becomes the remote holder of the corresponding endorsee and the subsequent transferee of the bill rights. To the endorsee, all the endorsers before him and the original drawer are his remote holders, while all the subsequent assignees are his successors, and the former endorser is liable to the latter endorsee for guaranteeing that the bill will be accepted or paid. As the debtor of the negotiable instrument, the endorser shall bear the same liability as the drawer for the negotiable instrument and the guaranty liability for the subsequent holder of the negotiable instrument after him. The subsequent holder may exercise the right of recourse against the prior holder. If the drawee (or acceptor) dishonor the draft, the endorser shall pay. In addition, the endorser's endorsement serves as a guarantee to any subsequent official holder that the entire endorsement of his prior holder is true. A bill may be transferred consecutively. The endorsee may transfer it by adding an endorsement to it, thus becoming the second endorser, and the third endorser is then created by the subsequent endorsement, and so on. If the endorser wishes to exonerate himself, he can add "without recourse to me" when issuing the endorsement. In this way, if the bill is dishonored, the holder, when exercising the right of recourse, can only skip the endorser and claim against the prior endorser. But such "no recourse" endorsements impede the liquidity of bills. Therefore no one is willing to accept them.

②Endorsee

The endorsee, i. e. , the transferee of the instrument, refers to the party who accepts the instrument and enjoys the rights on the instrument. If the endorsee transfers the bill again, he becomes another endorser, if not, he becomes the holder of it, and the last endorsee must be the holder. The endorsee is the creditor of the bill and has the right to demand payment from the drawee and the prior endorser up to the drawer.

③Acceptor

An acceptor is a person who promises to pay a bill when it is due. When the drawee agrees to accept the drawer's order and signs the bill, he becomes the acceptor. Upon acceptance, bill acceptor shall guarantee the payment in accordance with the accepted meaning, shall not refuse to pay to the office holder on the pretext that "the drawer does not exist", or that "the drawer's signature is forged", or that "the drawer has no capacity or authority to issue a draft", which is called "prohibiting the acceptor from reversing the verdict" in the bill law. The acceptor only exists in the usance draft relationship. Since there is no acceptance, there is no acceptor for sight draft, promissory note and check. Once the acceptor accepts the bill, he becomes the principal debtor of the bill, and the drawer abdicates to the subordinate debtor.

④Acceptor for honor

The acceptor for honor is the person who is not the debtor of commercial instruments but acts as the acceptor when the bill is rejected or cannot be accepted on presentation. The relationship between the acceptor for honor and the acceptee for honor is equivalent to that between the warrantor and the warrantee. The acceptor for honor is also the debtor of the bill. When the drawee refuses to pay when the bill is due, the acceptor for honor shall pay the bill to the holder.

⑤Guarantor

A guarantor is a person who signs a negotiable instrument in guaranteeing the acts of the debtor of the instrument. The guarantor shall assume the obligation of the bill. A guarantor may provide a guarantee for a drawer, an endorser, an acceptor or an acceptor for honor, who are all referred to as the person guaranteed. The liability of the guarantor and the guaranteed is exactly the same. After payment, the guarantor may make recourse against the acceptor, the guaranteed and his remote holder. When multiple guarantors provide guaranty for the same bill debt, each guarantor shall be jointly and severally liable. The guarantor may guarantee only part of the amount of the bill.

⑥Holder

A holder is a person who is currently holding a bill. As the subject of bill rights, the holder has the right to ask the drawee or other related parties to perform the obligations stipulated on the bill. The holder may be the payee of the bill or the endorsee or bearer in the circulation of the bill. A bill can be endorsed over and over again, so there may be several holders of the same bill. The payee is the first holder of the bill, the last endorsee is the last holder, and the other endorsers are the holders in between.

(3) The relationship between the parties to a bill

There are many parties to the bill, and due to the different status of the parties concerned, they have different rights and responsibilities to the bill. The person who holds the bill and has the right to exercise the bill right against the debtor is the creditor. The payee and the holder are the creditors of the instrument. The person liable for payment on the instrument is the debtor, for example, the drawer, the drawee, endorser and acceptor are all debtors on the instrument.

In addition to the rights and obligations of the instrument, there is a certain relationship between the parties. That is, the relationship between the drawer and the payee is a debtor-creditor relationship. The drawer is the debtor and the payee is the creditor. Therefore, the drawer shall issue a bill to the payee for payment. And the relationship between the drawer and the payer is also a debtor-creditor relationship. The payer is the debtor and the drawer is the creditor. The drawer may issue a bill to the drawee and order him to pay. The drawer becomes the principal debtor of the instrument after issuing the bill and is obligated to guarantee acceptance and payment. The drawee replaces the drawer as the principal debtor after accepting the bill. The endorser has an obligation to guarantee acceptance and payment to the endorsee and all subsequent parties.

[Task]

In the lead-in case, Nanhwa company opens a bank acceptance bill to Nam Kwong company. Nanhwa company is the drawer, Nam Kwong company is the payee and the Jiangsu branch of Bank of China is the drawee. All these three parties constitute the basic relationship of the negotiable instrument. As the drawer, Nanhwa company is the principal debtor of the bill and shall have an obligation to guarantee that the bill will be accepted by the drawee and paid when the bill is due. Upon accepting the bill, the Jiangsu branch of Bank of China becomes the acceptor, replacing Nanhwa company as the principal debtor of the bill. Since Nam Kwong company transfers the bill to the pharmaceutical company after indorsement. Nam Kwong company becomes the endorser, while the pharmaceutical company becomes the endorsee. Nam Kwong company assumes the guarantee liability for the subsequent pharmaceutical company, who has the right of recourse against its prior Nam Kwong company when the bill is dishonored. The pharmaceutical company does not transfer the bill to the other party, thus becoming the final bearer of the bill and having all the rights to the bill. When Bank of China pays the bill to the pharmaceutical company, it becomes the payer of the bill.

Task 8.1.3 Basic terms relating to bills

[Questions for discussion]

In international settlement, bill business has some special terms, therefore it is very important to understand the meaning of these terms correctly. Based on the bill business diagram and combined with the lead-in case, please think about the following questions:

(1) What acts are involved in bill business?

(2) What does a bill relationship comprise?

(3) How is a bill relationship related to a basic relationship?

After free discussion, the students summarize the connotation of key concepts such as acts under a bill, bill relationship and basic relationship under the guidance of teachers.

[Relevant knowledge]

(1) Acts under a bill

Acts under a bill refer to the legal acts that can produce, change and eliminate the rights and obligations on negotiable instruments, including drawing, endorsement, presentation, acceptance, guarantee and payment. In case of dishonor, the holder shall make a certificate of protest and claim for it according to the law. Among all the acts, issuing bill is the basic act under a bill, others are the subordinate acts.

①Issue/draw

Drawing a bill means the first delivery of a well-formed bill to the payee. It consists of three acts, namely, drawing bills, signing bills and delivering bills to payees. If drawer leaves the bill in his own hands instead of handing it to the payee after issuing it, the bill is not issued. A note must be signed before it is delivered to the payee. A negotiable instrument is a kind of a special formed security. When making a negotiable instrument, the drawer must record the legal contents on the negotiable instrument according to the provisions of the relevant state negotiable instrument law in order to have the effect of the negotiable instrument. When making a negotiable instrument, the drawer must record the content on it according to the provisions of relevant national negotiable instrument law so as to ensure its legal validity. If there is a lack of items required to be recorded in accordance with the law, the bill loses its validity. The act of drawing a bill obliges the drawer to guarantee the bill, including acceptance and payment. If the drawee refuses to accept or refuse to pay, the holder may make a certificate of protest and exercise the right of recourse against the drawer, requesting the drawer to pay back the bill.

②Endorsement/indorsement

Endorsement refers to the act of the bearer signing the bill on its back and giving it to the other party. The term endorsement comes from the way that the endorser signs his name on the back of the bill. Endorsement is a legal procedure to transfer the right of negotiable instruments. Order bills and order instruments must be transferred in endorsement. According to the principle of negotiable instrument law, once the endorser signs and endorses the bill, he becomes the debtor of the bill, and he shall be responsible for the bill and assume the responsibility to guarantee that the bill will be accepted or paid to all the subsequent endorsers. The endorsee owns the right on the instrument, and the endorsee who has paid consideration in good faith has the right over the endorser. According to *Negotiable Instruments Law* of each country, the holder should prove the establishment of bill rights by the continuity of endorsement, that is, an uninterrupted series of endorsements is evidence that the holder shall enjoy the rights on the bill. As long as the endorsement is continuous, the holder may, without any other proof, exercise his rights on the instrument, and the debtor shall pay him accordingly.

③Presentation

Presentment is the act of holder presenting the bill to the drawee for acceptance or payment. This is a kind of behavior that the holder must do to exercise and preserve the bill rights. A negotiable instrument is the proof of a kind of right only, while presentation is an act claiming bill rights. Presentation includes presentation for acceptance and presentation for payment. The presentation of a bill at sight is intended to be paid immediately against the bill, therefore functions as the presentation for payment; while usance bills generally have to be presented twice, first for acceptance, then for payment when due. Presentation must be made during normal business hours at the place of business of the drawee. Only in this way can the holder obtain the bill rights. According to the bill law of various countries, the holder should make a presentation to the payer for acceptance or payment within the specified time, otherwise, the holder will lose the right of recourse against his prior holder and the drawer. As to the specific time of presentation, each country has different regulations.

④Acceptance

Acceptance means that the drawee accepts the entrustment of the drawer and agrees to bear the obligation of paying the amount of the negotiable instrument, while expressing this intention in written form on the negotiable instrument. The function of acceptance is to determine the obligation of the drawee to pay the usance bill. If the act of drawing is the unilateral act of the drawer, while the payer fails to participate in it, the payer is not the debtor of the bill. Before acceptance, the principal debtor is the drawer, but the drawee becomes the principal debtor after acceptance. Usually, when signing the acceptance, the acceptor writes the word "accepted" on the bill. Acceptance must be written on the draft and signed by the drawee. The signature of the drawee without any other clause also constitutes acceptance. Acceptance shall not indicate that the drawee will fulfill his commitment in any other way than payment. Sight drafts, promissory notes and cheques need not be accepted. For a time draft, the holder makes a presentation for acceptance and asks the drawee to sign confirming that he will pay at the due date. For a usance draft, the holder should first make a presentation for acceptance and ask the drawee to sign confirming payment at the due date. If the payment is made after several days' sight, the date of acceptance by the drawee is the date of sight, from which the due date is presumed. At the due date, the holder shall make a presentation for payment and the acceptor shall pay against the bill.

Whether to require acceptance is generally a free right of the holder, and he is generally willing to prompt the payer for acceptance. On the one hand, it is conducive to the protection of the holder's right, because through acceptance he can obtain the acceptor's payment guarantee, on the other hand, it is conducive to the circulation of the bill.

⑤Guarantee or ava

Guarantee refers to the subordinate act on a negotiable instrument by a third party other than the debtor of the negotiable instrument for the purpose of guaranteeing the debts arising from the act of the principal negotiable instrument. The guarantor may provide guaranty for the drawer, endorser, acceptor and acceptor for honor. Guarantee is a formal act in that the guarantor shall state and sign the word "guarantee", indicating the date of the guarantee and the guaranteed. Guarantee is an independent act. Even if the principal debt guaranteed is invalid for any reason, the guarantor shall assume the obligation, except for the lack of the style of the instrument. The guarantor and the guaranteed bear the same liability. When multiple guarantors provide guaranty for the same bill debt, each guarantor shall be jointly and severally liable. The guarantor may guarantee all or part of the amount of the note. The guarantor shall have the right of recourse against the acceptor and the guaranteed after paying off the debt of the bill.

⑥Payment

Payment means that the payer pays the amount of the bill to the holder at the due date to eliminate the bill relationship. A sight note is payable upon presentation immediately, while a forward note is payable upon presentation at a due date. The act of payment eliminates the rights and obligations on the instrument, and the drawee shall take back the instrument after payment. Once the bill has been paid off in full by the drawee, the debtor-creditor relationship on the bill shall terminate. The holder shall sign the bill with the word "paid" and deliver it to the drawee, and all the debtors shall be discharged.

⑦Dishonor

Dishonor, also known as a refund, refers to the holder of the bill being refused by the payer when asking for acceptance or payment, including dishonor by non-acceptance and dishonor by non-payment. Dishonor means not only that the drawee expresses a clear refusal of acceptance or payment, but also that the drawee dies, flees or declares bankruptcy. In case of dishonor, the holder shall make a certificate of protest and give the notice of dishonor to his prior party, who as the prior endorser shall notify his prior party again, then all the way to the drawer. If the prior holder is not notified, the holder or endorser forfeits the right of recourse against the prior holder. If the debtor of the bill fails to receive the notice of dishonor, he can free himself from his debt. The certificate of protest is a legal document issued by the legal notary at the place of payment or other institutions that have the right to issue the certificate upon the request from the holder within the legal time limit, proving that the payer refuses to accept or dishonor the payment. The holder may exercise the right of recourse against the endorser and the drawer without making a presentation for payment after obtaining the certificate of protest.

⑧Recourse

Recourse refers to the act of the holder requesting the prior parties (endorser, acceptor, guarantor and drawer, etc.) to repay the amount of the bill when the bill is dishonored. When exercising the right of recourse, the holder must make a certificate of protest within the period of time required by law after the instrument has been dishonored. Notice of dishonor must notify the prior party of the fact of dishonor within the statutory period. In addition, the holder may, without any restriction of order, make recourse against any prior hand or drawer. If a prior hand indicates "without recourse to us" when transferring the bill, the bearer shall bypass that person instead of making a recourse against him. The amount of the claim shall include the amount of the bill, interests, expenses for making notice of dishonor and certificate of dishonor and other necessary expenses. According to *Negotiable Instruments Law* of our country, the time limit of recourse is 2 years.

(2) Bill relationship

Bill relationship refers to the relationship of rights and obligations on negotiable instruments based on negotiable instrument behavior. It is the inherent legal relationship of the bill itself. From the perspective of rights, there are three basic rights of negotiable instruments: circulation right, the right to demand a payment and recourse right, which all belong to the holder. Demanding payment is the main right on the bill, also known as the first claim right; while the right of recourse is the second one. Only when the main right is not obtained can the second claim be exercised. Whoever obtains the bill in good faith also obtains the title to the bill. The means of acquiring the rights to negotiable instruments include: obtaining them from the drawer; obtaining them through transfer from the holder; obtaining instruments by inheritance, gifts, etc. Acquiring negotiable instrument in good faith means obtaining negotiable instrument through an endorsement or direct delivery without malice or gross negligence, and with consideration paid beforehand. Unqualified record on a negotiable instrument, expiration or exceeding legal time limit of negotiable instrument preservation right shall all lead to the loss of bill right.

(3) Basic relationship

The basic relationship is closely related to bill behaviors but does not produce bill rights and obligations in law. In theory, the basic relationship of negotiable instruments can be divided into two types: causal relationship and capital relationship.

①Causal relationship

Causal relationship refers to the basis or cause of issuing or transferring negotiable instruments between the parties. Generally, this kind of basis is the creditor's right debt relation between parties, for instance, payment, loan, guarantee, bestowal, which normally have considerations. It is stipulated in all countries that once a bill relationship is established, it is separated from the causal relationship. Whether the causal relationship is valid or not, it does not affect the validity of the negotiable instrument.

②Capital relationship

Capital relationship refers to the capital compensation relationship between the drawer and the payer or between the drawer and the acceptor, such as debit and credit, fund deposit, etc. The capital relationship exists in the bill of exchange and the check, while the promissory note is a self-paying that has no capital relation at all. At present, most countries believe that the capital relationship should be separated from the bill relationship, and notes are valid regardless of whether the drawer provides funds to the payer. The relationship among the three basic parties of the bill is shown in figure 8.3.

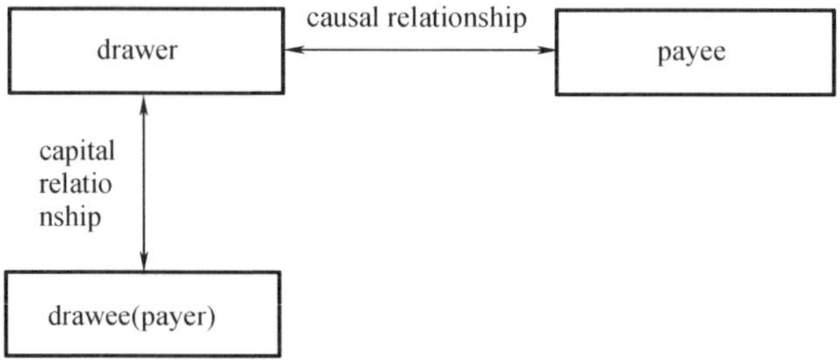

Figure 8.3 Relationship among three basic parties of the bill

It is a common practice in every country that bill relationship is separated from its basic relationship once it is established. Bill relationship is generated, changed and eliminated due to bill behaviors, and has nothing to do with the basic relationship, that is, the invalidation of the basic relationship will not result in the invalidation of the bill relationship. This principle plays an important role in promoting the circulation of notes and ensuring the security of their transactions.

(4) Types of endorsement

The transfer of bill rights is mostly carried out by endorsement, and the holder mainly completes transferring his rights by special endorsement, blank endorsement and restrictive endorsement. Special endorsement is also known as full endorsement, during which, the endorser shall write the name and trade name of the endorsee on the back of the bill and sign his name before giving the bill to the endorsee. There are two ways to write it: one is to write only the name of the endorsee; the other is to add "or order". Blank endorsement is also known as open endorsement or abbreviated endorsement. In other words, the back of the bill will only be signed by the endorser instead of the endorsee. This endorsed instrument is transferable upon delivery only. Restrictive endorsement means that the endorsement is annotated with "not negotiable" or "pay A only". Such bills are generally not allowed to be transferred again, otherwise, all subsequent parties will not be guaranteed. Endorsement can be divided into transferrable endorsement and non-transferrable endorsement according to the intention of endorsement. Transferrable endorsement refers to the endorsement for the purpose of transferring rights on bills and the endorsee can take the ownership of the bill. Such endorsement shall be indivisible and the amount of the bill shall be transferred to the same person at the same time. Non-transferrable endorsement is the endorsement not for the purpose of transfer or circulation. For example, the purpose of endorsement for collection is to entrust the endorsee to draw the money on his behalf instead of transferring the ownership of the bill and is usually marked with the words of "for collection" or "for procuration". Endorsement of pledge is for the purpose of setting the pledge, usually marked with "value in security" or "value in pledge". The endorsee may enjoy the rights on the bill when exercising the pledge according to law. In addition, there is a qualified endorsement, on which the endorser shall note the sentence "free from recourse" when endorsing so as to limit his liability, and after that the endorser shall generally be free from recourse. Conditional endorsement shall be invalid because of non-conformity with the unconditional payment order.

(5) The validity of bills

After the issuance of the instrument, the deadline of the presentation by the payee shall be the time limit of validity of the instrument. The period of validity of note is different from its tenor (spot or forward). The term of validity is the validity for presentation, that is, it should be considered overdue after the presentation. The drawee does not pay for an overdue note, or may ask the drawer for his consent before payment. With respect to the validity of a sight draft, *Negotiable Instruments Law* both in the UK and in the USA stipulates that the validity shall be within a reasonable time from the date of issue. As for the length of the reasonable time, there is no specific stipulation, therefore it depends on the nature of the note, bank or commercial practices and other specific circumstances. *The Uniform Act of Geneva* provides that the validity lasts for one year. As for the validity of usance draft, the law on negotiable instruments in the UK and the USA also provides that presentation for acceptance should be made within a reasonable time. According to *The Uniform Act of Geneva*, the presentation of acceptance should be made within one year from the date of issue. After the usance draft is presented for acceptance, it shall be presented for payment at the due date. If it is not presented for payment at the due date, it will be treated as the sight draft in its subsequent presentation.

(6) Acceptance for honor and payment for honor

Acceptance for honor means that the third party permitted by the holder accepts the bill for the benefits of the drawer when the bill is dishonored so as to prevent the exercise of the right of recourse. The purpose of it is to prevent the holder from exercising the right of recourse without acceptance so as to maintain the credibility of the drawer and the endorser. According to the law on negotiable instruments of each country, the acceptor for honor must mark the word "accept for honor", his signature and the date on the bill, and state the name of the acceptee for honor (otherwise, the acceptee for honor is regarded as the drawer). The relationship between the acceptor and the acceptee is equivalent to that between the guarantor and the guaranteed. Acceptance for honor shall be premised on non-acceptance and a certificate of protest. Unlike the acceptor, the acceptor for honor is not the principal debtor of the bill. He is only liable to pay when the payer refuses to pay. If the holder allows him to participate in the acceptance, the holder cannot exercise the right of recourse against the acceptee and his successors before the validity date of the bill.

Payment for honor refers to the payment made by a third party other than the payer when the payer or the acceptor does not pay to the holder. It also aims to preserve the credit of the debtor of the bill and prevent the holder from exercising the right of recourse. The payer for honor may be the acceptor for honor, the preparatory drawee or any third party, who obtains the right from the holder after payment, may claim against the payee for honor and its prior parties, but may not transfer the draft by endorsement. If the holder refuses the payment for honor, he will lose the right of recourse against the payee for honor and his subsequent parties. The payer for honor shall state the name of the payee for honor, or the drawer shall be deemed to be the payee for honor.

【Tasks】

In the lead-in case, Nanhwa company opens a banker's acceptance bill to Nam Kwong company. The bill conduct of Nanhwa company is to issue a bill, which is a principal bill act. When Nam Kwong company presents the bill to the Jiangsu branch of Bank of China for acceptance, the bill act of Nam Kwong company is a presentation for acceptance, while the bill act of the Jiangsu branch of Bank of China is acceptance. Nam Kwong company transfers the bill to the pharmaceutical company after endorsement. The bill act of Nam Kwong company is an endorsement. When the bill of exchange is due, the pharmaceutical company receives the bill payment from the Jiangsu branch of Bank of China. The bill act of the pharmaceutical company is a presentation for payment, while the bill act of the Jiangsu branch of Bank of China is payment. After payment, all claims and liabilities on the instrument are discharged. After acquiring the bill, Nam Kwong company and the pharmaceutical company become the holder of the bill and have the right to transfer the bill, the right to ask for payment and the right of recourse. Nanhwa company opens a banker's acceptance bill to Nam Kwong company, because these two parties have established a contract of sale and purchase, where Nanhwa company is the debtor (buyer), while Nam Kwong company is the creditor (seller), which constitutes the causal relationship of the bill. Nanhwa company orders the Jiangsu branch of Bank of China to make the payment because it has funds in the Jiangsu branch of Bank of China, which reveals the capital relationship between the two parties. The casual relationship and the capital relationship make up the basic relationship of the bill of exchange. Once the bill of exchange is legally opened, the relationship between rights and obligations on the bill will be separated from its basic relationship. No matter whether the sales contract is valid or not, the bill relationship is established.

Task 8.1.4 Understand the major laws on negotiable instruments

【Questions for discussion】

In an international settlement business, negotiable instrument is a tool to replace cash for payment and settlement. Laws of various countries have made specific provisions on the use and circulation of negotiable instrument and legalized the rules of negotiable instrument business. However, the law on negotiable instrument in each country also differs on the bill business operation. Therefore, understanding the world's major laws on negotiable instrument is essential for international settlement. Combined with the lead-in case, please think the following questions:

(1) What are the major laws on negotiable instrument in the world?

(2) How do they differ from each other in contents?

After a free discussion, students summarize the world's major negotiable instrument laws under the guidance of the teacher.

【Relevant knowledge】

(1) The concept of negotiable instrument law

Negotiable instrument law is the general name of legal norms that stipulate types, forms, acts of negotiable instruments and rights and obligations of parties to a bill. It can be understood from both broad sense and narrow sense. Negotiable instrument law in a broad sense refers to the general term of all legal norms regulating the relationship settled around negotiable instruments, including special legislation on negotiable instruments and legal provisions on negotiable instruments in civil law, commercial law, criminal law, procedural law and bankruptcy law. The bill law in the narrow sense refers to the special legislation on negotiable instruments, namely the legal norms on the circulation rules of bills of exchange, promissory notes and checks formulated by governments in order to promote the development of commodity trade. As negotiable instruments are a kind of securities with their own characteristics and particular legal relationship, special legislation should be made on them. The law on negotiable instrument that we refer to is normally the law in the narrow sense.

(2) The law of negotiable instruments in western countries

Western countries' negotiable instrument law originated from medieval Europe, but it wasn't until the middle of the 17th century that it became codified. In 1673, the provisions on negotiable instruments in *Land Business Ordinance* in Louis XIV period of France were the earliest written negotiable instrument law in modern times. Since then, each capitalist country formulated its own bill laws. In 1673, Germany enacted regulations on ordinary bills, which was promulgated and implemented in 1871. In 1882, the UK enacted *UK Bills of Exchange Act* on the basis of the original common law, and made three amendments in 1909, 1914 and 1917. In 1957, the UK separately enacted *Checks Act* as a supplement to *UK Bills of Exchange Act*. The great differences existing in bill legislation in various countries bring a lot of inconveniences to the circulation and use of bill in international economy and trade, thus affecting the smooth completion of international settlement. In the 20th century, the international unification of negotiable instrument law was formally put on the agenda. In 1930, more than 20 countries, including France, Germany, Switzerland, Italy, Japan and countries from Latin America, held a conference on the unification of international negotiable instruments Law in Geneva and signed *Uniform Law for Bills of Exchange and Promissory Notes signed at Geneva* 1930, and *Uniform Law for Cheques signed at Geneva* 1931, which are collectively known as *Geneva Uniform Negotiable Instrument Law*. It has been adopted by most European countries, Japan and Latin American countries. The law of negotiable instruments within the continental law system gradually tends to be unified, while the UK and the United States refuse to participate in the convention.

At present, there are two major legal systems of negotiable instruments in western countries, namely the continental law system represented by *Geneva Uniform Negotiable Instrument Law* and the Anglo-American law system represented by *UK Bills of Exchange Act*. The two have a lot of similarities on the whole, but specific terms vary due to different business practices in different countries, which are mainly reflected in the following aspects:

①Different classification of bills

The bill of exchange and the check in *Geneva uniform Negotiable Instrument Law* is independent, but *UK Bills of Exchange Act* incorporates the check into the bill of exchange. *Checks Act* in 1957 is actually a supplement to the check content in *UK Bills of Exchange Act* .

②Different rights of bill holders

According to *Geneva Uniform Negotiable Instrument Law*, as long as the endorsement is continuous on an instrument, the bearer is "the lawful holder", owns legal rights the instrument. In *UK Bills of Exchange Act*, holders are divided into three types: holder, holder for value, and holder in due course, who are endowed with different rights. Among them, holder in due course is the legal holder of the instrument, who enjoys complete bill rights and is fully protected by law.

③Different treatment of forged endorsement

Geneva Uniform Negotiable Instrument Law focuses on protecting bona fide holders. It stipulates that the risk of forged endorsement is ultimately borne by the owner of the bill, and the innocent bona fide holder is not liable. While the Anglo-American legal system focuses on the protection of the real owner of the bill. The endorsement with forged signature is invalid, and the risk of forged endorsement is ultimately borne by the person who obtains the bill directly from the forger.

④Different requirements on the bill form

Geneva Uniform Negotiable Instrument Law has strict requirements on the form of negotiable instruments so that a bill without specified requirements is invalid. However, the common law system has more flexible requirements, for example, the name of the bill is not required to be written on the bill.

(3) Uniform bill law

The Geneva Convention only unifies the differences among the continental law countries on *Negotiable Instruments Law*, but does not eliminate the differences with the common law system. The conflicts between these two legal systems seriously hinder the circulation of negotiable instruments. The Geneva conventions failed to achieve the goal of unifying instrument laws. In August 1987, the 20th session of the United Nations Commission on international trade law adopted *Convention on International Bills of Exchange and International Promissory Notes*, whose main purpose is to bridge as far as possible the differences between various countries, especially the Anglo-American legal system and the Geneva convention on negotiable instruments, so that it can become a uniform law generally accepted by countries with different legal systems. However, due to the small number of participating countries, the convention has not entered into force so far. Therefore a uniform law on the bill of exchange accepted worldwide has not come into being till now. In order to promote the transnational circulation and use of negotiable instruments, the principle of the place of conduct of negotiable instruments is internationally accepted, that is, whether the negotiable instrument is complete or not shall be subject to the national law of the place of issue, and the validity of other bill acts shall be subject to the national law of the place where such acts take place.

The differences between *Convention on International Bills of Exchange and International Promissory Notes* of the United Nations and *Geneva Uniform Negotiable Instrument Law* are mainly reflected in two aspects: first, the convention is only applicable to international bills of exchange and international promissory notes, but cannot be applied to the domestic norms of negotiable instrument law of a contracting state, while *Geneva uniform Negotiable Instrument Law* is applicable to both international norms of negotiable instrument law and domestic norms of negotiable instrument law of a contracting state; second, the convention has no coercive force on the parties of the contracting states, but only becomes effective when the parties choose to apply it, while *Geneva Uniform Negotiable Instrument Law* has the force of mandatory application on the parties of the contracting states.

(4) Laws of negotiable instrument in our country

Although negotiable instruments in China originated very early, they developed rather slowly. All the acts and disputes concerning negotiable instruments were dealt with in accordance with local customs. In 1928, the national government promulgated *Draft Bill on Negotiable Instruments*, which was formally implemented in 1929. It was the first formal bill law in China's history. Since the reform and opening up of the People's Republic of China, negotiable instruments have been widely used. Therefore the formulation of the bill law was put on the agenda. In 1988 *Bank settlement measures* were carried out. *Law of the People's Republic of China on negotiable instruments* was passed by the standing committee of the National People's Congress on May 10, 1995 and came into effect on January 1, 1996, after a careful consultation on *Geneva Uniform Negotiable Instrument Law* and the reasonable provisions in the Anglo-American negotiable instrument law system and a combination with the situation in China. Composed of 7 chapters and 111 articles, it is applicable to all the negotiable instrument activities in China.

It adopts the method of uniform legislation on bills of exchange, promissory notes and checks with relatively systematic and comprehensive contents, stipulating clearly not only the rights and obligations of the parties to the negotiable instrument, but also issuance, endorsement, acceptance, guarantee and payment behavior of negotiable instruments, emphasizing the characteristics of non-causation, formalism, literal meaning and independence of the bill.

【Tasks】

Before using negotiable instruments for international settlements, we have to decide whether the country concerned belongs to the continental law system or the Anglo-American law system and be clear about the differences of the legal provisions on negotiable instruments between these two legal systems, so that we can effectively safeguard our rights and interests in the case of disputes over negotiable instruments. It is a universally adopted principle that the note relationship is separated from the basic relationship, which is of great significance to promote the circulation and use of negotiable instruments in international settlements. In addition, in the transnational circulation and use of negotiable instruments, the principle of the place of act is internationally accepted, that is, whether the negotiable instrument is effective or not is subject to the law of the country where the bill act takes place. These rules are essential to our international payments and settlements by bills.

Task 8.2 Identifying, drawing and judging bills of exchange

【Tasks for analysis】

In international settlements, the bill of exchange is one of the most widely used bills, playing the most prominent role with the most complete performance. Therefore, identifying, issuing and judging bills of exchange are the basic skills of the business people in the international trade and economic industry. In particular, such questions as how to open bills of exchange, how to judge the validity of bills of exchange, how to use bills of exchange to complete settlements, what are the common types of bills of exchange, are often encountered in international settlements. Therefore, the tasks in this unit are divided into the following four sub-tasks:

Task 8.2.1 Definition of a bill and its basic parties

Task 8.2.2 Describe the entries in a bill of exchange

Task 8.2.3 Explain the behaviors of bills of exchange

Task 8.2.4 Master the types of bills of exchange

Task 8.2.1 Make clear the definition of bills and its basic parties

【Figures for demonstration】

A sample of two bills of exchange is listed in figure 8.4 for understanding their appearances and forms.

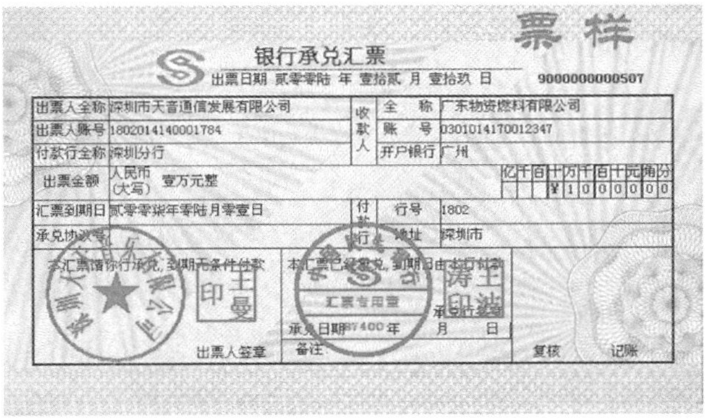

Figure 8.4 Sample bills of exchange

【Questions for discussion】

Please think after studying the above sample bills of exchange:

(1) What is bill of exchange?

(2) What are the characteristics of bills of exchange?

(3) What is the relationship among the three basic parties to a bill of exchange?

After a free discussion, students summarize the concept of bill of exchange, explain the characteristics of bills and the relationship between the parties to a bill under the guidance of the teacher.

【Relevant knowledge】

(1) Definition of bill of exchange

The definition of bill of exchange in *UK Bills of Excharge Act*, which has a wide influence in the international community, is a draft is a written order issued by the drawer to another person requiring unconditional payment of a certain amount to a person or his designee at sight, on a regular basis, or at a certain future time.

Article 19 in *Negotiable Instruments Law* in our country provides that: a bill of exchange is a bill signed and issued by the drawer, entrusting the payer to unconditionally pay the payee or bearer a certain amount at sight or on a specified date.

(2) The characteristics of bills of exchange

The definition of bill of exchange, whether in China or Britain, is essentially the same, that is, an unconditional payment order. Bills of exchange mainly have the following characteristics:

①A bill of exchange is a kind of security entrusting others to make payment. It has three basic parties. Instead of making the payment himself, the drawer entrusts the drawee (payer) to pay a certain amount to the payee. Therefore, the basic parties of a bill of exchange are drawer, drawee and payee.

②A draft is a written payment order from the drawer. A bill of exchange is a written instruction issued by the drawer ordering the payer to pay the payee. Signed by the drawer, it is in a written form, instead of in an oral form, and its content is an order rather than a request, a consultation, or a request for advice.

③The payment order of the bill is unconditional, which means that payment cannot be made with any restrictions or conditions attached, that is, without any preconditions. Otherwise, the bill is invalid and has no legal force.

(3) The relationship between three basic parties to a bill of exchange

Since a bill of exchange is an unconditional payment order, it is taken for granted that when it is used in foreign trade settlements, there must be both the party giving the order and the party receiving it, and there must be both the payee and the payer. In international settlements, the exporter issues a payment order to the importer when exporting goods or services. When the importer obtains the goods or services, he himself or his bank shall accept the order of payment, paying to the exporter himself or his bank. Therefore, a bill of exchange involves three parties—the basic parties, namely, the drawer, the drawee and the payee.

A drawer is a person who draws and issues drafts, usually the exporter or his nominated bank.

A payer, or drawee, is the person who accepts bills of exchange and carries out payment orders, usually an importer or his designated bank.

A payee is a person who receives the amount specified in a draft, usually the exporter (i. e., the drawer) or his designated bank.

The relationship among the above three parties clearly reflects their creditor's and debtor's relationship and settlement relationship, as shown in figure 8.5.

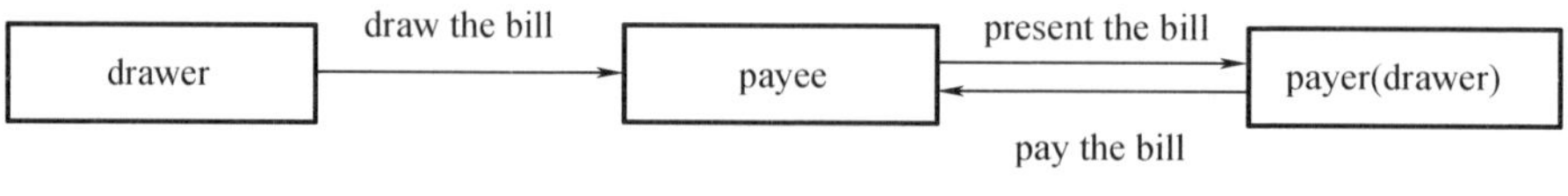

Figure 8.5 The relationship among the three basic parties to a bill of exchange

(4) British interpretation on the definition of bill of exchange in *UK Bills of Exchange Act*

UK Bills of Exchange Act of 1882 defined the nature of the bill, the relationship among involved parties and the method of payment. A bill of exchange is valid as long as it meets the definition. The key elements of this definition can be explained as follows:

①An unconditional order

Under this provision, a bill of exchange must be a payment order, not merely as a demand, nor with any conditions or restrictions attached.

②In written form

According to this provision, the order must be made in a written form, which means bills, whether written, printed, typed, or even mechanically made, are valid only if signed correctly.

③Addressed by one person to another

According to this provision, the person issuing the order is called the drawer of the bill, while the person who receives the order is called the drawee. A draft is invalid unless it is signed by the drawer or by an authorized person.

④Requiring the person to whom it is addressed to pay on demand or at a fixed or a certain time in the future

Under this provision, the demand for payment must be made during normal business hours and at the place of business of the payer. A bill payable on demand is often called a sight bill. A bill payable on a fixed date or a future date that can be determined is a usance bill.

⑤A specific sum of money

This stipulates the amount of the bill, which is an important item. The amount must be accurate in both numbers and currencies.

⑥Pay to the specified person or the designated person or the bearer

This article stipulates that, the payment shall be made to the person listed on the bill of exchange (payee) or to the person named by the payee. According to bill law, "bearer" refers to the person with the bearer bill, not any other party to the bill of exchange.

A bill payable to the specific person or the person designated by him is called an order bill; while the bill payable to the bearer is called a bearer's bill.

【Tasks】

In the lead-in case, Nanhwa company issues a bank acceptance bill to Nam Kwong company and orders its own bank, Bank of China Jiangsu branch, to pay. In other words, Nanhwa company issues an unconditional written payment order to Bank of China Jiangsu branch, which is a bill of exchange. In this settlement relationship, Nanhwa company does not make the payment by itself, but entrusts its own bank to make the payment. This entrustment is an order rather than a request, because with Bank of China Jiangsu branch Nanhwa company has signed the entrustment payment agreement, where Nanhwa company has the right to issue the order, while Bank of China Jiangsu branch has an obligation to accept the order, which is for payment and is unconditional. All these reflect the basic characteristics of the bill of exchange. In this settlement business, the three basic parties of the bill are: the drawer-the importer Nanhwa company; the payee—Nam Kwong company, the exporter; and the drawee—the correspondent bank of the importer Nanhwa company, Bank of China, Jiangsu branch.

Task 8.2.2 Describe the entries in a bill of exchange

【Figures for demonstration】

Figure 8.6 shows a bill of exchange in international settlement. Please pay attention to the main items.

Bill of Exchange

No.SNO1234

Exchange for $7,856.00 Hong Kong, 25th July,2008

At sixty days after sight of this FIRST of Exchange(Second of the same tenor and date being unpaid) Pay to the order of The Chartered Bank

The sum of POUNDS STERLING SEVEN THOUSAND EIGHT HUNDRED AND FIRTY SIX ONLY

Drawn under Standard Chartered Bank Ltd,London Letter of Credit No.4/4108 dated 12th July,2008

against shipment of Grey Shirting from Hong Kong to Liverpool per S.SGolden Star.

To:Standrd Chartered Bank Ltd.
London

For:Hong Kong Textiles Manufacturing
Company,Hong Kong
(Authorized Signature)

Figure 8.6 Bill of exchange

【Questions for discussion】

With the above figure, please think:

(1) What are the basic items of a bill?

(2) What is the specific meaning of each item?

(3) Based on the above example, please write the corresponding parties in the draft and the finish the specific contents of related items.

After a free discussion, the students ought to summarize the necessary items of a bill under the guidance of the teacher.

【Relevant knowledge】

The necessary items of a bill are requisites in the form of a bill. Bills stress forms. According to the international convention, the establishment and validity of the bill of exchange is based on the completeness of the necessary items and their compliance with the provisions of the bill of exchange law. According to its nature and importance, the content of a bill can be divided into three different categories.

(1) Essential contents of a bill of exchange

Essential contents are the contents that must be recorded on a bill of exchange. The completion of the content directly relates to the validity of the bill. According to our country's *Negotiable Instruments Law*, the content that must be recorded on a bill of exchange includes the following items.

①Mark of bill of exchange

According to *Geneva Uniform Negotiable Instrument Law Act*, bills of exchange must be marked with "Bill of Exchange" "Exchange" or "Draft", to indicate the variety of the bill, so as to be differentiated from promissory notes, checks and other means of payment, while *UK Bills of Exchange Act* does not have this requirement, but the mark of "bill of exchange" is commonly added in practice.

②Unconditional payment order

A bill of exchange is a written payment order, where payment cannot be restricted or subject to any conditions, otherwise, the bill is invalid. However, the terms of issue, methods of payment, or consideration statements on bills of exchange are not taken as conditional orders of payment. Of course, the simplest way is to write "pay... yuan". Bills of exchange must be in written form, including in types of printing, handwriting and typing, but shall not be made with pencil or similar writing instruments.

a. Payment order must be made in imperative or commanding tones. Courtesy expressions (e.g., please) can be used, but the tone of discussion or request is not advisable, for example:

Pay to C Co. or its designee the sum of ten thousand United States dollars.	—valid
We shall be glad if you would pay to...	—invalid
Would you please pay to...	—invalid

b. The order of payment must be unconditional and any conditional order will void the bill, for example:

Pay to ... provided that the goods are up to the standard of the contract.	—invalid
Pay to the order of ... on the condition that they submit certificate of quality.	—invalid

● Indicating the origin of the transaction, that is, the draft clause, does not constitute a conditional order of payment, the draft is valid. In collections and letters of credit, most drafts require a draft clause.

> Drawn under Standard Chartered Bank Ltd., London Letter of Credit No. 4/4108 dated July 12, 2008 against shipment of Grey Shirting from Hong Kong to Liverpool per S. S. Golden Star. —valid

● Where a bill of exchange is indicated as to how to obtain reimbursement after payment does not constitute a conditional order of payment, the bill shall be valid.

> Pay to C Co. or order the sum of ten thousand United States dollars and debit our a/c with you. —valid

● "Consideration received" or "consideration paid" shall not constitute an order of payment nor affect the validity of the draft.

> Pay to C Co. or order the sum of ten thousand United States dollars only for value received. —valid

● An order indicating payment after certain conditions have been met is a conditional order and the bill is invalid.

> Pay to C Co. or order the sum of ten thousand United States dollars only if / providing the goods they supply are complied with contract No. SN01234. —invalid

• An order specifying payment from a particular fund constitutes a conditional payment order and the draft is invalid.

Pay to C Co. or order the sum of ten thousand United States dollars only out of the proceeds in our No. 1 a/c with you. —invalid

③Money in specified amount

Bill of exchange is a kind of money negotiable instrument, where the subject of payment must be currency. The payment cannot be expressed with the number of goods and the amount must be specific. In practice, in order to prevent alteration, the amount of the bill must be indicated by both amount in words which comes after "the sum of" and amount in figures written after "Exchange for". If inconformity appears between the two records, different countries will deal with it differently. According to the regulations from our country's laws of negotiable instrument, both records must be consistent with each other. Otherwise the draft is invalid. *Geneva Uniform Negotiable Instrument Law* and *UK Bills of Exchange Act* stipulate that amount in words shall prevail in case of inconsistency. In practice, the bill is usually returned. The amount of the bill includes a definite amount or an identifiable amount, which cannot be expressed approximately or selectively. When interest is included in the bill or an equal amount is required to be paid by installments or in other currencies, the specific amount to be paid ought to be clearly calculated, otherwise the bill is invalid.

a. Selective or floating entries invalidate the bill

For example,

The sum of about ten thousand United States dollars. —invalid
The sum of circa ten thousand United States dollars. —invalid
The sum of one thousand United States dollars or two thousand United States dollars. —invalid

b. Interest clause

A bill of exchange can be marked with interests according to a certain interest rate or the market interest rate on a certain day, but must indicate the interest rate, the date of commencement and the date of termination of the interest. Otherwise the bill is invalid, for example:

Pay to C Co. or order the sum of ten thousand United States dollars plus interest. —invalid
Pay to C Co. or order the sum of ten thousand United States dollars plus interest calculated at the rate of 6.0% per ammum from the date hereof to the date of payment. —valid

c. Installment clause

When the bill of exchange indicates installments, the installment terms must be specific and workable. Otherwise the bill is invalid, for example:

Pay to C Co. or order the sum of ten thousand United States dollars by installment. —invalid
Pay to C Co. or order the sum of ten thousand United States dollars by four equal consecutive monthly installment. —invalid

d. Exchange rate clause.

When the bill of exchange is marked with payment by other currencies of equivalent value, the bill shall be paid after conversion at a certain or identifiable exchange rate, and be marked with interest rates. Otherwise the bill shall be invalid, for example:

Pay to C Co. or order the sum of ten thousand United States dollars converted into sterling equivalent. —invalid
Pay to C Co. or order the sum of ten thousand United States dollars converted into sterling equivalent at current rate of exchange. —invalid

When there is a decimal in the amount of the bill, there are several ways to express it (take US $2 356.89 as an example).

United States dollars two thousand three hundred and fifty six and cents eighty nine only
United States dollars two thousand three hundred and fifty six and eighty nine percent only
United States dollars two thousand three hundred and fifty six and point eighty nine only

④Name of the payer

The payer is the person who receives the order to pay, that is, the drawee, but the drawee may not pay because he may refuse to pay. The payer or the drawee, usually in the sentence beginning with "To…" in the bill of exchange, should be recorded with reasonable certainty to make sure that the payer can be found successfully without any mistakes. In practice, the payer must give full details of his or her address. The name and the address of the drawee must be clearly written so that the holder may present the drawee for payment or acceptance. Drawee and drawer should be two different parties, but *Geneva Uniform Negotiable Instrument Law* and *UK Bills of Exchange Act* stipulate that, the drawee of bill of exchange can be the drawer himself. There is usually only one drawee, but *UK Bills of Exchange Act* allows a draft to be drawn on two, however a bill drawn on A or B is not permissible, because the drawee is uncertain, for example, the payer may be recorded as "A and B", but not as "A or B".

⑤Name of the payee

Usually referred to as "order" in our country, the payee is the original holder of rights indicated on the bill of exchange, which should be recorded. Like the payer, it should be written with certainty. In practice, the address is not necessary, only a full name is required. Payee in the bill of exchange can be recorded in three ways, and its expression determines whether and how the bill of exchange is circulated.

a. Restrictive order

Restrictive order is a form in which the payee of a bill of exchange is written as the person paid only or as the person paid without transfer. In practice, it is often written as: "Pay A Co.

Only" "Pay A Co. not transferable/negotiable" or "Pay A Co." with the statement "not transferable" in the other place of the bill. Such bills of exchange are not negotiable. The debtor is only responsible to the named payee. Restricted order is not negotiable and therefore rarely used in practice.

b. Demonstrative order

Demonstrative order refers to a form where the payment of a bill of exchange is written as paid to a person designated by the payee. In practice it is written as "Pay A Co. Or order" "Pay to the order of A Co." or "Pay A Co." A demonstrative order may be endorsed by the payee before the payee delivers the bill for transferring his rights. If the drawer is the payee, the bill is self-indicting and transferrable after endorsement by the drawer. Being transferrable is one of the most basic natures of negotiable instruments. Notes are all negotiable in nature unless stated with "non-transferrable". Most bills of exchange issued in practice are drafts with demonstrative order.

c. Payable to bearer

This kind of bill does not record the name of the payee, but only "payable to the bearer". In practice, it is often written as: "Pay to bearer/holder" "Pay to A Co. Or bearer". Such bills of exchange are negotiable, and the right to the instrument is transferrable upon delivery, while endorsement is not necessary. Accordingly, in the circulation, the bill instead of the holder is recognized. Therefore the risk is relatively large. *UK Bills of Exchange Act* allows the bearer to act as the payee, while according to *Geneva Uniform Negotiable Instrument Law* and our country's *Negotiable Instruments Law*, a bill of exchange with the bearer acting as the order is not allowed.

⑥Date of issue

Date of issue is the date of issuing the bill of exchange. It is usually situated at the top right corner of the bill, adjacent to the place of issue. It is a necessary item of the bill of exchange, because if it is missing, the bill becomes invalid. The date of issue is of great importance because it plays a crucial role in the following three aspects:

a. It determines the validity of the draft

The date of issue determines the deadline of presentation, to be specific, it is the basis of presentation for payment and presentation for acceptance. The circulation of a bill of exchange has its time limit, namely the period of validity, which begins from the issuing date. The validity period of a bill of exchange cannot be determined if it is not dated. *Geneva Uniform Negotiable Instrument Law* stipulates that bills payable at sight must be presented within 1 year from the date of issue. Otherwise the bill becomes invalid and the drawee may refuse to pay. Our country's *Negotiable Instruments Law* provides that sight drafts shall be presented for payment to the drawee within 1 month from the date of issue.

b. It determines the maturity date of the bill

It is the basis for calculating the maturity date of a usance bill payable several days (months) after the date of issue. Suppose the deadline for paying the bill is at 30 days from the date hereof, if the bill is issued on "July 13, 2008," the maturity date of the draft shall be

August 12, 2008.

c. It determines the capacity of the drawer

If, when issuing the bill, the drawer has declared bankruptcy or liquidation, then the bill cannot be established. If the drawer issues the bill before declaring bankruptcy or liquidation, the holder can hold the bill as a general creditor into the drawer's bankruptcy liquidation procedures after the drawee refuses to pay.

To avoid confusion, it is recommended to use months (such as Jan., Feb., Mar., etc., or January, February, March, etc.) instead of numbers. Anglo-American bill laws do not consider the date of issue as a necessary item.

⑦Signature of the drawer

Signature principle is one of the most important and basic principles in *Negotiable Instruments Law*. The liability of negotiable instrument is assumed by signing. Whoever signs the bill shall be responsible for it. It is the fundamental basis to determine whether the debtor of the negotiable instrument must bear the debts of the negotiable instrument and the important formal element to determine whether the negotiable instrument is valid or not. When a drawer issues a draft, he must first sign his name on it, acknowledging his liabilities, before the draft is valid. If the signature is forged, the draft is invalid. Our country's *Negotiable Instruments Law* stipulates that, the signature on a negotiable instrument shall be in autograph or in seal or in autograph plus seal. *UK Bills of Exchange Act* stipulates that it must be signed manually. In the current practice, foreign-related bills should be signed by hand. If the drawer is a company, it shall be signed by the legal representative of the company (preferably signed by hand) together with the official seal of the company; while if the drawer is an individual, and the bill is signed by the principal acting on behalf of him, such as a company, an organization, a bank or a group, the name of the company shall be prefixed with "For" or "On behalf of" or "For and On behalf of" or "Per pro.", and the personal signature shall be followed with the job title, generally written at the right lower part of the draft, for example:

For ABC Co. Ltd., New York

John Smith, General Manager

The above items are necessary according to our country's *Negotiable Instruments Law*. Otherwise the bill of exchange is invalid. The provisions of *Geneva Uniform Negotiable Instrument Law* are basically the same as those of our country, while there are only 5 necessary items stipulated in *UK Bills of Exchange Act*, namely unconditional payment order, definite amount, name of drawee, name of payee and signature of drawer without the word "draft" and requirement on date of issue. The act holds that the absence of the word "bill" does not affect the validity of the bill, and the bill remains valid without the date of issue. If a usance draft is drawn, the bona fide holder may add the date of issue to ensure the maturity date so as to make it a full draft.

(2) Relatively essential contents of a bill of exchange

In addition to the above items that must be recorded, there are three relatively necessary items which are also important but do not affect the legal effect of bills of exchange if they are not recorded, because they can be concluded indirectly.

①Place of issue

The place of issue is the place where the drawer issues the draft, usually at the top right corner of the draft, which is next to the date of issue. The place of issue is of great significance to the international bill of exchange, because international practice follows the legal principle of the place of act. The establishment of the bill is judged by the law of the place of issue, that is, whether the necessary items are complete and whether the bill is established and effective are all based on the national law of the place of issue. International bills of exchange shall indicate the place of issue, which shall be the same as the address of the drawer, and the address of the drawer shall be the place of issue if the place of issue is not indicated. Our country's *Negotiable Instruments Law* stipulates, if the place of issue is not recorded on the bill of exchange, the place of issue shall be the business premises, domicile or habitual residence of the drawer.

②Place of payment

The place of payment is the place where the holder presents the draft and requests payment. The address next to the name of the drawee is the place of payment. It plays a very important role, because according to the "principle of the place of conduct" of private international law, such acts as "acceptance" "payment" "issuance of the certificate of protest" and determination of the maturity date are all applicable to the law of the place of payment. The address should be indicated in practice for the convenience of presentation. Our country's *Negotiable Instruments Law* regulates that where the place of payment is not specified on the bill of exchange, the business premises, domicile or habitual residence of the drawee shall be the place of payment.

③Tenor

Tenor, also known as the time of payment or maturity, is the due date on which the payer fulfills his payment obligation. In import and export trade, the exporter often voluntarily or passively gives the importer a certain period of time for payment, which is equivalent to giving the latter a certain period of credit time. Accordingly, bills can be payable at sight or after sight.

a. Payment at sight

Payment at sight is also known as payable at sight. Upon the holder claims his right of the bill after the completion of the drawing, and the drawee shall make payment to the holder immediately without accepting the bill. Our country's bill of exchange law stipulates that, bills of exchange, if the time of payment fails to be recorded on it, are sight bills. Payment at sight is usually expressed as "at sight" "on demand" "on presentation pay to...", for example:

At sight pay to C Co. or order the sum of ten thousand United States dollars. —sight draft
On demand pay to C Co. or order the sum of ten thousand United States dollars. —sight draft
On presentation pay to C Co. or order the sum of ten thousand United States dollars. —sight draft

b. Payable at usance

It means that when the holder first presents the bill to the drawee, the drawee only accepts the bill and the payment occurs at a fixed or identifiable time in the future. Usance bills require the drawee to confirm the obligation of payment due and the specific date of payment. The drawee should write "acceptance" on the bill, and then indicate the date of acceptance and sign his name. Upon acceptance, the drawee must pay at maturity. There are four common ways of recording forward payment:

- At a fixed date

Payment at a fixed date is also called board date. The due date of payment on the bill of exchange is specified as the fixed date of payment in the future, often expressed as "on × × × fixed pay to..." , for example:

On April 10, 2008 fixed pay to C Co. the sum of ten thousand United States dollars. —usance draft

- At a fixed period after date

Payment at a fixed period after date, also known as payment after date, refers to the payment made in a number of days or months after the date of issue in a bill of exchange. Such bills of exchange are first presented to the drawee by the holder for acceptance within the specified time, and then the due date is calculated from the date of issue. Such bills of exchange are frequently used in international trade settlements, expressed as "at × × × days (months) after date pay to..." , for example:

At 30 days after date pay to C Co. the sum of ten thousand United States dollars. —usance draft
At 3 months after date pay to C Co. the sum of ten thousand United States dollars. —usance draft

- At a fixed period after sight

Payment at a fixed period after sight, also known as payment after sight, refers to payment in a number of days or months after the date of sight. A bill of exchange of this kind is first presented to the drawee by the holder for acceptance within the specified time, and then the due date is calculated from the date of acceptance. This kind of bill of exchange is widely used in international trade settlements, expressed as "at × × × days (months) after sight pay to..." , for example:

At 30 days after sight pay to C Co. the sum of ten thousand United States dollars. —usance draft
At 3 months after sight pay to C Co. the sum of ten thousand United States dollars. —usance draft

- At a fixed period after the happening of a specified event

It refers to the payment in a number of days or months after the occurrence of a particular event (such as the date of bill of lading, the date of delivery). Such bills are separated from the date of issue and the date of sight, so the due date of payment demonstrates and also depends on the date on which the exporter delivers the goods to the carrier and obtains the transport documents from the carrier, or the date on which the beneficiary delivers the bill to the bank, expressed as "at × × × days (months) after B/L (presentation) pay to. . . ", for example:

> At 90 days after B/L pay to C Co. the sum of ten thousand United States dollars.
>
> —usance draft
>
> At 1 months after B/L pay to C Co. the sum of ten thousand United States dollars.
>
> —usance draft
>
> At 30 days after presentation of documents pay to C Co. the sum of ten thousand United States dollars. —usance draft

c. Calculation of the maturity date of payment for usance draft

For bills of exchange expressed with payment in several days or months after date, after sight, after bill of lading and after presentation, the specific time of future payment needs to be specified. In practice, the due date of payment of such bills is usually calculated according to the following principles.

- For the bill of exchange payable a few days after date or after sight, the principle adopted is: "the ending instead of the beginning is calculated and holiday is postponed accordingly". To make it more specific, the date of sight, the date of issue and the date of bill of lading are not included in the calculation of the payment date. Instead, the next day is calculated as the starting date, and the last day is the maturity date, which is included in the calculation, but if the due date is a statutory holiday, it shall be postponed to the next business day.

Case 8.1 The draft states "at 30 days after date pay to C Co. the sum of ten thousand United States dollars". If the date of issue is March 1, 2008, the date of March 1 will not be counted, instead, March 2 will be taken as the first day in the calculation, so the maturity date of the draft is March 31, 2008. If the date of issue is April 1 2008 and 30 days later it is a holiday; May 1 2008, the due date will be extended to the next business day i. e., May 4 2008.

- For bills of exchange payable several months after the date of issue or at sight, the "month to month principle" is adopted, i. e., the corresponding date of the corresponding month when due is the maturity date; if there is no corresponding date in the corresponding month when due, the last day of that month is the maturity date.

Case 8.2 The draft is stated as "At 2 months after sight pay to C Co. The sum of ten thousand United States dollars". If the date of acceptance (i. e., the date of sight) is June 8, 2008, then the maturity date of the draft is August 8, 2008. If the acceptance date is December 31, 2008, the corresponding date after 2 months is February 31, 2009, but February only has 28 days. Therefore the maturity date is February 28, 2009.

(3) Arbitrary items of a bill of exchange

The above basic content explains the general items of a bill of exchange, but it does not cover the whole items on a bill, because a bill still has a few arbitrary items. Arbitrary items refer to the items out of the above mentioned two categories, which state limitation or exemption of the liabilities recorded by the drawer as required. Once these items are accepted, they become binding.

①Draw clause

Draw clause is a clause indicating the origin of a bill of exchange, usually indicating the contract number of the buyer and the seller or the credit number of a bank. A bill of exchange is an unconditional payment order and a draw clause indicating the origin of the transaction shall not be deemed as an additional condition. It is recorded as follows:

Drawn under:	
DC No. :	Date:

②Pay this first / second bill (second / first of the same tenor and date being Unpaid to …) clause

A bill of exchange may be drawn in duplicate but represents only one debt. The reason for this is that a bill of exchange, as a payment order, is usually accompanied by shipping documents representing property rights, as a documentary bill of exchange, which is mailed by the exporter to the importer. Therefore two sets of documentary bills of exchange with content exactly the same are sent by two consecutive flights in case of being lost in the mail. If the first set of documentary bills (including the first bill) does not arrive due to flight problems, the delivery of goods, settlement and payment will not be delayed, because the second set of documentary bills (including the second bill) will arrive. It should be noted that these two bills of exchange with identical contents are neither the original nor the copy. Both of them are valid payment orders. When the first bill of exchange is paid, the second bill of exchange automatically becomes invalid, and vice versa.

③Person designated as payer

The person designated as payer is the one who replaces the drawee to perform the payment as indicated at the time of drawing or designated by the drawee at the time of acceptance according to the agreement with the drawee for the purpose of convenience. The person designated as payer is not the debtor of the instrument, but the entrusted drawee based on presumption, who is not liable for the instrument. The holder shall first demand acceptance from the drawee and on the due date present the person designated as payer for payment.

④Referee in case of need

Referee in case of need is equivalent to the second drawee, to whom the holder may request acceptance or payment when the drawee refuses acceptance or payment. When referee in case of need has presented the bill, he becomes the debtor of the bill after accepting it and pays the bill on the due date. The referee in case of need is generally indicated on the front of the bill in the position where the drawee is located. A detailed address should be indicated so that it is convenient for the holder to present the bill to him.

To: A Co.
Payable by B bank.

To: A Co.
In case of need refer to B bank.

⑤A set of bill

In order to prevent the bill from being lost in mail, bills of exchange are often drawn on a group of identical bills at the same time. However, sometimes only one draft (marked with "solo", meaning only one draft) is drawn for the negotiating bank nominated by L/C to claim against the nominated reimbursing bank. In a set of bills, each bill is identical to each other in value and content. Therefore, to avoid repeat payment, each bill must be numbered and the number of the full set should be crossed. For the bill of exchange in duplicate forms, the first is the first of exchange, sometimes marked with the word "Original" below; while the second one is called the second of exchange, sometimes indicated with the word "Duplicate" below. For the bill of exchange in triplicate, the first two bills are the same as above, and the third bill is the third of exchange. In a set of bills of exchange, each bill is valid, but after anyone is paid, the other will automatically become invalid and will not be paid anymore. The above content is indicated in each bill of exchange, which is marked with "Pay this first (second of the same tenor and date being unpaid)" on the first of exchange, and marked with "Pay second bill (first of the same tenor and date being unpaid)" on the second of exchange. Bills of exchange used in international settlements are most common in single and in duplicate.

⑥Notice of dishonor excused or protest waived

The bill can have the statement of "notice of dishonor excused" or "protest waived", which is recorded by the drawer or the endorser next to their signatures to express their waiving of such a demand on the holder, so as to save the cost of the certificate of protest and notice of dishonor. When the bill is dishonored, the holder may directly exercise his right of recourse without giving the notice of dishonor or the certificate of protest. If the statement of "protest waived" is indicated on the bill of exchange and holder still made a certificate of protest, his behavior is valid, however, the production cost is not borne by the drawer, but paid by the holder himself.

John Smith notice of dishonor excused. John Smith protest waived.

⑦No recourse clause

According to *UK Bills of Exchange Act*, the drawer or endorser can exempt themselves from the liability of recourse after the bill is dishonored through a non-recourse clause, which, in effect, exonerates the drawer or endorser from their liabilities for the draft. Non-recourse clauses can be specified in the bill as "Pay to C Co. or order the sum of ten thousand United States dollars without recourse to me", or in the blank of the draft as "without recourse". According to *Geneva Uniform Negotiable Instrument Law*, the drawer can relieve his obligation of guaranteeing acceptance, but any provision of relieving the drawer's obligation of guaranteeing payment shall be regarded as invalid.

In addition to the above, arbitrary items of a bill of exchange also include any specified payment terms of currency, interest, interest rate and exchange rate, presentation for acceptance required or acceptance prohibited, and the value received, etc.

(4) The general format of bills of exchange in international trade

The general format of bills of exchange used in international trade is shown in figure 8.7.

Drawn under ____________________

L/C No. ____________________

Date ____________________

Payable with interest@ ______%Per annum

No, ______ Exchange for ____________ Shanghai,China.Date: ______ **1**

At ____________ sight of this First of Exchange(Second of exchange being unpaid)

Pay to the order of ____

The sum of ____

To ____________________

____________________ For ____________________

____________________ (*Authorized signature*)

Figure 8.7 General format of draft

【Tasks】

In the case for study at the beginning of this section, the corresponding parties and related items in the bill are as follows:

(1) Three basic parties to the bill

Drawer and place of business: Hong Kong Textiles Manufacturing Company, Hong Kong.

Payer and place of payment: Standard Chartered Bank Ltd., London.

Payee: The Chartered Bank.

(2) Other items of the bill

Number: SN01234.

Amount: (in figures) £ 7 856.00; (in words) pounds sterling seven thousand eight hundered and fifty six only.

Drawn under: Standard Chartered Bank Ltd., London Letter of Credit No. 4/4108 dated July 12, 2008 against the shipment of Grey Shirting from Hong Kong to Liverpool per S. S. Golden Star.

Payment term: Sixty days after sight.

Date and place of issue: Hong Kong, July 25, 2008.

Task 8.2.3 Behaviours of bills of exchange

【Questions for discussion】

Bill behavior includes drawing, endorsement, acceptance, guarantee, presentation, payment, acceptance in honor, payment in honor, dishonor, recourse, etc. Featuring formality as the form and the content of bill of exchange, bill behavior must comply with the provisions of bill law. Bill of exchange act is the complete act in the whole bill act, bill of exchange act except individual act, apply to promissory note and check. Bill of exchange behavior is the most complete in the whole bill behaviors and can apply to promissory notes and checks except individual acts.

In international settlements, mastering the main acts of the bill of exchange is one of the basic skills for international traders. Combined with the lead-in case, please think:

(1) What are the main acts of bills of exchange?

(2) How can we put them into practice?

(3) Please complete the main bill behavior according to the lead-in case.

After free discussion, the students summarize the main acts of the bill of exchange under the guidance of the teacher.

【Relevant knowledge】

(1) Draw a bill

The drawing of a bill of exchange includes making a bill of exchange, signing and delivery. When making a bill of exchange, we shall strictly comply with the formality of the bill. The drawer must record legal contents on the bill according to the regulation of relevant bill law. Under the letter of credit settlement, the draft should be drawn as follows:

①The parties should be clearly indicated with a detailed address, and both these two items should comply with the provisions of the letter of credit or the contract.

②The amount of the draft shall not exceed the amount of the credit, with the amount in words the same as the amount in figures and the currency name in a draft consistent with it in the invoice and the letter of credit. When making a draft, it is a common practice to add "say" before the sum and "only" after the sum to prevent the addition of content.

③The date of issue should be accurate and conform to the requirements of the letter of credit or the contract. The term of payment should be in accordance with the letter of credit.

④Number of a bill of exchange. The number of a bill of exchange is compiled by the drawer himself. Generally, the corresponding invoice number is used as the number of the bill of exchange for reference. It can also be compiled by the seller in proper order from the first bill of exchange based on the actual needs of the exported goods. Some overseas bills of exchange have no numbers, our country often uses the uniform number of the bank.

⑤Draw clause. If there are specific provisions in the letter of credit, the draft should be drawn in accordance with the specific provisions of the L/C. If the terms of the draft are not specified in the L/C, the drawer may prepare the terms of the draft at his own discretion, including the name and place of the issuing bank, the L/C number and the issuing date of the L/C, for example, "Drawn under Bank of China Jiangsu branch, L/C No. 06 – 1234 dated June 10, 2008". If the draft is drawn on a collection basis, the contract number and date should be indicated, together with "for collection".

⑥The bill of exchange (payee) is usually written in three ways with different expressions determining different negotiability and ways of circulation of the bill, as is shown in table 8.1.

Table 8.1 Expressions and relevant negotiability of drafts

Classification	Expression	Transferable	Mode of transfer
Demonstrative to order	The order of C Co. Pay to C Co. or order C Co.	Yes	By endorsement
Restrictive order	C Co. only Pay to C Co. not transferable C Co. not negotiable	No	–
Payable to bearer	Bearer Pay to C Co. or bearer The order of C Co. or bearer	Yes	By delivery

(2) Endorsement

The bearer signs the bill in person and gives it to the other party to complete the endorsement. Not all bills of exchange need to be endorsed by the holder to transfer the right, only the bill of exchange with demonstrative order must be endorsed in order to transfer the right to receive the bill. Generally, the bill can be transferred in the market after re-endorsement, but the endorsement must be done in succession to preserve the bill rights. The types and expressions of endorsement is shown in table 8.2.

Table 8.2 Classification and expressions of endorsement of bills of exchange

Classification	Expression	Transferrable
Special endorsement	Pay to the order of B Co. For C Co. Nanjing Signature	Transferable by endorsement
Open endorsement	For C Co. Nanjing Signature	Transferrable by delivery or endorsement
Restrictive endorsement	Pay to B Co. only /not transferable / not negotiable For C Co. Nanjing Signature	No transferrable
Endorsement with attached conditions	Pay to B Co. on delivery of B/L No. 1234 For C Co. Nanjing Signature	Transferrable by endorsement
Endorsement for collection	Pay to B Bank for collection For C Co. Nanjing Signature	Transferrable by endorsement

Note: take "Pay to the order of C Co." as an example, the payee C Co. is the endorser.

(3) Presentation

Sight drafts only have a presentation for payment, while usance drafts usually have to be presented for acceptance before presentation for payment at maturity. The holder must make a presentation to the payer at the specified time and the stated place of payment, or will lose the right of recourse against his remote holder and the drawer. *Geneva Uniform Negotiable Instrument Law* stipulates that the bill payable at a fixed period after sight shall be presented for acceptance within 1 year; while drafts payable at sight shall be presented for payment within 1 year. The drawer may extend or shorten the term, while the endorser may shorten the time limit only. *UK Bills of Exchange Act* does not provide for a specific period of presentation, only requiring presentation in a "reasonable time". Our country's *Negotiable Instruments Law* regulates that the bill of exchange payable at a fixed date or at a fixed period after date shall be presented for acceptance to the drawee before the date of maturity. For bills of exchange payable at a fixed period after sight, presentation for acceptance shall be made to the drawee within 1 month from the date of drawing. For bills of exchange payable at sight, presentation for payment shall be made to the drawee within 1 month from the date of drawing. For bills payable at a fixed date, a fixed period after sight or a fixed period after date, the acceptor shall be presented for payment within 10 days from the due date.

(4) Acceptance

When accepting, the drawee should write "accepted" on the front of the bill, mark the date of acceptance and sign. Only the signature of the payer without other words also constitutes acceptance. Acceptance can also be accomplished by issuing a notice of acceptance. There are two ways of acceptance: one is general acceptance, according to which, the contents of the draft shall be accepted without any restriction; and the other is qualified acceptance, which is the acceptance of a bill of exchange payable at maturity with some reservations, such as conditional acceptance, partial acceptance, acceptance as to time, local acceptance, payment not accepted by all the drawees, etc. Acceptance under normal circumstances is general acceptance. For qualified acceptance, the holder has the right to refuse, which can be regarded as the acceptor's refusal to accept. If the holder accepts qualified acceptance and the drawer or the endorser, however, neither has authorization nor agrees afterward, the holder cannot exercise the right of recourse against them. The classification and expression of acceptance are shown in table 8.3 (Take the indication of "At 30 days after sight, pay to the order of Bank of China, Nanjing the sum of United States dollars ten thousand only" on the front of the bill of exchange as an example, and the payer is C Co.).

Table 8.3 Classification of acceptance

Classification	Expression	Effect of acceptance
General acceptance	Accepted June 10, 2008 For C Co. Nanjing Signature	It is an effective acceptance. The payer after acceptance becomes the principal debtor of the bill and must make payment when due

Table 8.3(continued)

Classification		Expression	Effect of acceptance
Qualified acceptance	Conditional acceptance	Accepted payable on delivery of B/L No. 1234 June 10, 2008 For C Co. Nanjing Signature	●The holder has the right to refuse and takes qualified acceptance as dishonor so as to exercise the right of recourse. ● The payer shall be responsible for the attached conditions and be bound by the acceptance attached to conditions. ●The accept qualified acceptance and request payment according to the attached conditions, but if the drawer or the endorser neither gives authorization nor agrees afterward, the holder loses the right of recourse
	Partial acceptance	Accepted payable for US $ 8, 000.00 only June 10, 2008 For C Co. Nanjing Signature	
	Local acceptance	Accepted payable at Bank of China, Shanghai only June 10, 2008 For C Co. Nanjing Signature	
	Acceptance as to time	Accepted payable at 60 days after sight June 10, 2008 For C Co. Nanjing Signature	

(5) Guarantee

China's Negotiable Instruments Law stipulates that only the third party other than the debtor of the bill can act as the guarantor, because the purpose of guarantee of bills is to increase the credibility of the bill, and the debtor of the bill of exchange should be responsible for the bill of exchange in the literal sense. If they act as guarantor, the credit of the bill cannot be increased. The guarantor may provide a guaranty for the drawer, the endorser, the acceptor and the acceptor in honor, and shall indicate the word "aval/guarantee" and sign, indicating the date of guaranty and the guaranteed. If the date of guaranty is not indicated, the date of drawing shall be deemed as the date of guaranty. If the guaranteed is not indicated, the drawer shall be the guaranteed for the bill not accepted and the acceptor shall be the guaranteed for the bill accepted. No conditions shall be attached to the guaranty, and if there are such conditions, they shall not affect the guaranty liability of the guarantor for the bill of exchange. The expression of guarantee is shown in figure 8.8.

Per Aval	Guarantee
For: C Co.(name of the guaranteed)	For: C Co.(name of the guaranteed)
Signed by: A Co.(name of guarantor)	Signed by: A Co.(name of guarantor)
Dated on June 10.2008(date of guarantee)	Dated on June 10.2008(date of guarantee)
Signature(signature of guarantor)	Signature(signature of guarantor)

Figure 8.8 Expression of guarantee

(6) Payment, dishonor and recourse

At the maturity date of the bill, the drawee shall pay the amount of the bill upon presentation by the holder, and the holder shall sign "paid" on the bill and deliver it to the drawee, then the liability of all debtors of the bill is discharged. If the payer refuses to pay, the holder may exercise the right of recourse. When exercising it, the holder must make a certificate of protest within the statutory period after the instrument has been dishonored, and the notice of dishonor must inform the remote holder of the fact of dishonor within the statutory period after dishonor. In recourse, the holder may recourse against any remote holder or drawer, regardless of the order. The procedure of bill recourse is shown in figure 8.9.

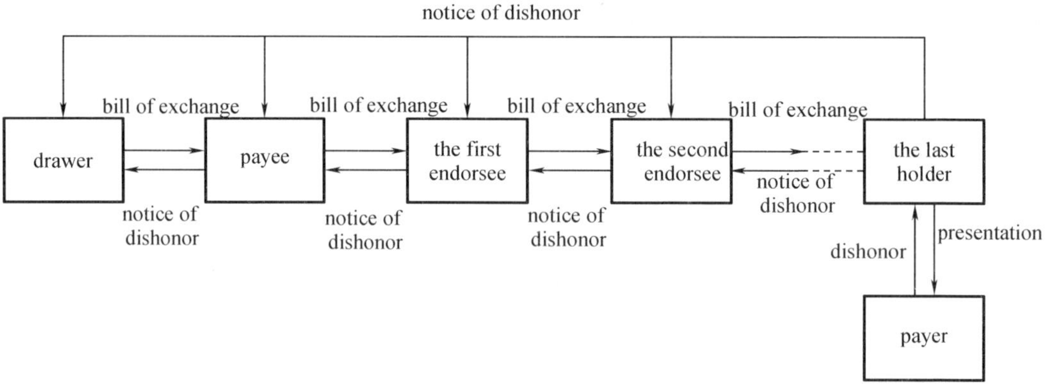

Figure 8.9 Procedure of bill recourse

(7) Acceptance in honor and payment in honor of draft

Acceptance in honor refers to the acceptance of dishonored bills by the non-debtor of the bills to prevent the exercise of the right of recourse and maintain the credibility of the drawer and the endorser under the premise of the consent of the holder. The acceptor in honor is only a secondary debtor, who is only responsible for paying when the principal debtor does not pay and thus becomes the payer in honor. *UK Bills of Exchange Act* stipulates that the acceptor in honor is a third party other than the debtor of the bill, while *Geneva Uniform Negotiable Instrument Law* stipulates that the acceptor in honor or the payer in honor may be any person other than the acceptor, including the drawer, the endorser, the guarantor, and the preparatory payer. Our country's *Negotiable Instruments Law* does not have this provision. Acceptance in honor shall be recorded on the bill, which shall be signed and sealed by the acceptor in honor (in the absence of such record, the drawer shall be deemed to be the acceptor in honor). The general expression of acceptance in honor is shown in figure 8.10.

Accepted for honour of B Co.
June 10,2008
For C Co.
Signature

Figure 8.10 General expressions of acceptance in honor

(8) Discount of bill of exchange

Discount is a kind of financial transaction in which a commercial enterprise or an individual exchanges an undue note for cash and the bank deducts interests in advance when making payment.

For a bank, a discount is actually a loan with interests deducted in advance. Since commercial bills have trade backgrounds and banks have goods as collateral, it is safe for banks. Therefore they do not need to take any other collateral. In addition, the bank can sell the bills bought as a discount when their funds are tight, so that there is great flexibility in the use of funds.

For commercial enterprises or individuals, it is quite convenient to get cash in advance and get access to funds through bill discounts. Generally speaking, a discount does not need collateral and the procedure is relatively simple. Therefore, bills of exchange are often used in discounts.

Discounts of commercial paper in progress are a very good source of financing. Only those bills with higher credit can be discounted, since the notes of those debtors with lower credit will bring great risk to the bank. Generally speaking, small and medium-sized manufacturers are of less capital and lower popularity. Therefore, the draft signed by them is less possibly accepted. But if the bill is signed by a bank, the price of the bill will increase and its acceptability will also grow. Banks and discount houses are usually willing to discount only bills of exchange from large enterprises, while bills issued by small and medium-sized enterprises can generally get discounts after acceptance by the bank.

【Tasks】

In the lead-in case for study, Nanhwa company opens a bank acceptance bill to Nam Kwong company. When Nanhwa company issues the bill, it is necessary for it to make the bill first and then hand it to Nam Kwong company after signing the bill. Nam Kwong company then sends the draft to Bank of China Jiangsu Branch for acceptance. When Bank of China Jiangsu branch makes the acceptance, it should make the corresponding record on the front of the bill. Nam Kwong company transfers it to the pharmaceutical company after endorsement. When making the endorsement, Nam Kwong company should make the corresponding record on the back of the bill.

(1) When Nanhwa company issues the draft, it makes the draft as follows:

Exchange for CNY 500 000.00 Hong Kong, March 15, 2008

At two months after the date of this of exchange (second of the same tenor and date unpaid), pay to the order of Jiangsu Nam Kwong International Trading Corp.

The sum of SAY CHINESE YUAN FIVE HUNDRED THOUSAND ONLY

To: Bank of China, Jiangsu Branch, Nanjing

For: Hong Kong Nanhwa International
Trading Co., Ltd, Hong Kong
(Authorized Signature)

(2) When Bank of China Jiangsu branch makes acceptance, the content recorded on the

front of the bill is as follows:

Accepted March 20, 2008 For Bank of China, Jiangsu Branch, Nanjing Signature

(3) When making an endorsement, Nam Kwong company records the corresponding contents on the back of the bill as follows:

Pay to the order of Nanjing Pharmaceutical Co. ,Ltd For Jiangsu Nam Kwong International Trading Corp. Signature

Task 8.2.4 The classification of bills of exchange

【Questions for discussion】

The bills of exchange used in international settlements can be classified into different categories from different perspectives. Different kinds of bills of exchange have different characteristics and can apply to different situations in practice. Being familiar with the main types of bills of exchange is the basis for international traders to conduct international settlements. Combined with the lead-in case, please consider the following questions:

(1) What are the main types of bills of exchange?

(2) How can we use them in practice?

After a free discussion, students can summarize the main types of bills of exchange under the guidance of the teacher.

【Relevant knowledge】

(1) According to different drawers

Commercial draft is a draft issued by an industrial and commercial enterprise or an individual. Its payer may be a company, an enterprise, an individual or a bank. Commercial bills of exchange are based on commercial credit, and the risk is borne by the payee or the bearer is relatively large, but the risk can be reduced to a certain extent by acceptance. A commercial draft is usually a draft drawn by an exporter, which is used when the exporter commissions a local bank to collect payment from a foreign importer or a bank. Most commercial bills of exchange are attached by shipping documents.

Banker's draft is a draft drawn by a banker to entrust a foreign branch or a correspondent bank to make payment. Both the drawer and the payer are banks. In the method of remittance settlement, the bank draft is used for the negotiable instrument business. The importer purchases the draft issued by the bank from the bank and sends it to the exporter abroad. The exporter holds the bill of exchange to the paying bank to get payment. When a bank issues a draft, it must send a notice of payment to the paying bank for checking. The credit basis of bank bills is bank credit, which is less risky than commercial bills.

(2) According to whether attached by shipping documents

A clean bill, also known as a white bill, is a bill of exchange without any shipping documents representing property in goods. Its circulation is entirely based on the credit of the parties to the bill (drawer, payer, endorser), so it is generally not used to collect payment for goods. In international trade settlements, clean bills are generally limited to the incidental expenses (such as freight, insurance, interest, etc.), payment balance, commission, etc. Because banks have high credit, bank drafts are usually clean bills.

Documentary bill, also known as credit bill, refers to the bill of exchange that needs to be attached by commercial documents (commercial invoice, bill of lading, warehouse receipt, insurance policy, packing list, etc.) before payment.

Commercial bills of exchange are mostly documentary bills, which embody the principle of cross-flow between payment for goods and documents and provide a certain security for both the import and the export. They are commonly used in international trade settlements.

(3) According to different time of payment

Sight /demand bill is a bill of exchange payable by the drawee immediately after the presentation by the holder. It does not require acceptance. A draft without a specific date of payment is generally regarded as a sight draft. The holder of a sight draft must make a presentation to the drawee for payment within the prescribed time, otherwise, the drawer and all endorsers shall be relieved of their liabilities, however, provided that the delayed presentation is not caused by the drawer, the delayed presentation is allowed.

A time/usance bill is a bill payable by the drawee at a specified period after the date of issue or a specified date. It must be accepted by the drawee. To be specific, the draft payable at the maturity date recorded on it is the fixed bill of exchange, the bill payable in a certain period after the date of issue is the dated bill of exchange, the bill payable in a certain period after sight is the note dated bill of exchange, and the bill whose face amount is divided into several shares with each share designated a maturity date is the installment bill of exchange.

(4) According to different acceptors

Banker's acceptance bill is a usance draft drawn by companies, enterprises or individuals on a bank and accepted by the paying bank mainly for commercial bills. The acceptance of commercial bills of exchange by banks changes the credit basis of bills of exchange and converts commercial credit into bank credit. The holder can usually get paid when it is due, thus enhancing the acceptability and negotiability of bills of exchange. In international trade settlements, it is usually authorized by the bank of the importing country to issue a usance bill with that bank or its nominated bank as the drawee. Upon acceptance the drawee becomes the principal debtor of the bill and the holder presents the bank for payment at the due date.

Commercial acceptance bill is a usance bill accepted by an industrial and commercial enterprise other than a bank or an individual. It is built on the basis of commercial credit and its drawer and payer are companies, enterprises or individuals (for example, the export enterprise issues the bill, the import enterprise accepts the bill), so commercial acceptance bill is a kind of commercial bill. Commercial acceptance does not change the credit basis of the bill. If the acceptor is bankrupt or unable to pay for other reasons, the holder cannot get the payment at the due date.

Although bills can be classified according to their characteristics, it does not mean that a bill can only have one of the characteristics, instead, a bill usually has several attributes at the same time, such as commercial bill, usance bill, documentary bill, and so on.

(5) Other categories of bills of exchange

The above is only part of the classification of bills, bills can also be classified as follows:

①Home currency bill and foreign currency bill

According to the use of currency, bills are divided into home currency bill and foreign currency bill. The currency amount on a foreign currency bill is foreign currency, while the currency amount on a domestic currency bill is domestic currency.

②Inland bill and foreign bill

Bills can be divided into inland bill and foreign bill according to whether the place of issue and the place of payment are the same. The drawer, the payer and the payee of a domestic bill reside in the same country where the bill circulates, while the drawer, the payer and the payee of a foreign bill of exchange do not all live in the same country and the bill circulates between two different countries. Most bills of exchange used in international settlements are international bills of exchange.

③General bill and variant bill

According to different basic relations of bills of exchange, they can be divided into general bills of exchange and variant bills of exchange. General bills of exchange are the bills with different drawers, drawees and payees. Variant bills of exchange are bills of exchange in which one of the basic parties has two or more identities. If the drawer is the payee, the bill is called the self-directing bill or the received bill; while if a drawer takes himself as the payer, the bill is called the draft drawn on oneself or the paid bill, and the bill of exchange payable to the payer is called the acceptance bill.

Besides, according to different payees, bills of exchange are divided into order bills and bearer bills. According to whether the place of acceptance and the place of payment are the same, bills of exchange can be divided into direct bills and indirect bills. The place of acceptance and the place of payment are the same in a direct draft, while acceptance and payment of an indirect draft are not in the same place. The draft in international settlements is generally a direct draft.

【Task】

In the lead-in case, Nanhwa company issues a bank acceptance bill to Nam Kwong company. The acceptance bank is the Jiangsu Branch of Bank of China, and the payment period is 2 months. This bill of exchange is drawn by Nanhwa company in favor of Nam Kwong company. Both are companies, so the bill belongs to the category of commercial bills of exchange. This bill of exchange is accepted by Jiangsu Branch of Bank of China, so it belongs to the bank acceptance bill. This draft is payable for 2 months. Therefore it is a usance draft. In addition, for Nanhwa company, the amount of the bill is expressed in RMB, which is a foreign currency, so the bill is a foreign bill. From the above, we can see that this bill has several properties at the same time.

Task 8.3 Identify, issue and judge promissory notes

【Tasks for analysis】

In international settlements, promissory notes can also be used as a tool for payment and settlement. Identifying, issuing and judging promissory notes is a basic skill that international traders need to master. In particular, how to issue promissory notes, how to judge the validity of promissory notes, how to use promissory notes to complete the settlement, what are the common types of promissory notes, these are frequently encountered problems in international settlements. Therefore, the task in this unit is divided into the following three sub-tasks:

Task 8.3.1 Definition and characteristics of promissory notes;

Task 8.3.2 Entries of promissory notes;

Task 8.3.3 Types of promissory notes.

Task 8.3.1 Definition and characteristics of promissory notes

【Figures for demonstration】

A sample of a promissory note is listed in figure 8.11 for demonstrating its form.

Figure 8.11 The sample of a promissory note

【Questions for discussion】

Based on the sample of the promissory note, think about the following questions:

(1) What is a promissory note?

(2) What are the features of a promissory note?

(3) What is the relationship between the basic parties to a promissory note?

After a free discussion, the students are required to summarize the concept of a promissory note, explain the characteristics of a promissory note and the relationship between the parties to a promissory note under the guidance of the teacher.

【Relevant knowledge】

(1) Definition of a promissory note

According to *UK Bills of Exchange Act*, a promissory note is an unconditional written promise signed by one person to another to guarantee a sum of payment at sight, at a fixed date or at a specified time in the future to a specified person, or to the person designated or to the bearer. In short, a promissory note is a note in which the drawer promises to pay a certain amount of money to the payee unconditionally.

Article 73 in our country's *Negotiable Instruments Law* provides that: "a promissory note is a note issued by the drawer promising to pay a certain amount of money to the payee or the bearer unconditionally at sight." A promissory note in this act refers to a banknote only.

(2) Characteristics of a promissory note

①A promissory note is a note paid by the drawer himself with only two basic parties. A promissory note is the promise made by the drawer to guarantee his payment, so the drawer is the payer. There are only two basic parties to the promissory note, namely, the maker and the payee. This is the most significant difference between a promissory note and a bill of exchange or a check. Bills of exchange and checks are entrusted to a third party to pay the bill, they have three basic parties.

②A promissory note is an unconditional promise to pay and a usance promissory note need not be accepted. A promissory note is a written promise issued by the drawer to the payee that payment will be made at the due date. Therefore the drawer is the principal debtor in all cases. A usance promissory note does not require acceptance, and the bearer may immediately request a court order if payment is dishonored. The court only needs to examine the contents of the bill, and if the record is qualified, the bill is established, and the court can order the drawer to pay. However, a usance bill of exchange needs to be accepted to preserve the bill rights. For bills of exchange in a set, only one bill needs to be accepted to avoid repeated payment. A promissory note is like an accepted bill of exchange, so it is drawn only once.

(3) Basic parties to a promissory note

The drawer and the payer of a promissory note are the same people, so it has only two basic parties, namely the drawer and the payee.

The drawer is the person who issues the promissory note. He is the payer (debtor) of the promissory note. His main responsibility is to keep his promise to pay the payee or the holder when it is due. After delivery, the drawer shall have no rights to interfere with the holder. The maker of a promissory note is in every case the absolute principal debtor.

The payee is the creditor of the promissory note. He may endorse a promissory note and guarantee payment to the subsequent parties. If the drawer refuses to pay, the subsequent parties may exercise the right of recourse against the prior endorser.

(4) Acts relating to a promissory note

①Issue

A promissory note is self-paid security. The drawer becomes the principal debtor of the promissory note immediately after the note is issued and has an absolute obligation to pay. Even if the holder does not make a presentation for payment, a presentation at sight or a certificate of protest within the prescribed time limit, the drawer shall not be exempted from liabilities within the term of validity of the promissory note. The holder may make a presentation for payment directly to the drawer on the due date, and the drawer shall pay unconditionally. At the same time, the drawer's payment obligation is final. Once the payment is made, the rights and obligations on the promissory note also disappear. If the drawer has the ability to pay but is unwilling to perform the payment obligation, the holder may apply to the court for enforcement.

A promissory note may be issued by two or more makers who are jointly responsible for the note by using the words "We promise to pay." Sometimes they can be responsible for the promissory notes together, and also be responsible for the promissory notes respectively by indicating "We jointly and severally promise to pay". Such promissory notes for which makers are responsible both together and jointly may be written as "I promise to pay", but signed by each drawer respectively.

②Demand

Demanding refers to the act of the promissory note holder presenting the bill to the drawer, which records the word of sight and date of sight and signs the bill on the promissory note. Demanding is special for promissory notes payable at a fixed date of after sight. There are two steps in the procedure of demanding: presentation at sight by the holder and the drawer's record and signature. Presentation at sight should be made in the term of validity of promissory notes, which is one month from the date of issue according to our country's *Negotiable Instruments Law*, and 1 year from the date of issue according to *Geneva Uniform Negotiable Instrument Law*. Failure to present the draft in accordance with the provisions shall forfeit the holder's right of recourse against the prior endorser, but the drawer shall still be liable for payment to the holder. If the drawer refuses to make the relevant record and signature, the holder shall, within the time limit for presentation of the draft, make a certificate of protest of the draft so that he can directly exercise the right of recourse against the prior endorser.

③The stipulation that a promissory note may be used as a bill of exchange

Bill laws in most countries are centered on bills of exchange. For promissory notes, except for some special regulations due to their own characteristics, exampled by the sight system, no acceptance, no acceptance in honor and no discount to the promissory note bank, the rest provisions are the same as those in bills of exchange, namely, the provisions on issuing, endorsement, guarantee, the due date, payment, payment in honor, the right of recourse are the same as the provisions of the draft.

(5) Application of promissory notes in trade settlements

Compared with bills of exchange, promissory notes are more frequently used in China, but seldom used in international trade settlements. Because it is less efficient in international trade to have promissory notes issued by the importer than to have bills of exchange issued by the exporter. A promissory note is generally used in the buyer's credit business in international trade. The bank of the exporting country lends money to the importer for opening an L/C to pay for the imported goods. Then the importer issues a usance promissory note, which is endorsed by the bank of the importing country as a note to repay the loan. In addition, a promissory note may be used as a voucher for money lending to raise funds abroad, make a bank remittance, or to be issued to a large withdrawal customer as a payment instrument instead of cash. Therefore, promissory notes are widely used in international credit, international financing and other fields.

【Task】

In the lead-in case, in order to pay the contract payment, Nanhwa company does not need to open a bank acceptance bill, but opens a promissory note to Nam Kwong company, promising to pay the sum of 500 000 yuan when due. Nanhwa company, as the drawer, is also the payer of the promissory note, and Nam Kwong company is the payee. Therefore, the basic parties of this promissory note are only Nanhwa company and Nam Kwong company. When Nanhwa company issues a promissory note, it means that it has made a promise of payment, thus becomes the principal debtor of the note and therefore assumes an absolute obligation to pay. Consequently, this note does not need to be accepted. Of course, after obtaining the promissory note, Nam Kwong company can also transfer it to Nanjing pharmaceutical company by endorsement, which is the same as the bill of exchange.

Task 8.3.2 Entries of promissory notes

【Figures for demonstration】

The following is a sample of a promissory note in international settlement, which is exhibited for knowing the major entries.

PROMISSORY NOTE

&50,000.00 London,March 15,2008

On the August 8,2008 fixed by the promissory note.I promise to pay C Co. or order the sum of POUND STERLING FIFTY THOUSAND ONLY for value received.

For A Co.London

(Signature)

Figure 8.12 Sample promissory note

【Questions for discussion】

Based on the above sample of a promissory note, think about the following questions:

(1) What are the basic entries of a promissory note?

(2) What is the specific meaning of each entry?

(3) Please make a promissory note to replace the bill of exchange as a means of payment and settlement based on the lead-in cases.

After free discussion, students are required to summarize the necessary entries of a promissory note under the guidance of teachers.

【Relevant knowledge】

Same as the bill of exchange, the producer of a promissory note also must sign and issue the promissory note that accords with legal requirements according to the relevant regulations of *Negotiable Instrument Law*. A promissory note that does not meet the statutory requirements is invalid. According to *Geneva Uniform Negotiable Instrument Law*, a promissory note shall have the following entries:

①Indicating "promissory note";

②Promise to pay unconditionally;

③Name of the payee;

④The specified amount;

⑤The place and date of issue (written in the upper right corner, if the place of issue is not specified, the place written next to the drawer is regarded as the place of issue);

⑥The drawer's signature;

⑦The term of payment (if the term of payment is not specified, the note is deemed to be payable at sight);

⑧The place of payment (if the place of payment is not specified, the place of issuing shall be deemed as the place of payment).

Since the drawer of a promissory note is the drawee, there is one absolutely necessary item missing compared with the bill of exchange—the drawee. Article 76 in our country's *Negotiable Instruments Law* regulates that: "a promissory note must record the following items: indication of 'promissory note'; unconditional payment commitment; the specified amount; the name of the payee; the date of issue; the signature of the drawer." Compared with the provisions of *Geneva Uniform Negotiable Instrument Law*, except the place of payment, the payment term and the place of issue, all other items are absolutely necessary items stipulated in China's *Negotiable Instrument Law*. A promissory note shall be invalid if it fails to record any of the above prescribed items.

As can be seen from the above provisions on the promissory note, it is absolutely necessary to indicate the words of "promissory note", the unconditional payment commitment, the specified amount, the name of the payee, the date of issue and the signature of the drawer; while the maturity date, the place of issue and the place of payment are the relatively necessary items for a promissory note. Apart from this, a promissory note also can have a few arbitrary entries, for example, the person designated as payer, interest and interest rate, non-negotiability record, a special record of an extension or shortening of the period of payment at sight and for presentation, the record of protest waived and the entry of the notice of dishonor excused.

【Task】

In the sample promissory note, the following items are included:

(1) The amount of the promissory note is £ 50 000.00;

(2) The place of issue is London;

(3) The date of issue is March 15, 2008;

(4) The payment term is August 8, 2008;

(5) The payee is C Co;

(6) The drawer is A Co.

In the lead-in case, in order to pay the contract payment, Nanhwa company does not need to open a bank acceptance bill, but opens a promissory note to Nam Kwong company, promising to pay the amount of 500 000 yuan when due. The contents of the promissory note made by Nanhwa company shall be:

Promissory note for CNY 500 000.00 Hong Kong, March 15, 2008

At two months after date, We promise to pay Jiangsu Nam Kwong International Trading Corp. or order the sum of SAY CHINESE YUAN FIVE HUNDRED THOUSAND ONLY.

For and on behalf of Hong Kong Nanhwa International
Trading Co. ,Ltd, Hong Kong
(Signed)

If Nam Kwong company transfers the promissory note to Nanjing pharmaceutical company through endorsement, the transfer shall be recorded on the back of the promissory note, and the endorsement shall be made in the same way as the endorsement of the bank acceptance bill.

Task 8.3.3 Classifications of promissory notes

【Questions for discussion】

Promissory notes can be divided into different categories from different perspectives. Different kinds of promissory notes have different characteristics and different applications in practice, so it is necessary for international traders to be familiar with the main types of promissory notes. Based on the lead-in case, please think about the following questions:

(1) What are the main types of promissory notes?

(2) How are they used in practice?

After free discussion, students are required to summarize the main types of promissory notes under the guidance of teachers.

【Relevant knowledge】

(1) According to different drawers

A trader's note, also known as a general note, is a promissory note issued by an industrial and commercial enterprise or an individual. Because a commercial promissory note is established on the basis of commercial credit, its acceptability is weak. Except for large companies with a good reputation, common enterprises seldom issue promissory notes. They are mainly used when businessmen issue a guarantee or financing.

Banker's note is a promissory note issued by the bank. When a customer deposits money in a bank, the bank may, at the customer's request, issue a promissory note for transfer settlement or cash withdrawal. Banker's note is based on the bank credit, so its acceptability is strong, thus usually used to replace cash in payment. The bank issues a promissory note to pay an order payee or a bearer. The promissory note can be given as cash to the customer who takes a deposit. The banknote that does not indicate payee can replace cash to circulate. Since the issuance of a banknote at sight will increase the supply of money in a certain sense, countries generally restrict the issuance of bank notes in order to strengthen their management on cash and money market.

(2) According to different payment terms

Sight note is a promissory note payable at sight. A banker's note is usually at sight, and most of the notes used in international trade settlements are banker's notes.

A time note is a promissory note payable at a fixed date, at a fixed period after date, or at a fixed period after sight. Commercial promissory notes can be divided into sight notes and usance notes, among them, usance notes don't need acceptance. Each country has strict restrictions on the time limit of usance banker's notes. Our country's *Negotiable Instruments Law* regulates: the maturity of the promissory note shall not exceed 2 months from the date of issue.

(3) According to different payees

A special note is a promissory note bearing the name or the firm of the payee. The promissory note shall be made with a restrictive order, for example, indicating "promise to pay A Co. Only".

Note payable to order is a promissory note bearing "by order", i. e., a promissory note with a demonstrative order bearing not only the name or the firm of the payee, but also the word "order", such as "promise to pay A Co. Or order".

A bearer note is a promissory note on which the name or the firm of the payee is not recorded. Such promissory notes are transferable upon delivery. Some countries and territories have placed restrictions on the denomination of such notes in case they replace money into circulation. Bearer promissory notes are not recognized in our country.

Our country's *Negotiable Instruments Law* has made provisions toward special sight banker's notes only, and excluded trader's notes, time notes, and bearer notes.

【Task】

In the lead-in case, in order to pay the contract payment, Nanhwa company does not need to open a bank acceptance bill, but opens a promissory note to Nam Kwong company, promising to pay the sum of 500 000 yuan when due. What Nanhwa company opened is a trader's note, which is based on the reputation of Nanhwa company, thus belongs to commercial credit. Since it is due in 2 months, this trader's note is also a time note and does not need to be accepted. When Nanhwa company issues a promissory note, the name of the payee—Nam Kwong company will be written on it. Therefore, this note is a special note, and Nam Kwong company needs to make an endorsement before transferring it.

Task 8.4 Identify, issue and judge checks

【Tasks for analysis】

This unit will help you master the basic knowledge of checks and how to use checks. In international settlements, checks can also be used as a tool for payment and settlement. Identifying, issuing and judging a check is also a basic skill that international traders need to master. In particular, questions like how to open checks, how to judge the validity of checks, how to use checks to complete a settlement, what kind of checks are commonly used, what are the differences between the three major bills are often encountered in international settlements. Therefore, the task of this unit is divided into the following four sub-tasks:

Task 8.4.1 Definition and characteristics of checks;

Task 8.4.2 Entries of a check;

Task 8.4.3 Classification of a check;

Task 8.4.4 A comparison between bills of exchange, promissory notes and checks.

task 8.4.1 Definition and characteristics of checks

【Figure for demonstration】

Figure 8.13 is a sample of a check for you to know its appearance.

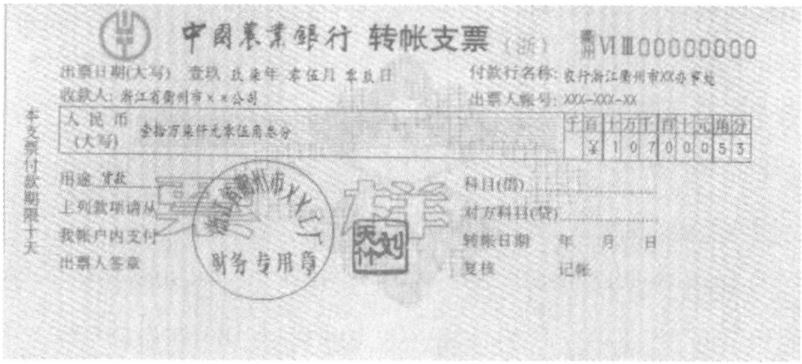

Figure 8.13 Sample check

【Questions for discussion】

Based on the above sample, please think about the following questions:

(1) What is a check?

(2) What are the characteristics of checks?

(3) What is the relationship between the basic parties to a check?

After a free discussion, students should summarize the concept of checks and explain the characteristics of checks and the relationship between the relevant parties under the guidance of teachers.

【Relevant knowledge】

(1) Definition of a check

According to *UK Bills of Exchange Act* of Britain, a cheque is an unconditional written payment order, issued by a bank account to a bank, authorizing the bank to pay a certain sum of money at sight to or to the order of a specified person or to a bearer. Briefly speaking, a cheque is a bill of exchange drawn on a bank payable at sight.

Article 82 of our country's *Negotiable Instruments Law* defines a check as: "a check is a note signed and issued by the drawer that entrusts a bank or other financial institution that handles check deposit business to pay a definite amount unconditionally at sight to the payee or bearer."

From the definition, we can know that a check is essentially a special kind of bill of exchange and a note ordering a third party to pay. A check is similar to a bill of exchange in many respects, for example, both are unconditional payment orders, both have three basic parties of drawer, payee and payer, and both can be endorsed and transferred. Because of this, the bill of exchange law of each country has the regulation that the relevant items of a check also applies to a bill of exchange, while the provisions concerning presentation, endorsement, payment, right of recourse and certificate of protest of a bill of exchange can also apply to a cheque. For example, *UK Bills of Exchange Act* of Britain clearly provides that, except as otherwise provided by the cheque law, any provision applicable to sight drafts shall apply to cheques.

(2) Characteristics of cheques

Compared with the bill of exchange, the check still has its own characteristics.

①The drawer of a check must meet certain conditions. First of all, a check is an unconditional payment order issued by a bank deposit account to the bank in which it has opened an account. Therefore, the drawer of a check must be a bank deposit account, that is to say, the drawer must have enough deposit in the bank, a person who has no or insufficient money in a bank can never be the drawer of a check. Secondly, there is an agreement between the drawer and the bank on using the check, that is, the deposit bank allows the depositor to use a check. Finally, the drawer of the check must use the check printed uniformly by the deposit bank. The check cannot be made by the drawer himself, like the bill of exchange and the promissory note.

②A check is a note payable at sight. Cheques are payable on demand and the paying bank must pay them at sight. Since there are no usance checks, checks do not need to be accepted, and unlike a bill of exchange which can be drawn in multiple copies, checks can only be made one at a time.

③Cheques are paid by banks only, but the payer of the bill of exchange and the promissory note can be the bank, the enterprise or the individual.

In addition, checks have some characteristics that are different from bills of exchange. Checks generally do not carry interest clauses, and even if there is a record of interest, the record is invalid and no payment is required. The drawee may not pay for a late presentation of a check which has exceeded the legal or reasonable time limit for circulation, but the drawer shall not be relieved of his obligation to the holder unless the late presentation causes loss to the drawer.

(3) The basic parties to a check

①Drawer

A drawer is a person who has a certain financial relationship with the drawee. By drawing a cheque, the drawer promises to pay the bank when the cheque is presented and to compensate for any dishonour. Normally, the drawer of a check is the principal debtor, except for a certified check, whose principal debtor is the paying bank.

②Payee

Checks can be obtained not only through transactions, but also through endowment, inheritance, so they are widely payable. Sometimes, the customer does not take a check to withdraw money, but gives it to his bank and entrusts the bank to collect the money, and this bank is called the collecting bank.

③Drawee

The drawee under the check is the drawer's bank of deposit.

(4) Kiting check

A kiting check is a check issued by a drawer but refused by the bank because it exceeds its actual balance in the bank account. If the drawer and the payer do not have a financial relationship and have not entered into an overdrawn credit contract or the check amount exceeds the bank balance, the check issued is a kiting check. Banks, of course, don't pay kiting checks. However, the issuance of kiting checks can not be prevented in advance, only after the payer sees the check, sanctions can be imposed on the drawer. The drawer that opens a kiting check should assume legal responsibilities. The sanctions imposed by various countries on those who issue kiting checks are generally stipulated in their bill laws. Our country's *Negotiable Instruments Law* prohibits the issuance of kiting checks. The bank has the right to impose fines on the client that opens kiting checks and can move the person that opens kiting checks repeatedly and maliciously to judicatory organizations for fraud.

【Task】

In the lead-in case, Nanhwa company may not open a bank acceptance bill to pay the contract payment, but opens a check to Nam Kwong company from its deposit bank Jiangsu branch of Bank of China, which will pay 500 000 yuan. Nanhwa company is the drawer of the check, while Bank of China jiangsu branch is the payer of the check, and Nam Kwong company is the payee. Therefore, there are three basic parties to this check. Unlike a bill of exchange, the cheque issued by Nanhwa company is drawn on a bank and payable at sight. When Nanhwa company issues the check, it becomes the principal debtor of the note and undertakes the absolute payment obligation. As it is a sight note, the check does not need to be accepted. Of course, after obtaining the check, Nam Kwong company also can transfer it to Nanjing pharmaceutical company through endorsement, this is the same as with the bill of exchange.

Task 8.4.2 Entries of a check

【Picture for demonstration】

Figure 8.14 is a sample of the check for you to know its appearance.

Check for &5 000.00　　London, Jan 1,2008

Pay to the order of British Trading Company the sum of Pounds Sterling Five Thousand Only.

TO:National Westminster Bank Ltd.

London

For London Export Corporation London

(Authorized Signature)

Figure 8.14 Sample check

【Questions for discussion】

Based on the sample of the check, please think about the following questions:

(1) What are the basic items of a check?

(2) What is the specific meaning of each item?

(3) Based on the lead-in case, please make a check to replace a bill of exchange as a means of payment and settlement.

After a free discussion, students are required to summarize the necessary items of the check, and write down the corresponding parties in the check and the specific contents of related items under the guidance of teachers.

【Relevant knowledge】

(1) Basic items of a check

The requirements on the necessary items of a check are generally the same as a bill of exchange. Generally speaking, a cheque must contain the following information:

①Mark of "Check"

②Unconditional payment order

③A specific amount

④Name of the payer

The drawee of the check must be the drawer's deposit bank. Because there are restrictions on the qualification of the check payer, it cannot be omitted. The drawee must be unique and specific with a clear indication of the bank and its business office. In practice, checks are designed and printed by the paying bank with complete name of the bank and its detailed address.

⑤Date of issue

A check is a sight note, what's more, the term of presentment for payment is short and calculated from the date of issue. So the date of issue of the check determines the period of validity of the check, therefore it must be clearly indicated. *Geneva Uniform Negotiable Instrument Law* sets the time limit of a check for presentation as following: if issue and payment are in the same country, the period of validity lasts 8 days from the date of issue, if issue and payment are not in the same country but on the same continent, the validity period is 20 days from the date of issue; if issue and payment are neither in the same country nor on the same continent, the check is valid for 70 days from the date of issue. The term of recourse shall be 6 months from the above due dates. Our country's *Negotiable Instruments Law* regulates that, the holder of a check should present the check for payment within 10 days from the date of issue, while other countries like Britain, the United States, France only provides presentation within a reasonable period, without specifying the exact number of days.

⑥Signature of the drawer

The drawer should hold deposits in his deposit bank and have the right to write checks under the agreement. Checks issued by the drawer without deposits or with deposits but without check agreements will not be paid.

Article 85 in China's *Negotiable Instruments Law* stipulates that the above 6 items are absolutely necessary in a check, and the check with one of the above items missing is invalid. Nevertheless, the amount on the check can be added afterwards under the drawer's authorization. In addition to the above Necessary items, the payee, the place of issue, the place of payment are all important items of a check. If the name of the payee is not recorded in the check, it can be added with the authorization of the drawer, and the drawer can also record himself as the payee on the check. Where the place of payment is not specified, the business premises of the payer shall be the place of payment. If the place of issue is not recorded, the business premises, the domicile or habitual residence of the payer shall be the place of issue. It should be noted that a cheque must be paid at sight, so there is no need to specify its term of payment.

(2) Dishonour of a cheque

The dishonour of a cheque means that the paying bank refuses to pay the cheque and returns the cheque because it fails to meet the payment conditions. Checks are usually returned for following reasons: signature differs; orders not to pay; insufficient deposit fund; words and figures differ, amount in words requires drawer's confirmation; amount required in words; the check is not regularly drawn; out of date or stale cheque; payee's endorsement required; material alterations to be confirmed by the drawer; post-dated checks; refer to drawer, etc.

(3) Countermand and certification of a check

Countermand of a cheque means that the drawer withdraws the cheque (countermand) or notifies the paying bank to stop the payment before the cheque is paid. A check is a note on which the drawer authorizes his deposit bank to pay at sight. Therefore the check itself is a letter of authorization. However, if the drawer wants to revoke his authorization, that is, stop payment on the check, the drawer shall send a written notice to the paying bank, requiring the bank to do it. At this time, all obligations and authorizations of the drawee bank to honour the cheque are terminated, and instead of suing the drawee bank, the holder can only make recourse against the drawer or his remote holders. The reason behind the countermand of a check is often that the cheque is lost or stolen. When the holder loses the check and reports the loss, the paying bank shall help the holder to contact the drawer immediately, and then the drawer shall send a written notice to the paying bank, requesting countermand. When the check is presented, the payer shall mark "orders not to pay" on the check and return the check. But in order to prevent the drawer from escaping the debt by opening a kiting check first and then requesting countermand, *Geneva Uniform Negotiable Instrument Law* prohibits countermand of a check within the period of validity, and *UK Bills of Exchange Act* of Britain stipulates that payment of a check stops only after the bank receives the written notice signed by the drawer.

Confirmation of a check is to require the drawee bank to certify a check in order to prevent the drawer from withdrawing the check or notifying the drawee to stop payment. Upon certification of the check, the paying bank undertakes the absolute payment obligation and becomes the only debtor.

【Task】

In a cheque, the following items are included:

①The amount of the check: 5 000.00 pounds.

②The place of issue: London.

③The date of issue: January 1, 2008.

④The payee: British Trading Company.

⑤The drawee: National Westminster Bank Ltd.

⑥The drawer: London Export Corporation.

In the lead-in case, in order to pay the contract payment, Nanhwa company may not open a bank acceptance bill, but opens a check from its deposit bank, Bank of China, to Nam Kwong company, and the Jiangsu branch of Bank of China will pay 500 000 yuan for the goods. The contents of the cheque printed by the Jiangsu branch of Bank of China shall be written by Nanhwa company as follows:

Cheque for Bank of CHINA, Jiangsu branch

A/C No. ________

Nanjing, May 15, 2008

Pay to the order of Jiangsu Nam Kwong International Trading Corp. the Sum of CHINESE YUAN FIVE HUNDRED THOUSAND ONLY (CNY 500 000.00)

Cheque No. 031250808

For Hong Kong Nanhwa International Trading Co., Ltd, Hong Kong

(Signed)

If Nam Kwong company transfers the cheque by endorsement to Nanjing pharmaceutical company, it shall make the relevant record on the back of the cheque, and the form of endorsement shall be the same as that of the bank acceptance draft.

Task 8.4.3 The classification of checks

【Questions for discussion】

Checks may be classified from different perspectives. Different kinds of checks have different characteristics and different applications in practice, so it is necessary for international traders to be familiar with the main types of checks. Based on the lead-in case, please think about the following questions:

(1) What are the main types of checks?

(2) How are they used in practice?

After a free discussion, students are required to summarize the main types of checks under the guidance of the teacher.

【Relevant knowledge】

(1) According to different ways of indicating payees

Cheque to order means the drawer marks "Pay to..." or "Pay to the order of..." in the payee column. Such checks must be endorsed by the holder when transferred for circulation and signed by the payee at the back when withdrawn.

A cheque to bearer, also known as a blank check, is marked with "Pay bearer" in the payee column. These checks do not need to be endorsed. They can be transferred upon delivery. Therefore the bearer does not need to sign the back of the check when withdrawing money.

(2) According to whether the check is crossed

An ordinary check, also known as an uncrossed check or an open check, is a common uncrossed check that can be transferred through a bank or withdrawn for cash.

A crossed check refers to the check with two parallel lines on the face to indicate that cash cannot be withdrawn at the counter of the paying bank but only paid to the payee's account. The holder of such a check cannot draw cash but can only entrust the bank to collect the money into his account. The person who draws the crossed line shall be the drawer or the bearer. Crossed checks are used mainly to meet the requirements of bank transfer and settlements, and to prevent the check from being falsely claimed. The crossed line is to protect the benefit of the drawer and the bearer. Once the check is lost and falsely claimed, the drawer or the bearer can recover the money through the clues of the collecting bank.

(3) Certified cheque

A certified cheque is a check signed and marked by the paying bank with "certified to pay". The payee or the holder of a check may require the bank to certify payment in order to prevent the drawer from writing kiting checks so as to guarantee payment upon presentation. A certified check indicates that the drawer has a sufficient balance in his deposit account, so the bank certifies it. After the check is certified, the paying bank becomes the main debtor and must pay on presentation, which exempts the drawer and the endorser from their responsibilities and recourse. A certified check is usually non-refundable and there is no notice of countermand of it.

(4) Banker's cheque

A banker's check is a check issued and paid by a bank. It is essentially a bank draft at sight, a written order issued by one bank to order another bank to pay to a person or his designee or a bearer. Both the drawer and the payer of a banker's check are a bank, thus its credit is high. Therefore it is usually used by the bank in remittance business for customers.

Our country's *Negotiable Instruments Law* classifies checks into three types, ordinary checks, cash checks and transfer checks. Ordinary checks can be drawn for cash or transferred. When used for transfer, the check should be indicated on the front. Where a cheque is specially used for withdrawing cash, a cash cheque may be made separately, which can only be used for cash withdrawal. Where a cheque is specially used for transferring payment, a transfer cheque may be made separately, which can only be used for transfer but not for withdrawal. The transfer check of our country is equivalent to the crossed check. The drawer or the bearer clearly indicates "transfer payment" in the ordinary check, then the payee can only transfer the money instead of withdrawing cash.

(5) The way of crossing a check

A crossed check can be divided into ordinary crossed check and special crossed check. An ordinary crossed check is a check that any bank can collect and transfer money on its behalf (figure 8.15). The drawer shall draw two parallel lines on the cheque without any markings or markings of "& Co." or "not negotiable" in between. A specially crossed cheque is a cheque marked with the name of a bank when the cheque is crossed, i.e., a cheque specially drawn on the bank (figure 8.16). The drawer draws two parallel lines on the check and adds the name of a bank in the middle. Only this bank can act as the collecting bank for check payments.

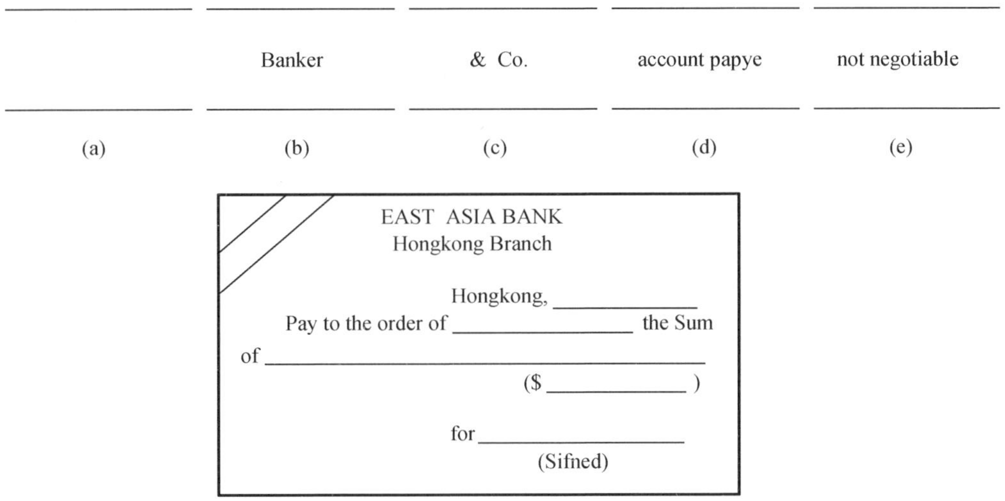

Figure 8.15 Form of ordinary crossing and ordinary crossed cheque

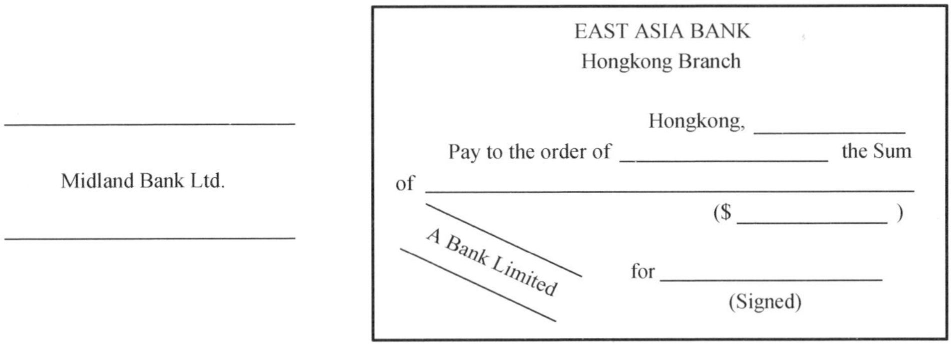

Figure 8.16 Form of special crossing and special crossed checks

【Task】

In the lead-in case, Nanhwa company may not open a bank acceptance bill to pay the contract payment, but issues a check to Nam Kwong company, and Bank of China, Jiangsu branch, will pay the sum of 500 000 yuan for the goods on the payday. When the cheque is drawn by Nanhwa company, the name of the payee Nam Kwong company is recorder on it, thus it is a cheque to order. Nanhwa company does not cross the cheque, so it is an un-crossed cheque, which can be transferred by bank and withdrawn for cash. If the cheque is crossed, it becomes a crossed cheque and can only be transferred by bank, but not withdrawn for cash.

Task 8.4.4 Compare bills of exchange, promissory notes and checks

【Questions for discussion】

The tasks of the previous units have clarified the concepts and characteristics of the three basic notes in international settlements, described their recorded items, main behaviors, and their classifications. Through these tasks, we have mastered the basic methods and skills of using them. Therefore, in the practice of international settlements, it is necessary for international traders to correctly distinguish the three bills before applying them. Based on the lead-in cases and the previous unit tasks, please consider the following questions:

(1) What's the difference between a bill of exchange, a promissory note or a check?

(2) How do they relate to each other?

After a free discussion, students are encouraged to compare a bill of exchange, a promissory note and a check under the guidance of the teacher.

【Relevant knowledge】

(1) A comparison between a promissory note and a bill of exchange

As a main form of bills, both promissory notes and bills of exchange are expressed with a certain amount of money, made in the unconditional written form. Both can be divided into sight drafts and usance drafts in the term of payment and may have registered or anonymous payees. The endorsement, guarantee, payment and recourse of a promissory note are the same as that of a bill of exchange. The drawer of the promissory note is similar to the acceptor of the bill of exchange, the payee of the promissory note is the same as the payee of the bill of exchange, and the first endorser of the promissory note is similar to the payee of the accepted bill of exchange. The differences between a promissory note and a bill of exchange is shown in the following aspects:

①The nature of the note is different

Promissory note is a document by which the drawer undertakes and warrants payment, an unconditional payment promise, while a bill of exchange is an unconditional payment order ordered by the drawer or entrusted to the payer.

②The basic relationship is different

There are only two parties to a promissory note, namely the drawer and the payee. The drawer is the payer, while a bill of exchange has 3 basic parties, namely the drawer, the payee and the drawee.

③The principal debtor is different

The principal debtor of a promissory note is always the drawer, while the principal debtor of the bill of exchange is the drawer before acceptance and the acceptor after acceptance.

④Acceptance is different

The drawer of the promissory note and the payer of the promissory note are the same person. After the promissory note is issued, the drawer is the principal debtor, who undertakes the unconditional, absolute and final responsibility for the instrument, so the promissory note does not need to be accepted. But the bill of exchange is the bill that orders the third party to pay. The bill of exchange at sight need not be accepted, while the usance bill of exchange must be accepted before the liability of the drawee to the bill and his status as the principal debtor can be determined.

⑤The number of copies issued is different

A promissory note is issued separately and bills of exchange may be issued in sets of two or more copies.

⑥Bill behavior is different

A promissory note has the act of drawing, endorsement, presentation, payment, recourse and guarantee, but no acceptance and acceptance in honor, because there is no acceptor and acceptor in honor, while a bill of exchange has above all bill behaviors.

(2) A comparison between a check and a bill of exchange

A check is a special kind of money order. There is no essential difference between a check and a bill of exchange, except that the drawee must be a bank and the term must be at sight in a check. The common practice of bills of exchange, like drawing, endorsing, paying, recourse, dishonor, etc. also applies to checks. The difference between the two is mainly reflected in the following aspects.

①The payers are different

The drawee of a check is limited to banks only, but the drawee of a bill of exchange can be a bank, a business or an individual.

②The time of payment is different

Cheques are payable at sight and have no record of maturity date. But bills of exchange can be payable at sight or after sight generally with the record of maturity date.

③The relationship between the parties is different

The drawer of the check is the bank customer, and the payer is the bank in which the drawer has opened an account, so the drawer and the payer must have a financial relationship in advance; while for a bill of exchange, its drawer and drawee do not need to have financial relation before the bill is issued.

④Acceptance is different

Cheques are payable at sight and do not require acceptance, while the bill of exchange, except for the case of payment at sight, generally need acceptance.

⑤The main debtor is different

the main debtor of the check is the drawer, while the principal debtor of the bill of exchange is the drawer before acceptance and the acceptor after acceptance.

⑥The content of bill behavior is different

The check has the crossing and the certifying system, but no acceptance, guarantee and other behaviors, however, although the bill of exchange does not have a crossing system, it has acceptance, guarantee and other behaviors. In addition, the payment of a check can be stopped. When the drawer notifies a bank to stop payment, the drawer's deposit is insufficient or the drawer is dead or bankrupt, the payment can be stopped. But the payment is irrevocable for a bill of exchange after it is accepted.

⑦Different Numbers of copies

a check can only have one copy, but a bill of exchange may be drawn in several copies.

⑧Different functions

A check is a means of payment, but a bill of exchange has the function of a credit instrument as well as a means of payment.

A comprehensive comparison of bills of exchange, promissory notes and cheques is shown in table 8.4.

Table 8.4 A comprehensive comparison of bills of exchange, promissory notes and cheques

Items \ Notes		Bill of exchange	Promissory note	Cheque
Similarities	Nature	Bills with necessary contents and certain behaviors and for the purpose of paying a certain amount		
	Circulation	All of them are negotiable instruments, among which special bills and those with demonstrative order may be transferred by endorsement, while bearer's bill may be transferred upon delivery		
Differences	Nature	Unconditional written payment order	Unconditional written payment commitment	Unconditional written payment order
	Immediate parties	Drawer, drawee, payee	Drawer, drawee	Drawer, drawee, payee
	The basic relationship between parties	It's not necessary for the drawer and the payer to establish financial relationship first	The drawer and the payer are the same person, so there is no financial relationship between them	Financial relationship must exist between the drawer and the payer before the cheque is issued
	The nature of the payer (drawee)	Banks, enterprises, individuals	Banks, enterprises, individuals	Banks only

Table 8.4 (contiuned)

Items \ Notes		Bill of exchange	Promissory note	Cheque
Differences	Liabilities of the drawer	Guarantee the acceptance and payment of the drawee	Assume the liability for payment by himself	Guarantee the payer to pay
	Deadline	Bills are sight bills or usance bills, so the maturity date should be recorded	Bills are sight bills or usance bills, so the maturity date should be recorded	Only sight draft, therefore no maturity date recorded
	Acceptance	A usance bill needs to be accepted	No acceptance	No acceptance
	The principal debtor	Drawer in case of sight draft or usance draft before acceptance; acceptor in case of usance draft after acceptance	Always the drawer	Always the drawer
	Acts under a bill	Bill acts are relatively comprehensive without crossing and certifying payment systems. Bills are irrevocable after acceptance and discountable	No acceptance, acceptance in honor, and stop of payment, but can be discounted	No acceptance, acceptance in honor, guarantee, payment in honor, and discount, but can be crossed and certified and payment can be stopped
	Number of copies	In duplicate or more copies (original and duplicate)	One copy (original only)	One copy (original only)
	Right of recourse	In case of dishonor within the validity period and with the certificate of protest, the holder shall have the right of recourse against the drawer, the endorser and the acceptor, while in case of dishonor out of date the holder loses the right of recourse against all the debtors on the bill	There is no need to make a certificate of protest if the bill is dishonored within the validity period. The holder only has the right of recourse against the drawer. If the bill is dishonored out of the validity period, the holder shall lose the right of recourse against the endorser, but may exercise the right of recourse against the drawer	There is no need to make a certificate of protest if the bill is dishonored within the validity period. The holder only has the right of recourse against the drawer. If the bill is dishonored out of the validity period, the holder may still exercise the right of recourse against the drawer

Table 8.4(contiuned)

Items \ Notes		Bill of exchange	Promissory note	Cheque
Differences	Function	Settlement instrument, credit instrument	Settlement instrument, credit instrument	Settlement instrument

(3) Different functions of three kinds of negotiable instruments

The above three kinds of bills are used as means of payment, means of circulation and means of settlement, but they have different functions in practice. Bills of exchange are both instruments of settlement and credit. As a settlement tool, bills of exchange are mainly used for international remittance, that is, to transfer funds by issuing bank bills of exchange. As a credit instrument, it is mainly a commercial draft issued by the manufacturer against the background of import and export trade, which is easily discounted after bank acceptance. Therefore, commercial bills have become an important tool for importers and exporters to obtain financing.

Promissory notes are basically credit instruments. Large enterprises with good credit may raise funds by issuing commercial promissory notes. Banks may also raise funds or take deposits by issuing bank promissory notes.

Checks are basically settlement instruments. As an ideal settlement tool, it brings convenience to people in the receipt and payment of funds. As long as the drawer issues a check, the payer can make the payment, and the payee can collect the payment soon only by sending the check to the correspondent bank.

(4) The different scope of application of the three bills

Bills of exchange are the most widely used in international settlements. The bank draft drawn and paid by the bank is the most reliable for the payee. Commercial bills of exchange issued by manufacturers are also widely used in international trade settlements. Documentary bills of exchange are sent together with trade documents to the payer as a payment order, which is less risky because the importer will pay against the documents only. Therefore bills of exchange are a safe settlement tool. In addition, countries generally encourage import and export, and commercial papers with import and export trade as the background are easy to discount. Therefore, commercial bills are a convenient financing tool, which is much easier than ordinary financing tools.

Checks are mainly used for domestic settlements. It is very convenient for the drawer to issue a check to the payee, because there is no need to count the banknotes or go to the bank. It is also quite convenient for the payee to simply send the check to the corresponding bank and collect the account soon. Therefore, checks are widely used in domestic settlements in western countries. However, as checks are payable at sight, they can not be used as financing instruments, moreover private checks are more likely to be returned, which greatly limits the use of checks in international settlements.

Promissory notes are rarely used in both domestic and international settlements. Commercial promissory notes are often dishonored by the drawer, consequently, people are generally unwilling to accept commercial promissory notes. Currently, commercial promissory notes are only occasionally used by large enterprises to raise funds. As to banknotes, because countries usually have many restrictions on its issuance, they are rarely seen.

【Task】

In the lead-in case and the previous unit task, Nanhwa company can draw a bill of exchange, a promissory note or a check to Nam Kwong company to pay the contract payment. On the payment date of the contract, Bank of China, Jiangsu branch or Nanhwa company itself will pay 500 000 yuan. All the three kinds of bills are negotiable instruments with the purpose of paying a certain amount, with necessary contents and certain acts, and are settlement tools that can be transferred. If Nanhwa company issues a bank acceptance bill, it issues an unconditional payment order to the Jiangsu branch of Bank of China, the opening bank. In that case three basic parties are involved. Since it is a usance bill, it has to be accepted. If Nanhwa company issues a promissory note, it is an unconditional payment commitment issued to Nam Kwong company, which involves two basic parties. Since Nanhwa company has promised to pay when issuing the note, acceptance is not needed. If Nanhwa company issues a check, it issues an unconditional payment order to the Jiangsu branch of Bank of China, the opening bank. There are three basic parties involved. The payer is the Jiangsu branch of Bank of China, the opening bank, and the payment is at sight, so there is no acceptance needed. Since cheques are payable at sight and the date of payment is 2 months later. Therefore the date of issue should be written directly as the date of payment in the future when the cheque is issued, i. e. , the date of payment May 15 should be written as the date of issue when the cheque is issued by Nanhwa company on March 15. This is obviously different from drawing a draft or a promissory note.

Task 9 Different methods for international settlements

【Learning objectives】

(1) Be familiar with the parties, classifications and business procedures of remittance;

(2) Be familiar with the parties, classifications and business procedures of collection;

(3) Be familiar with the parties, classifications and business procedures of the letter of credit;

(4) Understand the basic knowledge concerning the bank guarantee and the standby letter of credit.

【Tasks】

(1) The method of settlement by remittance;

(2) The method of settlement by collection;

(3) The method of settlement by letter of credit;

(4) The method of settlement by bank guarantee and standby letter of credit.

[Requirements]

(1) Can describe the remittance process correctly and use the remittance method for international settlements;

(2) Be able to describe the collection process correctly and adopt the collection method to deal with international settlements;

(3) Can understand the letter of credit and use the letter of credit for international settlements.

The international settlement method, also known as the international payment method, refers to the way of transferring funds from the paying party to the receiving party in international economic transactions, in order to settle claims and debts. The settlement of international trade grows gradually with the increase of production and economy and the development of international trade. Beginning in the 1860s, the first industrial revolution greatly promoted the establishment of the big machine industry in Europe and the United States, which led to the rapid development of international trade, and trade-related finance, maritime transportation and insurance. As a settlement tool, various bills, especially bills of exchange gained their popularity. The Marine bill of lading became a document of property rights which can be transferred by endorsement. Payment against documents was widely used in international trade settlements. With the full play of banks' role in international trade settlements, banks' credit and financing functions were widely used, and the bank letter of credit emerged at the right moment. Especially in the late 19th century, documentary letter of credit was comprehensively promoted and applied all over the world, which not only gave full play to the guarantee role of the bank, but also made it more and more convenient for banks to conduct financing by undertaking documentary bills. With the development of international trade and transnational banking, international settlement has changed from simple cash settlement in the early days to modern non-cash settlement centered on banks. Modern international settlement is to realize the transfer of convertible currencies through the non-cash settlement method of international commercial banks, so as to achieve the purpose of paying off the creditor's rights and debts between international enterprises. Developed according to the basic principles of notes, remittance, collection, letter of credit, letter of guarantee and other settlement methods now basically meet the needs of different forms of trade. In particular, collection and letter of credit are widely used in international trade settlements for integrating bills and documents. After completing this task, you can master the methods of three basic international settlements, and easily choose different ways of settlement in your future work so as to realize the payment and settlement of international goods.

Task 9.1 Settlement by remittance

[Case for demonstration]

On August 1, 2008, Nam Kwong company signed an import contract with Nanhwa company for importing a batch of wool fabrics with the contract value of HK \$1 000 000. 00. How can Nam Kwong company pay the goods to Nanhwa company to complete the settlement of the contract payment? There are three basic ways: first, Nam Kwong company can directly pay the money to Nanhwa company through its own correspondent bank which connects to the channels of international banks, that is, remittance; second, Nanhwa company can entrust its own correspondent bank to collect the money through the channels of international banks, namely collection; third, the importer Nam Kwong company can apply to its own bank to open a letter of credit and notify the exporter Nanhwa company of the letter of credit through the channels of international banks. Nanhwa company can obtain the money paid by the advising bank upon delivering the documents representing property rights, that is, the letter of credit. In addition, NamKwong company can also realize payment and settlement through bank guarantee or standby letter of credit.

【Task for analysis】

In international settlements, remittance is the earliest and simplest method of settlement. Remittance business generally involves four parties, which closely relate to each other. Remittance can be classified into different types, different ways of remittance have different characteristics and applications. In practice, remittance business in international trade has a specific form of application.

Task 9.1.1 The concept of remittance and the parties involved

【Case for demonstration】

JNK imported a batch of wool fabrics from Hong Kong Nanhwa company. On August 4, 2008, NamKwong company applied for T/T outward remittance contract balance payment 100 000 Hong Kong dollars from the opening bank, Jiangsu branch of Bank of China (paying bank), which sent a telex to its correspondent bank, Bank of China, Hong Kong branch (receiving bank) according to the telegraphic transfer application and entrusted the receiving bank to remit the remittance to Nanhwa company. After receiving the telex, the receiving bank checked the test key, made out the telegraphic transfer notice and informed Nanhwa company to collect the money. After receiving the notice, Nanhwa company collected the payment from the receiving bank, sealed the receipt and gave it to the receiving bank. The receiving bank debited the paying bank account to take out the position, remitted the remittance to the payee, and sent the debit note to the paying bank to inform it that the remittance had been settled. So far, the two trading companies completed a settlement by telegraphic transfer.

【Questions for discussion】

After reading the above case, you can understand the basic situation of remittance business. Please think about the following questions:

(1) What is remittance?

(2) What are the characteristics of remittance?

(3) What are the general procedures for remittance?

(4) What are the parties to the remittance business and how do they relate to each other?

【Relevant knowledge】

(1) Concept and characteristics of remittance

Remittance is a way of settlement by the bank (remitting bank) at the request of the customer (remitter) through its branch or agent in foreign countries (clearing bank) to pay a certain amount of money to the foreign payee. In short, remittance means that the payer takes the initiative to remit the payment for the goods through the bank by using a variety of settlement tools.

In remittance, the payer takes the initiative to send funds to the bank to pay the foreign payee, so the funds flow in the same direction as the settlement tools do. Therefore it is a typical way of favorable exchange. In international trade practice, remittance settlement means that the importer takes the initiative to remit the funds to the exporter through the bank, which is mainly used for payment in advance and payment on delivery. Remittance is the earliest settlement method in international trade and the basis of other settlement methods. Remittance settlement has the following characteristics:

①Simple procedure and low cost

Remittance is developed to solve the problems of cash settlement. It is the oldest settlement method but has the simplest procedure compared with other settlement methods. The seller sends the goods directly to the buyer, and the buyer pays the seller through the bank. The bank does not need to process bills or documents, and charges the least. Therefore, remittance is the most ideal in a transaction where both parties trust each other, or between different subsidiaries of a multinational company.

②Belong to commercial credit with big risks

The essence of remittance is that the two sides of a trade use the channel of fund transfer between banks to pay off their credit and debt. The bank only acts as an agent, providing services only but not bearing the payment responsibilities. Therefore, remittance is a settlement method based on commercial credit. For the buyer of payment in advance and the seller of cash on delivery, once the payment or delivery is completed, there is no way to restrict the other party. Whether the goods or the payment can be received in time depends entirely on the credit of the other party, which of course brings great risk.

③Unbalanced financial burden

For the buyer who pays in advance or the seller who receives payment on delivery, they bear heavy burdens because a lot of funds are tied up, while the other party's financial burden is much lighter.

(2) The principal parties of the remittance

In remittance business, there are generally four parties, namely the remitter, the remitting bank, the receiving bank and the payee. Among them, the remitter and the payee may be the same person. For example, in bill collection, the remitter may go abroad to withdraw money after the remittance.

①Remitter

Namely payer, is the person who pays the bank and entrusts the bank to remit the money to foreign creditors or payees. In international trade, remitter is usually the importer, who shall pay the goods to the exporter through the bank according to the time and payment stipulated in the contract. When the remitter entrusts the bank to remit the money, he/she should fill in the application for remittance, provide the cash or payment voucher equivalent to the amount of remittance and pay the relevant fees.

②Remitting bank

Also called paying bank, which is entrusted by the remitter to remit the remittance. The remitting bank is usually in the place where the remitter is located. In international trade, it is usually the bank where the importer is located, that is, the importer's bank. It mainly deals with the outward remittance business. The remitting bank shall carefully examine the application for remittance and relevant documents submitted by the remitter, and if the contents do not meet the requirements or have adverse effects on the smooth settlement of the payment, the remitting bank shall require the remitter to do the modifications before making the payment authorization letter and remitting the money to the bank according to the way entrusted by the remitter. The remitting bank shall be liable for any error caused by its failure to comply with the application for remittance.

③Receiving bank

A bank entrusted by the remitting bank to make payment directly to the payee. The receiving bank is usually the affiliated bank or the agent bank of the remitting bank, usually situated where the payee is located. In international trade, the receiving bank sits in the place where the exporter is located, that is, the exporter's bank. It deals with the inward remittance business. After receiving the authorization letter of payment, the receiving bank must verify its authenticity and strictly comply with its requirements. It cannot change the content of the authorization letter of payment without being authorized. Otherwise, the receiving bank shall bear the consequences caused thereby. For remittances that cannot be remitted, the receiving bank shall promptly give reasons to the remitting bank.

④Payee

Also called beneficiary, refers to the person designated by the remitter to receive the remittance. In international trade, the payee is usually the exporter. When receiving the remittance bank notice, the payee may provide the related materials to withdraw money according to the request.

(3) The relationship among the parties to the remittance

①The relationship between the remitter and the payee

In practice, it can be demonstrated in two aspects: first, in trade settlement, due to the commodity trading, both the remitter and the receiver show a debt-creditor relationship; second, in non-trade settlement, due to the unilateral transfer of funds, the remitter and the receiver show the relationship of the provider and the recipient of funds.

②The relationship between the remitter and the remitting bank

The relationship between remitter and remitting bank is based on entrustment. When the remitter entrusts the remitting bank to handle the remittance business, the remitter should issue the application for remittance, which is the contract voucher between both parties with the rights and obligations of both parties clarified in this business.

③The relationship between the remitting bank and the receiving bank

The relationship between the remitting bank and the receiving bank is based both on agency and entrustment, and generally speaking, their agency relationship comes before their entrustment relationship. That is, two banks have signed a business agency contract or have account current relationship in advance, and then perform their respective duties in the scope of the agency contract. For a remittance, the remitting bank transmits the entrustment information through the remittance voucher, and the receiving bank accepts the entrustment and undertakes the obligation of remittance settlement.

④The relationship between the payee and the receiving bank

Usually, the relationship between the payee and the receiving bank is based on account transactions, that is, the payee has a deposit account in the receiving bank. However, there is possibly no such relationship between the two parties. But if the above situation is true, the receiving bank is still responsible for the payment to the payee. The relationship between the main parties to the remittance is shown in figure 9.1.

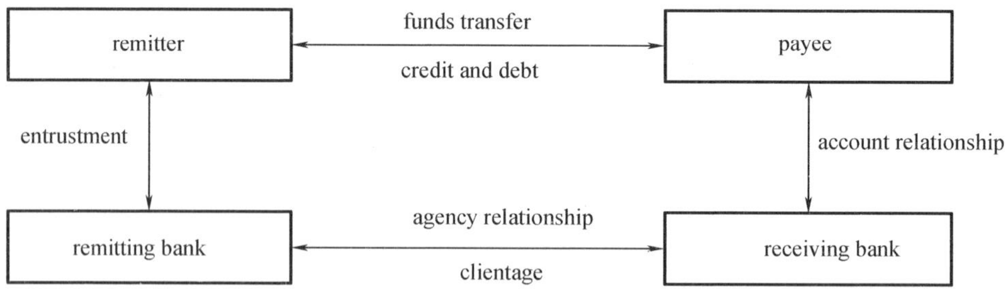

Figure 9.1 Relationship between parties in remittance business

(4) The general procedures of remittance business

In international trade, after signing the contract, the seller sends the goods directly to the buyer. And the buyer takes the initiative to remit the payment to the seller through the bank according to the time agreed in the contract, which leads to the remittance business. When handling the remittance business, we should follow the following steps:

①Application

Before paying the money, the remitter submits to the remitting bank the application for remittance, which is the contract between the remitter and the remitting bank, and also the instruction of the remitter. The remitting bank is obliged to send the order of payment to the receiving bank according to the instructions of the application for remittance. The remitter shall fill in the application form of remittance accurately according to the actual situation, and shall be liable for any delay or fault caused by the error in the application for remittance. The content of the application for remittance mainly includes: the amount of remittance and currency, name and address of the remitter, name and address of the payee, name and account number of the payee's bank, method of remittance, details of payment, etc.

②Receipt

The remitting bank shall send the receipt to the remitter and debit the remitter's account. The remitting bank shall carefully examine and verify the application for remittance and relevant documents submitted by the remitter, and require the remitter to make modifications if the contents do not meet the requirements or have an adverse impact on the smooth settlement of the payment. If the application for remittance meets the demands after a careful examination, the receipt shall be given to the remitter and the amount of remittance shall be debited from the remitter's account.

③Instruction

After accepting the entrustment, the remitting bank shall prepare the payment order as required by the remitter, send the instruction of payment to the receiving bank in the form of texted telex, telegram, MT advice or bill of exchange notice, and entrust the receiving bank to make the payment to the payee. The remitting bank shall be liable for any error caused by its failure to comply with the requirements of the application for remittance

④Payment

The receiving bank shall remit the funds to the payee after checking the instructions correctly. After receiving the authorization letter of payment, the receiving bank must verify its authenticity and strictly comply with its requirements. It cannot change the content of the authorization letter of payment without authorization, otherwise, it shall bear all the consequences caused thereby. For remittances that cannot be remitted, the receiving bank shall promptly give reasons to the remitting bank. After checking the instruction correctly, the receiving bank is obliged to pay the payment to the payee. However, both the remitting bank and the receiving bank shall not be liable for any loss that is not due to their own faults (such as the inability or late receipt of the payment due to the loss or delay of the payment order in the mail), nor shall the remitting bank be liable for any fault in the receiving bank's work.

⑤Debit

After the payment, the receiving bank shall debit the remitting bank's account or claim a position from the remitting bank.

The process of remittance business is shown in figure 9.2.

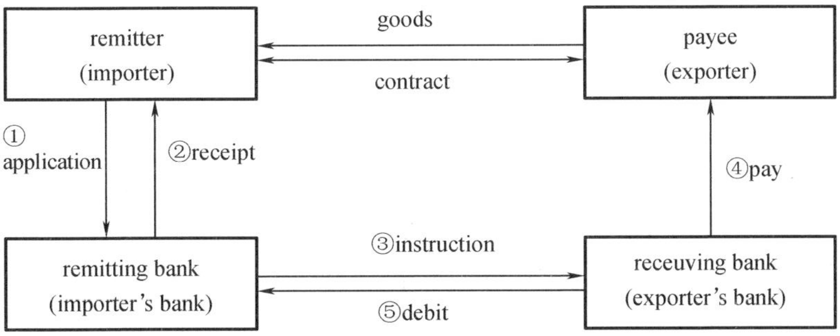

Figure 9.2 Flow chart of remittance business

According to whether the capital flows in the same direction as the settlement tool does, remittance can be classified into two categories: direct remittance and reverse remittance.

①Direct remittance

A way in which the debtor voluntarily gives money to the local bank, and entrusts the bank to remit the remittance to foreign creditors or payees through the use of certain settlement instruments, also known as remittance method. It is characterized by the same direction of movement of settlement tools and capitals from payer (debtor) to payee (creditor). In international settlements, remittance is usually done in the way of direct remittance, as is shown in figure 9.3.

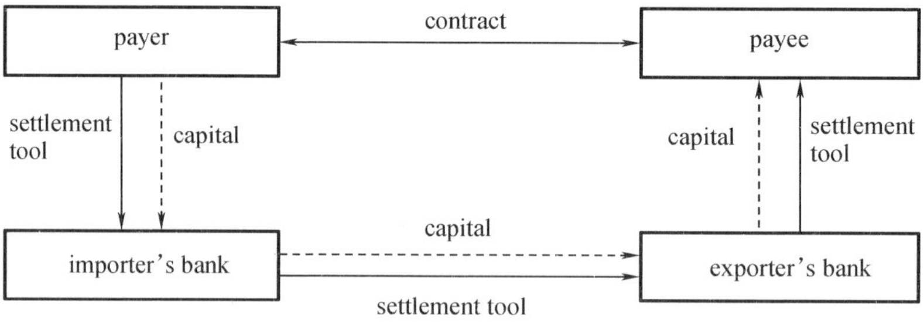

Figure 9.3 Settlement by direct remittance

②Reverse remittance

Also known as the method of issuing, refers to the settlement method that the creditor entrusts the domestic bank to collect the draft amount from the foreign debtor by issuing the bill. It is characterized by the opposite movement of settlement tools and capitals. In international settlements, collection and letter of credit are usually carried out in the way of reverse remittance, which is shown in figure 9.4.

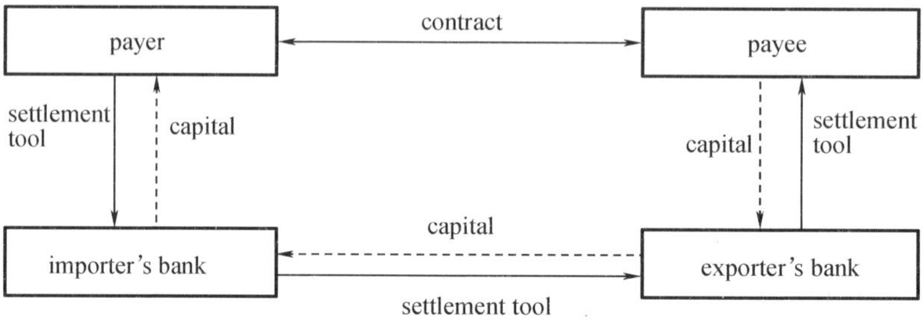

Figure 9.4 Settlement by reverse remittance

【Task】

In the case of this sub-task, Nam Kwong company. entrusted its bank of deposit, the Jiangsu branch of Bank of China, to remit the money to Nanhwa company in order to pay for the imported goods. Remittance, as the settlement method, is used here. In this settlement, Nam Kwong company is the remitter, while Nanhwa company is the payee, Jiangsu branch of Bank of China is the remitting bank and Hong Kong branch of Bank of China is the receiving bank. Among them, the credit and debt relationship between Nam Kwong company and Nanhwa company is caused by the trade contract. The relationship between Nam Kwong company and Jiangsu branch of Bank of China is based on the entrustment through telegraphic transfer application. The relationship between the Jiangsu branch of Bank of China and the Hong Kong branch of Bank of China is an entrustment relationship based on the agency contract. Bank of China's Hong Kong branch may or may not have an account relationship with Nanhwa company. Since both the capital and the settlement instrument (i. e., the authorization of payment in telex form) flow in the same direction, from the importer to the exporter, it is the settlement by direct remittance.

Task 9.1.2 The classification and process of remittance

【Questions for discussion】

Based on the above case, please consider the following questions:

(1) What are the main types of remittance service?

(2) What are their respective characteristics and operating procedures?

【Relevant knowledge】

When the remitter entrusts the bank to remit the money, he/she shall fill in the application form for remittance and submit it to the remitting bank. After receiving the amount of remittance and relevant fees, the remitting bank shall, according to the instructions on the application form, issue the order of payment to the receiving bank and authorize it to remit the money to the payee. According to the way of sending the order of payment by the remitting bank to the receiving bank, remittance can be divided into three types: M/T, T/T and D/D.

(1) Telegraphic transfer

Telegraphic transfer (T/T) refers to remittance by tested cable, telex or the society for worldwide inter-bank financial telecommunication (SWIFT). The remitting bank, requested by remitter, instructs the overseas receiving bank by tested cable, telex or SWIFT to pay a certain sum of money to beneficiary. It is often used when the remittance amount is large and the transfer of funds is subject to a time limit. Thus, 90% remittance is done through T/T.

Featuring safety and high speed, telegraphic transfer has become the remittance method most frequently used. Telegraphic transfer rate may be used as the base rate in the foreign exchange market and as the basis for the calculation of other exchange rates. Telegraphic transfer has the following characteristics:

①Fast speed

As payment instructions are transmitted by telecommunication, telegraphic transfer is extremely fast and hence enjoys a high priority for business processing. As a result, the bank usually handles the remittance on the same day so that the payee can receive the payment quickly.

②Safety and reliability

Wire transfer is a direct communication between banks, the possibility of error and loss is very small. In order to ensure the authenticity of telegrams and telex messages, the remitting bank usually encrypts the message or uses the automatically encrypted standard message format in the form of SWIFT. After receiving the notice, the receiving bank first checks whether the test key is correct and whether the format of SWIFT message is valid and then notifies the payee to withdraw money after confirmation.

③High cost

Because telegraphic transfer can not occupy client capitals, it costs more than mail transfer and demand draft, so the bank charges higher, and consequently, the remitter has to bear a heavier burden.

In telegraphic transfer, the remitter must fill in the application for telegraphic transfer and pay to the remitting bank, and then the remitting bank informs the receiving bank by cable, telex or international clearing network, entrusting it to pay the payee. After receiving the notice, the receiving bank shall notify the payee (creditor) to withdraw the money by telegraphic transfer notice after verifying the test key. After the payee withdraws money, clearing occurs between the remitting bank and the receiving bank, so far, a telegraphic transfer remittance business is completed. The basic procedure of remittance by telegraphic transfer is shown in figure 9.5.

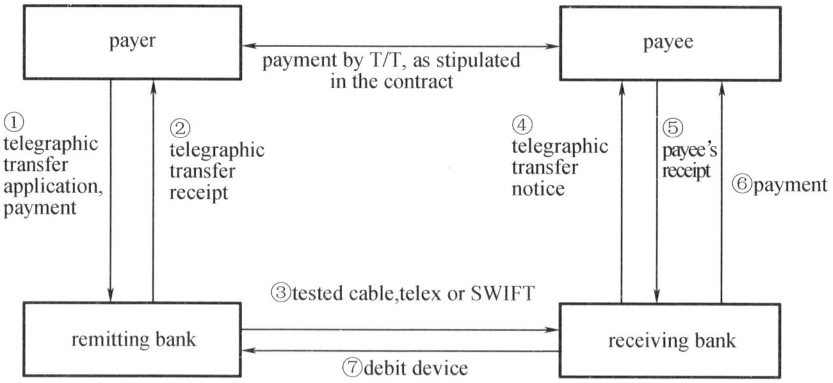

Figure 9.5 Flow chart of telegraphic transfer

(2) Mail transfer

A mail transfer (M/T) is a method of remittance in which the remitting bank sends a payment order or mail transfer advice by airmail to the receiving bank on the request of the remitter, instructing the receiving bank to make payment to the named payee.

Mail transfer is a traditional way of remittance, characterized by low cost and long time. The bank charges a relatively low fee because the fund is on the way for a long time and the remitting bank can occupy the funds for the length of one mail delivery. Due to many transit links in the mail process, unexpected events, such as loss or delay are likely to occur. And once the seal is illegally used, great risks will come with it. Therefore, mail transfer can only be used for a small amount of remittance, which is not urgent, but cannot meet the demand for transferring large urgent capitals. With the development of telecommunications, the use of mail transfer has decreased greatly.

There is no bill used in mail transfer, only the letter of order of payment is adopted. Therefore, the letter should be signed by the authorized signatory of the remitting bank. After receiving the order of payment, the receiving bank should carefully check the seal and make the withdrawal notice immediately after confirmation so as to notify the payee to withdraw the money. Basic procedures of remittance by mail transfer are shown in figure 9.6.

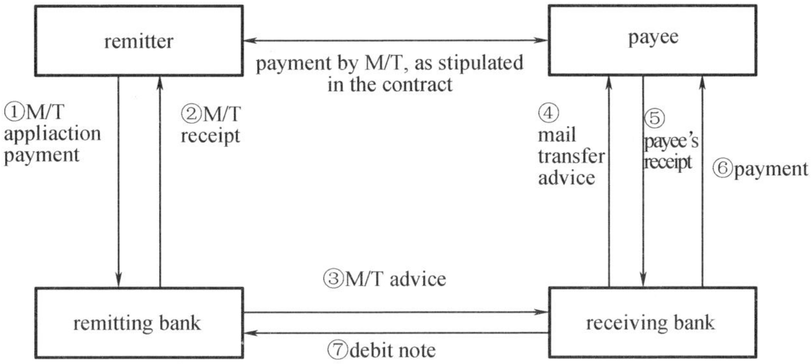

Figure 9.6 Procedure of remittance by mail transfer

(3) Demand draft

Demand draft (D/D) is a form of remittance in which the remitting bank, at the request of the remitter, draws a sight draft on the drawee to pay a certain amount to the payee.

In demand draft, the remitter actually buys the bank demand draft to deliver it to the payee. The payee of the draft is the payee of the remitter, and the drawee is the receiving bank. Demand draft is mainly used for small remittance and settlement of subordinated expenses in international trade. In addition to the use of drafts, other instruments (such as banknotes and checks) are also increasingly used. It is also frequently used in the foreign trade business of both the mainland of China and the Hong Kong special administrative region. Due to the great improvement of communication method, the use of large-denomination drafts is decreasing.

Compared with mail transfer and telegraphic transfer, demand draft has great flexibility in that so long as the draft is drawn to the extent allowed, the beneficiary can be the remitter himself or a foreign creditor. The payee of mail transfer and telegraphic transfer can only receive remittance after receiving the remittance advice from the receiving bank, while the payee of the demand draft can take the initiative to collect the payment by holding the draft. In addition, mail transfer and telegraphic transfer means withdrawal by remittance notices, which cannot be transferred in the market, while demand draft uses bank drafts, which can be endorsed before transfer or discounted on foreign banks, demonstrating its flexible way of payment.

In remittance by demand draft, the remitting bank shall send the letter of advice (advice of drawing) to the receiving bank at the same time it draws the bank demand draft and hands it to the remitter. After obtaining the bank demand draft, the remitter may send it to the foreign payee or take it out of the country in person to withdraw money. The basic procedures of remittance by demand draft are shown in figure 9.7.

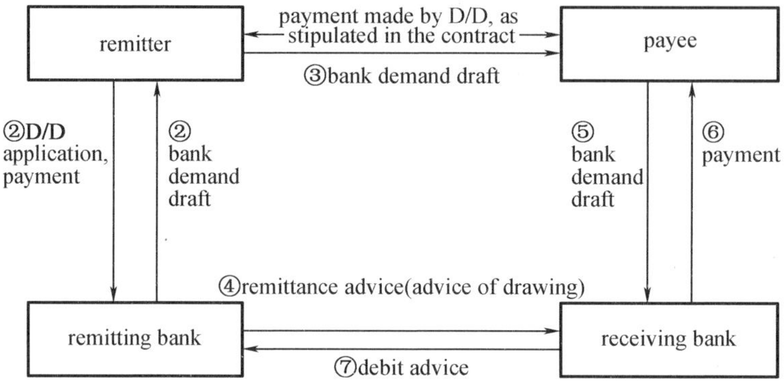

Figure 9.7 Procedure of remittance by demand draft

(4) A comparison of the above three remittance methods

Telegraphic transfer, mail transfer and demand draft are the 3 kinds of means of remittance, where the remitter needs to issue the application for remittance, and the payment instrument flows in the same direction as the capital, therefore all belong to the way of favorable exchanges, these are their shared common characteristics. However, they have their own specific features, and the comparison between them is shown in table 9.1.

Table 9.1 Comparison of the three methods of remittance

Classification	Payment tools	Verification	Capital safety	Can capital be used by banks	Cost for remittance	Business speed
T/T	Telegram, telex, SWIFT	By test key	High safety	No	High	Fast
M/T	M/T or payment order	By signature	May be lost or delayed	Only by receiving banks	Low	Slow
D/D	Bank demand draft	By signature	May be lost or delayed	Only by receiving banks	Low	Slow

(5) SWIFT

Founded in 1973 and headquartered in Belgium, SWIFT is an inter-bank international cooperative organization and one of the most important financial communication networks. By the end of 2001, more than 7 000 financial institutions in more than 200 countries and regions had connected to SWIFT. Bank of China in our country officially used SWIFT in May 1985. SWIFT implements membership, requiring each member to have a dedicated network terminal and pre-approved software, and to use a standard message format. Through this system, we can connect all the financial institutions that are not in contact with each other in series to carry out information exchange on a global scale, providing safe, cheap, fast, standardized and automatic communication services for bank settlement, thus greatly improving the speed of bank settlement.

Case 9.1 The remittance clause in the contract

(1) D/D

The buyer shall pay 100% of the payment in advance to the seller by demand draft no later than August 1.

(2) T/T

The buyers shall pay the total value to the sellers in advance by T/T before × × ×.

(3) M/T

The buyers shall pay the total value to the sellers in advance by M/T not later than × × ×.

【Tasks for implement】

In the case of the above sub-task, Nanhwa company paid the money to Nam Kwong company through the telegraphic transfer remittance. Nanhwa company shall submit the application for telegraphic transfer to the remitting bank, and the remitting bank shall send the payment instruction to the receiving bank by telex according to the telegraphic transfer application, and then the receiving bank shall verify the test key and send the telegraphic transfer advice to Nanhwa company, who then shall collect the payment from the receiving bank after receiving the notice. Of course, Nanhwa company can also complete the remittance through M/T and D/D. In the remittance by M/T, the remitting bank shall, according to the application for mail transfer submitted by Nanhwa company, send the payment order or M/T order by airmail to the receiving bank to issue the payment instruction. In the remittance by demand draft, the remitting bank shall, according to the application for demand draft submitted by Nanhwa company, draw the bank demand draft to Nanhwa company and mail the advice of drawing to the receiving bank. Nanhwa company can send the bank demand draft to Nam Kwong company by itself, or take the draft to Nanjing in person, and then pay to Nam Kwong company after the withdrawal. In the three kinds of remittance, the remitter (Nanhwa company) submits an application for remittance, and the remitting bank (Bank of China Hong Kong branch) sends the payment instructions to the receiving bank (Bank of China, Jiangsu branch), which then pays the payee (Nam Kwong company), therefore, payment tools flow in the same direction as the capital. Their differences lie in that, telegraphic transfer is safe and fast, and the remitting bank cannot use remittance capitals, so charges high fees; while M/T and D/D are slower, with the risk of loss or delay. As the remitting bank can make use of the funds during a postal journey, the cost is much lower.

Task 9.1.3 The application of remittance in international trade

【Questions for discussion】

In international trade, remittance settlement has specific forms of application, different forms have different characteristics and suit for different situations. According to the flow chart of remittance business and based on the lead-in case, please consider the following questions:

(1) What are the main forms of application for remittance in international trade?

(2) What kind of situations are they suitable for?

After a free discussion, students are advised to summarize the situations that remittance can be applied in.

【Relevant knowledge】

Remittance mainly acts as a way of transferring funds, so it is widely used in non-trade international fund transfer business, such as credit, foreign exchange transaction, donation, private remittance, etc. It can also be used for international trade settlement, mainly the payment of small fees such as deposit, balance payment and commission. Remittance can also be used for some bulk transactions in international trade by installment or deferred payment. In international trade, when settling the creditor's rights and debts between the buyer and the seller by remittance, according to the time sequence of payment and goods delivery, remittance can be divided into two types: payment before delivery and payment after delivery. The former is called prepayment and the latter is called cash on delivery.

(1) Payment in advance

Payment in advance, also known as settlement before export, means that the importer first transfers all or part of the payment to the exporter through the bank. After the exporter receives the payment, the goods are transported to the importer within a certain period of time or immediately according to the contract signed by both parties.

Payment in advance is a kind of remittance settlement which is favorable to the exporter but unfavorable to the importer. The exporter gets the payment for goods before the export, and does not need to advance the payment by himself, which is equivalent to getting the interest-free loan, therefore it is conducive to the turnover of funds. Receiving payment before delivery reduces the risk of goods being sold. However, the importer receives the goods after making the payment, which leads to a backlog of funds, and in turn will bring about problems in capital turnover and cause interest losses. If the exporter fails to deliver the goods or the goods are of poor quality, the importer will suffer huge losses.

Therefore, payment in advance only applies to the situations in which two parties are sharing close relationships, the goods are sold well or the supply of goods is limited. When importers adopt the way of prepayment, in order to protect their own capital security, they usually manage to reach the terms of payment with the bank and the exporter, namely the conditions of settlement. In international trade, payment in advance is mainly applied in the following situations:

①The goods traded between two sides are in short supply, and the buyer is in urgent need of high profits, so prepayment is adopted at all costs.

②The importer and the exporter share a very close relationship and know each other's credit standing very well, so the importer is willing to pay in advance.

③Because the importer has a poor credit standing, or the exporter does not know much about the importer's credit standing, the exporter preconditions the shipment with payment in advance.

④The exporter is in short of funds, and therefore need the payment in advance to buy raw materials, organize production and organize the source of goods before sending goods to the importer.

⑤In the bulk trade such as large machinery and equipment, transport facilities, or the goods ordered specially for the importer, exporters often require a certain proportion of advance payment, i. e. , the deposit, and the bulk trade generally adopts payment by installment, both deposits and installments are mostly paid by remittance.

(2) Cash on delivery

Cash on delivery, also known as settlement after export, is a kind of remittance settlement in which the exporter delivers the goods first and the importer remits the payment to the exporter immediately or within a certain period of time after receiving the goods. This is actually an open account transaction or deferred payment transaction.

Compared with payment in advance, cash on delivery is favorable for the importer and unfavorable for the exporter. Cash on delivery means the seller delivers the goods first and then collects the payment. The buyer does not need to bear the financial risks. If the goods fail to arrive or the quality of the goods is inconsistent with the contract, the buyer shall not pay, therefore the buyer always takes the favorable position in the whole transaction. As buyers often pay sellers after a period of time of receiving goods, they in fact occupy the seller's funds. While sellers deliver goods first, they must assume the risk that buyers refuse to pay, therefore it is possible for them to lose both the goods and the payment. Because the payment for goods often cannot be collected in time, the seller's capital is occupied, which causes a certain loss to the seller.

Cash on delivery (cod) is widely used in trade practice, although it is unfavorable for the exporter. Because most export commodities are in buyer's market, the competition is fierce, and since developed countries such as Europe and the USA adopt group purchase mode, their huge import volume creates a great attraction for exporters. In international trade, cash on delivery is often used in the following business:

①Goods sold

It means that when both the importer and the exporter reach an agreement on the terms of transaction and sign a contract, the price of goods and the time of payment are determined. Upon receipt of the goods, the importer shall remit the payment to the exporter at a price agreed upon. As the price has been determined in advance, the situation is called goods sold. At present, this way of payment is only applicable to the settlement of exporting fresh goods from Chinese mainland to Hong Kong and Macao.

②Consignment

It means that the exporter entrusts the foreign importer to sell the goods for him after delivering the goods with the price undetermined and sometimes the lowest price set. After the importer sells the goods, he deducts the commission and remits the money to the exporter. In consignment, both the importer and the exporter must first sign a consignment agreement, and the documents for the goods can be sent either through the bank or directly to the overseas trustee. Consignment is usually used in the following situations: the promotion of unmarketable goods; expanding overseas markets for new products; disposal of surplus goods at a trade fair.

(3) The difference between payment in advance and deposit

Payment in advance and deposit are two concepts of different natures, there is a distinctive difference between them.

According to relevant legal regulations in our country, "deposit" and "payment in advance" are two kinds of completely different funds. The deposit has the nature of a guarantee. Whether for the side offering deposits or the side receiving deposits, they promise each other at the time of giving and receiving that, if there is any non-fulfillment of obligations under the contract in the future, that is, a breach of the guarantee, the party in fault shall accept corresponding punishment on the basis of "deposit penalty" stipulated in the law. If the contract is implemented smoothly, the "deposit" which acts as a guarantee shall either be recovered by the payer or be used to set off against the price. That is to say, before the contract is performed, the "deposit" should be an independent payment unrelated to the contract.

Payment in advance is totally different. As part of the payment for the goods, it is paid to the seller before the implementation of the contract, and the rest of the payment for the goods is paid after the contract is fully performed, or according to the specific provisions of the contract about payment terms. Therefore, no matter pay first or later, it is the payment under the contract.

If the contract only stipulates "payment in advance" and fail to stipulate "deposit", then in the case of breaching the contract by any party, only the breaching party can be sentenced to pay "liquidated damages", while "the deposit penalty" cannot be applied on the "payment in advance". "Liquidated damages" is a kind of sanction to the breaching party and a kind of compensation to the observant party.

Are "deposit penalty" and "liquidated damages" penalty both applicable in the case of both "deposit" and "payment in advance" stipulated in the contract, if one party breaches the contract? According to relevant regulations and provisions in our country, they can be applied at the same time. The basic principle of "deposit penalty" is, the party offering the deposit has no right to claim a refund of all or part of the deposit, if it fails to fulfill or fully fulfill obligations of the contract. And the other party receiving the deposit shall return all or part of the deposit in double or even the liquidated damages, which can be specified by both parties within the scope of law, if it fails to fulfill or fully fulfill the obligations stipulated in the contract.

【Tasks for implementation】

In the case of the above sub-task, Nam Kwong company remitted the contract balance payment 100 000 Hong Kong dollars by T/T, at this moment, it has followed the contract and paid most of the payment to Nanhwa company, which has delivered the wool fabric to Nam Kwong company. The remitted balance payment is equivalent to the settlement business of cash on delivery. If Nanhwa company requires Nam Kwong company to pay the full amount of goods before delivery when signing the contract, at this moment, Nam Kwong company remits the contract amount by T/T or M/T or D/D, then the remitted amount is the settlement of payment in advance. Payment in advance is beneficial to Nanhwa company, because it can receive payment before delivery therefore frees itself from the risk of non-payment or delayed payment by Nam

Kwong company; However, it brings troubles to Nam Kwong, because it must pay the fund in advance, and may suffer the risks of non-delivery by Nanhwa company or inconsistency in quality between the goods delivered and the stipulation in the contract.

Task 9.2 Settlement by collection

【Task for analysis】

In international settlement, collection is often used as one of the methods. Collection business generally involves four parties, who share a certain relationship with each other. Collection can be classified into different types, and different types have different characteristics and can be applied to different situations.

Task 9.2.1 The concept of collection and the parties involved

【Case for demonstration】

On August 4, 2008, Jiangsu Nam Kwong International Trading corp. JNK exported fashion T-shirts worth 100 000 United States dollars to Hong Kong Nanhwa International Trading Co. , Ltd and entrusted Jiangsu branch of Bank of China (remitting bank) to handle collection with terms of D/P at sight and specified Bank of China, Hong Kong branch (collecting bank) as the collecting bank. Nam Kwong company draws a draft and delivers it together with documents to the remitting bank, who in turn shall send the collection order and the full set of documents to the collecting bank, who then shall present the draft to Nanhwa company, asking it to fulfill its obligations on the bill. Nanhwa company shall perform its payment responsibility immediately after the sight of the bill and take delivery of the goods against the receipt of the documents. After receiving the payment, the collecting bank shall remit the payment to the remitting bank according to the instructions by the remitting bank. And then the remitting bank shall make payment to Nam Kwong company. So far, the two trading companies have completed the settlement of payment by means of collection.

【Questions for discussion】

Based on the lead-in case, please try to understand the basic knowledge of collection business and think about the following questions:

(1) What is collection?

(2) What are the features of collection?

(3) What are the general procedures for collection?

(4) What are the parties involved in the collection business and how do they relate to each other?

【Relevant knowledge】

(1) Concept of collection

Collection, entrusted collection of payment, is an arrangement whereby the goods are shipped and the relevant bill of exchange is drawn by the seller (creditor) on the buyer (debtor), and/or document(s) is sent to the seller's bank with clear instructions for collection through one of its correspondent banks located in the domicile of the buyer(debtor).

International chamber of commerce publication No. 522 "uniform rules for collections" (URC522) defines collection as following: collection refers to the bank, in accordance with the instructions, dealing with financial documents (bills of exchange, promissory notes, checks, etc.) and/or commercial documents (invoice and transport documents, documents of title, etc.), in order to: obtain payment and/or acceptance, or deliver documents against payment and/or acceptance, or other terms and conditions. The definition is a broad definition of collection used for international trade settlement and non-trade settlement.

(2) Characteristics of collection

In the current international trade, collection, a settlement by non-letter of credit, occupies an increasing proportion, and is the most important international trade settlement method second only to letter of credit. Collection has the following characteristics.

①It is a kind of inverse settlement

In collection business, funds are transferred in the opposite direction from the clearing instrument. The fun is always transferred from the debtor to the creditor, while the clearing instrument (bill of exchange, etc.) is transferred from the creditor to the debtor through the bank.

②It belongs to business credit

In collection business, payment is entirely up to the importer, and the bank is only the agent of the documents and is not responsible for payment. If the importer refuses to pay, goes bankrupt, or becomes insolvent, etc., the seller needs to find a new buyer, warehouse, insurance and backhaul, etc., all of which will cost a lot of money. And all these responsibilities and expenses are borne by the exporter.

③Compared with remittance, it features higher security, requires higher cost and demands more procedures

In the way of remittance, whether by credit sale or advance payment, it is impossible to make two sides clear. Therefore, the other party is hard to be restrained and the risk is relatively high. Collection turns a transaction into payment upon delivery (presumptive delivery, of course), with less risk than remittance. Collection requires the presentation of bills and documents through the bank, so the service charge required is higher than remittance. But since collection is safer than remittance, it is cost-effective.

④The financial burden is unbalanced

In collection, the exporter bears a heavy financial burden. The exporter needs to advance his own funds to prepare the goods, arrange the shipment and collect money through the bank. The importer, on the other hand, can obtain qualified documents only by payment and then can take delivery of the goods against these documents. If the distance between the import and the export is very close, it is almost equivalent to "payment upon delivery". At the same time, some banks are willing to settle the payment by paying for the bills because of the documents, so exporters can get financing, while remittance cannot be negotiated at all. Therefore, collection is widely welcomed by importers, which can increase the motivation of importers and improve the competitiveness of exporters.

(3) Basic parties involved in collection business

There are four basic parties in collection business, namely, principal, remitting bank, collecting bank and payer.

①Principal

A principal is a person who draws a draft together with shipping documents and commissions a bank to collect money from a foreign importer (buyer). In international trade, the principal is the creditor, the drawer of the bill of exchange, and generally the exporter (seller). On the one hand, the principal assumes the responsibility under the trade contract, that is, the goods are delivered according to the quality, the quantity, the time and the place, and the documents in accordance with the contract are provided, on the other hand, it takes the responsibility under the agency contract, that is, filling in the collection application, giving instructions to the remitting bank clearly and timely, and bearing the relevant fees.

②Remitting bank

Also known as the entrusting bank and the sending bank, is a bank that accepts the entrustment of the creditor to collect money from the foreign debtor. In international trade practice, the remitting bank is the exporter's bank, usually the bank where the exporter opens an account. The remitting bank carries out the instructions of the principal and is fully in the position of an agent in the collection business. Therefore, the collection advice giving instructions must be attached when documents are sent to the collection bank. The remitting bank's responsibility is mainly to carry out the instructions of the principal, and the contents of the printed "collection advice" must be strictly consistent with the contents of the principal's application. The collecting bank is not responsible for the compliance of the documents provided by the principal with the sales contract. The collection bank is liable for its faults.

③Collecting bank

The collecting bank is the bank which situates at the place of import and accepts the entrustment from the remitting bank to collect money from the debtor. In the practice of international trade, the collecting bank is designated by the principal or the remitting bank, usually the bank where the importer opens an account, generally the remitting bank's affiliated bank or agent bank in the place where the payer is located. The collecting bank collects the payment from the payer and hands the bill to the payer. The collecting bank is also an agent and bears the same basic responsibilities as the remitting bank. In addition, the collecting bank should keep the documents well and inform the principal of the situation of collection in a timely and rapid manner through the remitting bank, such as refusal of payment and non-acceptance. The collecting bank is not obliged to take any action against the goods under collection.

④Payer

The payer is the person who makes payment to the collecting bank. The payer is the debtor and the drawee of the bill of exchange. In international trade, the payer is usually the importer (buyer). The basic responsibility of the payer is to make payment according to the contract under the premise that the principal has fulfilled the contractual obligations.

Among the above parties, the relationship between the principal and the payer is the buyer-seller relationship based on the sales contract; the relationship between the principal and the remitting bank is the principal-agent relationship based on the application for collection, which is essentially an agency contract between both parties; the relationship between the remitting bank and the collection bank is the principal-agent relationship based on the collection order, which is essentially the agency contract of both parties. There is no legal relationship between the payer and the collecting bank. The payer makes the payment according to the obligations in the sales contract between him and the principal, therefore, whether the principal can receive the payment depends entirely on the credit standing of the importer, and both the collection bank and the remitting bank do not assume any responsibilities.

(4) General business procedures for collection

①The exporter shall deliver the goods according to the contract and prepare the documents. In the case of documentary collection, the exporter shall first ship the goods according to the contract and obtain the bill of lading and other documents required in the contract.

②The exporter draws a draft and presents the documents to the collecting bank for collection. When going through collection procedures, the principal shall submit an application for collection to the remitting bank. The application for collection is generally provided by the bank and filled in by the exporter in duplicate, one copy to the remitting bank and one copy to be left on file, where the format varies from bank to bank. The application for collection shall include: a. The full name, detailed address, telephone and fax number of the foreign collecting bank, the payer and the principal, etc.; b. the amount and the currency of the collection; c. a list of the documents to be sent, which includes the name and number of copies of the documents; d. the date and the deadline of the draft; e. contract number; f. collection clauses, etc.

③The remitting bank prepares a collection order according to the application for collection and sends the order and documents to the collecting bank, instructing it to collect the money from the payer. The content of the collection order is basically the same as the application for collection.

④According to the instructions of the collection order, the collecting bank presents the draft to the importer when it is due and demands the importer to accept or pay.

⑤After checking the bill and performing the bill obligations, the importer obtains the bill, and can take delivery of goods against the bill.

⑥After collecting, the collection bank shall deliver the payment to the remitting bank in the manner specified in the collection order.

⑦The remitting bank shall deliver the payment to the exporter upon receipt of the payment.

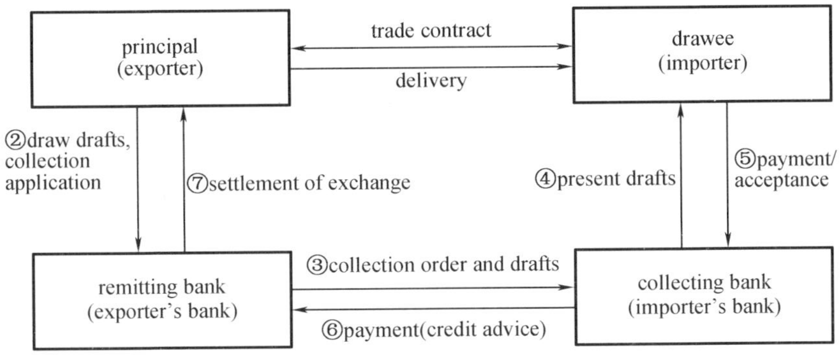

Figure 9.8 The flow chart of collection business

(5) Collection bill

When receiving payment in the way of collection, bills with the same terms of payment as the letter of credit shall be used. The collection bill is also in duplicate. Two copies have the same legal effect, but when the first bill takes effect, the second one will be void automatically and when the second draft becomes effective, the first draft becomes void automatically. There are the following differences in the way of filling in bills:

①It is not necessary to fill in the three columns of the reasons for drawing drafts, L/C number and L/C date, so leave them blank.

②In the "payment term" column, fill in D/P at sight or D/P × days; D/A × days.

③In the "payee" column, fill in the name of the collection bank.

(6) Other parties to the collection business

Collection business may have other parties besides the principal, the remitting bank, the collection bank and the payer.

①Presenting bank

It refers to the bank that presents drafts and documents to the debtor (payer) under documentary collection. In general, the presenting bank and the collecting bank are the same bank. However, if the collecting bank has no current relationship with the debtor, it may, on its own initiative or at the request of the payer, entrust the payer's correspondent bank to act as the presenting bank.

②Principal's representative in case of need

It is the agent appointed by the principal in advance at the place of payment for the purpose of preventing the occurrence of unattended goods due to the payer's refusal to pay. Its function is to accept the documents and handle the goods on behalf of the principal when the payer refuses to pay or accept the goods.

(7) "Uniform rules for collection" (URC522)

In international settlement, when handling collection business, banks from various countries often have different interpretations of the relationship between the bank and the principal, the relationship between the remitting bank and the collecting bank, and the rights, obligations and responsibilities of the parties, which easily causes misunderstandings in the business process. As a result, disputes and disagreements occur, which, to a certain extent, affect the development of international trade settlement.

To solve such problems, the International Chamber of Commerce (ICC) drafted *Uniform Rules for the Collection of Commercial Paper* in 1958 and suggested that banks from different countries adopt it in the collection business so as to make it a universally accepted international practice. In 1967, the ICC reformulated and published this rule. In 1978, according to the change and development of collection practice, the International Chamber of Commerce revised and supplemented the collection rules, and changed its name to Uniform Rules for Collection (URC), namely the international chamber of commerce publication No. 322 (URC322).

【Tasks for implementation】

In the case of this task, Nam Kwong company exported goods to Nanhwa company, entrusting Jiangsu branch of Bank of China to collect the payment for goods, which in turn entrusted Hong Kong branch of Bank of China to collect money from Nanhwa company, which was a business settled by means of collection. This business involves four parties, the exporter Nam Kwong company is the principal, Bank of China Jiangsu branch is the remitting bank, Bank of China Hong Kong branch is the collection bank, the importer Nanhwa company is the payer. Among them, the relationship between Nam Kwong company and Nanhwa company is a buyer-seller relationship, and the relationship between Nam Kwong company and Jiangsu branch of Bank of China and the relationship between the Jiangsu branch of Bank of China and the Hong Kong branch of Bank of China are both a principal-agent relationship, while there is no direct legal relationship between the Hong Kong branch of Bank of China and Nanhwa company.

Task 9.2.2 The classification and business procedures of collection

【Questions for discussion】

In practical operation, collection business can be divided into different categories. Different collection methods have different characteristics and operation procedures, and are also different in practical application. Based on the above case, we can consider the following questions:

(1) What are the main types of collection services?

(2) What are their characteristics and operating procedures?

【Relevant knowledge】

Settlement by collection can be classified into clean collection and documentary collection according to the nature of the documents involved. Among them, documentary collection can be divided into documents against payment collection and documents against acceptance collection according to different conditions of presentation. And depending on the time of payment, documents against payment collection can be divided into two categories: D/P at sight and D/P after sight.

(1) Clean collection

Clean collections are collections on financial instruments (bills of exchange) without being accompanied by commercial documents, such as invoice, bill of lading, insurance policy etc. It is a method of settlement where the principal entrusts the bank to collect payment from the payer only on the strength of financial documents.

Clean collection does not necessarily come without any documents. The collection of such a bill of exchange also belongs to clean collection if the bill is accompanied only by non-shipping documents (such as invoice, advance payment list, etc.). In the international trade of goods, if clean bill collection is adopted, the shipping documents are usually sent directly by the exporter to the importer. In this case, the exporter loses his control of the goods and often falls in a passive position when the importer refuses to pay. Therefore, in the import and export trade practice, the amount of money used in clean bill collection is usually relatively small, and most of the clean bills are payable at sight, mainly used for collection of trade incidental expenses (such as freight, insurance premium, commissions, etc.), the remainder of the payment, claims and recovery of the overpayment, also used for collection of non-trade donations, support payment and other charges.

Bills of exchange under clean collection can be divided into sight and usance. When sight draft is adopted, the collecting bank shall immediately present to the drawee for payment upon receipt of the draft. When a usance draft is adopted, the collecting bank, upon receipt of the draft, shall immediately make a presentation to the payer for acceptance, so as to confirm the liability of payment due. After acceptance, the collecting bank takes back the draft and presents for payment on the due date. If the payer refuses to pay or refuses to accept, unless otherwise provided in the collection order, the collecting bank shall inform the remitting bank of the refusal of payment within the legal time limit and inform the principal.

Bill collection needs no shipping documents and therefore does not involve transferring and processing of goods. The bank only collects money according to the bill, so the business procedure is relatively simple. The remitting bank shall forward the financial documents delivered by the principal to the collecting bank abroad and ask it to collect the money from the payer on the bill. Upon receipt of the payment, the collecting bank may notify the principal to withdraw the money or credit the principal's account. The business procedures for clean bill collection are shown in figure 9.9.

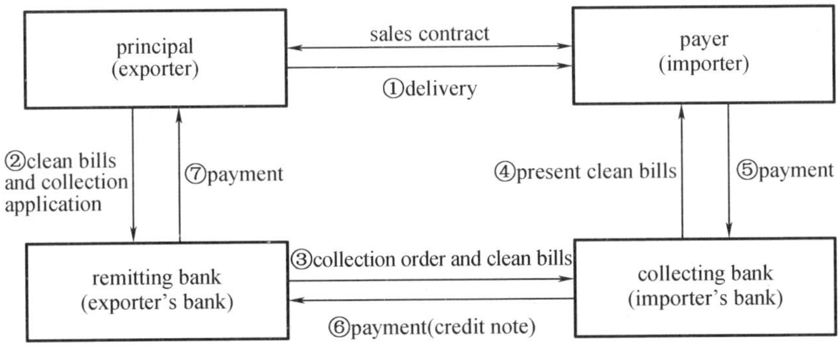

Figure 9.9 Flow chart of clean bill collection procedure

(2) Documentary collection

Documentary collection is the collection of commercial documents. It is a method of settlement in which the exporter issues a draft together with a complete set of shipping documents to the domestic remitting bank after loading the goods and entrusts it to collect the payment for goods.

Documentary collection may be a collection of financial instruments accompanied by commercial documents or a collection of commercial documents without financial instruments attached (i. e. , an invoice instead of a bill of exchange). The collection of a bill of exchange with commercial documents attached belongs to payment by bill. Commercial documents are the subsidiary documents to the bill of exchange. In some countries, stamp duty is required for the use of bills of exchange. Therefore, in order to free themselves from the tax, people have established a new form of collection within multinational companies and between customers who have been in contact with each other for many years, which involves only commercial documents but no bills of exchange. Once this kind of collection encounters refusal from the drawee, it is difficult for the bank to make a certificate of protest, which puts the principal in a disadvantage in his prosecution against the drawee in the future, therefore should be avoided as far as possible. In international trade, the payment for goods is mostly collected by documentary collection.

The business procedures of documentary collection are listed as follows:

①According to the contract, the principal (exporter) shall ship the goods to the payer (importer) and obtain the bill of lading and other documents required in the contract.

②The exporter issues the bill of exchange, fills in the application for collection, and sends the full set of documents (including the bill of exchange, the invoice, the bill of lading, etc.) to the remitting bank for collection.

③After accepting the commission, the remitting bank shall verify the documents submitted by the exporter before filling in the order of collection, and send the draft and the full set of documents to the collecting bank, which shall present the draft to the importer according to the instructions in the order of collection.

④The importer shall make payment immediately after seeing and examining the documents, or make acceptance first and perform the obligation of payment on the due date.

⑤The collecting bank shall deliver the bills to the importer, and the importer shall obtain the full set of documents and then take delivery of the goods from the shipping company.

⑥The collecting bank will transfer the amount of money to the remitting bank, and the remitting bank will immediately transfer the sum of money to the exporter.

The shipping document in the commercial paper represents the ownership of the goods, and its transfer represents the delivery of the goods. Therefore, the condition of the presentation of documents is an important link for the exporter to control the collection. The terms of delivery of documents in documentary collection shall be determined by the principal (exporter) in the collection order and shall be complied with by the remitting bank, the collecting bank and the payer. If the payer requests to change the way of presentation of documents in the original collection order, he must consult the principal, and both the remitting bank and the collection bank have no right to change it without authorization. Documentary collection can be divided into D/P and D/A depending on the conditions of presentation. The business procedure of documentary collection is shown in figure 9.10.

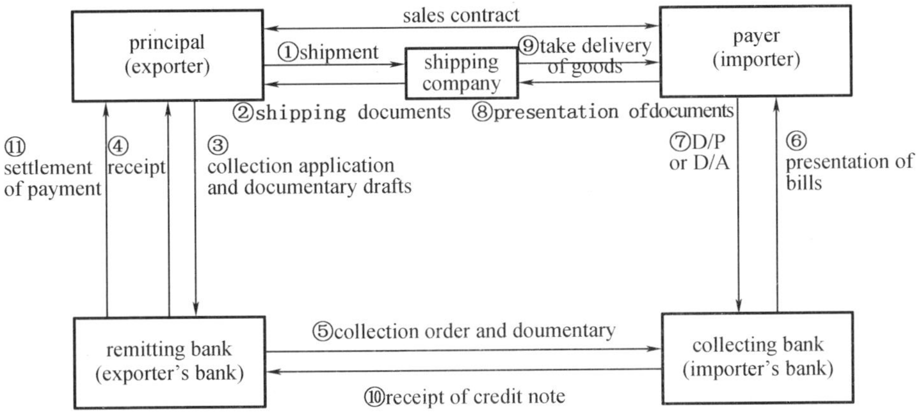

Figure 9.10 Business procedure of documentary collection

(3) Documents against payment

Documentary against payment collection refers to the collection method whereby the collecting bank delivers shipping documents to the importer on the basis of payment by the importer. In other words, the collecting bank gives shipping documents to the importer after the payment has been paid by the importer according to the instructions of the principal.

In D/P collection, the exporter may draw a sight draft or a usance draft. But either at sight or after sight, the importer must pay up before obtaining the shipping documents, which is called "redemption documents". According to the time of payment, D/P collection can be divided into D/P at sight and D/P after sight.

①D/P at sight

It is a collection method in which the exporter, after the shipment according to the contract, issues a draft at sight (or no draft) together with the shipping documents and presents them through the bank to the importer, who then shall pay for the documents immediately after checking them.

In principle, payment should be made when documents are presented for the first time in D/P at sight. According to international practice, the term for the importer to redeem the documents is 24 hours, so that the importer can make payment within the next working day after the first presentation of the documents. In practice, however, some importers often insist on payment after the arrival of the goods in order to reduce the risk. In the practice of international trade, the two parties shall sign a contract stipulating that the payment shall be settled by D/P at sight. Its business procedures are shown in figure 9.11.

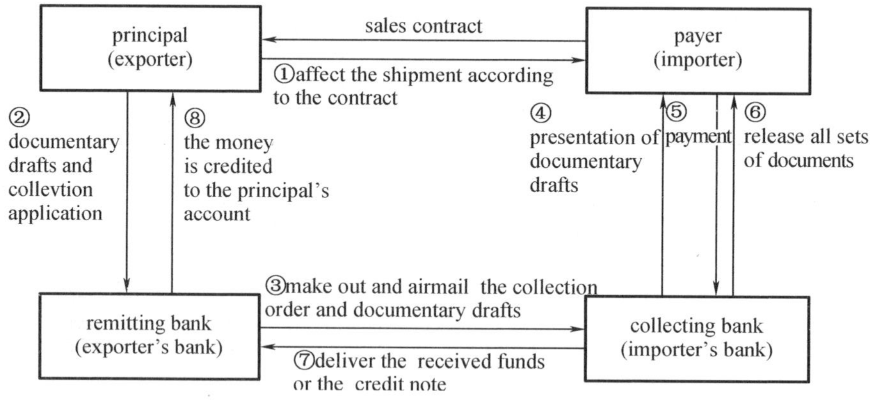

Figure 9.11 Procedure of D/P at sight

②D/P after sight

Documentary against payment at sight means that the exporter issues a usance bill of exchange attached with the commercial documents after delivery and presents them to the importer through the collecting bank. After acceptance, the collecting bank will keep the full set of commercial documents which shall be collected by the importer when the bill is due for payment.

The purpose of acceptance is to give the importer time to prepare the money and at the same time to protect the interests of the exporter. Before payment, the document of title is still in the hands of the bank entrusted by the exporter. The allotted time shall be shorter than the voyage time of the carrying vessel, generally lasting between 30 days and 45 days, up to a maximum of 60 days. Since the importer, as the drawee of the bill of exchange, has accepted the bill but cannot obtain the shipping document which represents the property right, the shipping documents are still in charge of the collecting bank before payment, which therefore is of no practical significance to the importer. This method is seldom used in practice.

In contrast to D/P at sight, the exporter of a usance D/P draws a usance draft and usually has to draw a draft, which the importer shall accept first. The bill of exchange and documents after acceptance shall be collected by the collecting bank. While in D/P at sight, a sight bill of exchange for the exporter is a free choice and the acceptance is omitted.

In the case of adopting such a way of collection, both parties shall sign a trade contract and stipulate that the payment shall be settled by D/P after sight. After shipment, the exporter issues a usance draft and delivers it together with a full set of shipping documents to the bank for collection. The collecting bank immediately presents the usance draft and documents to the importer and takes back the draft and documents after the acceptance by the importer. When the draft is due, the collecting bank shall make another presentation to the importer for payment and deliver the documents to the importer after receiving the payment. Its business procedures are shown in figure 9.12.

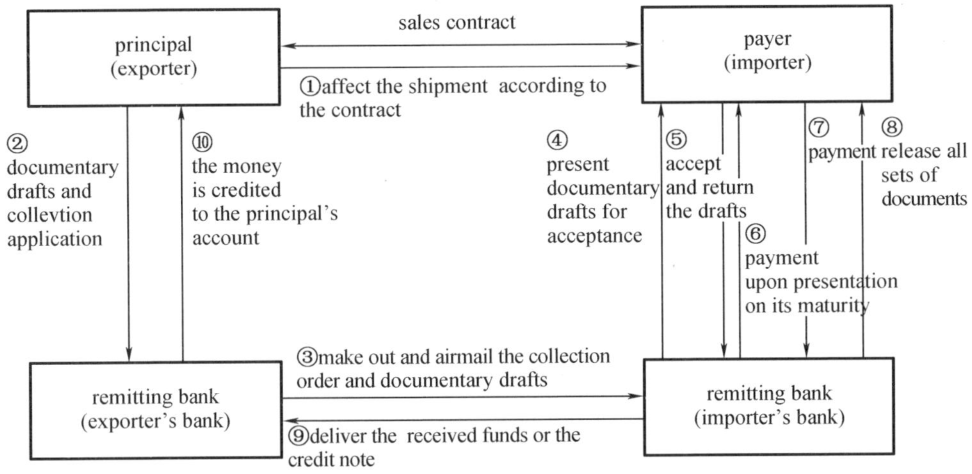

Figure 9.12 Procedure of D/P after sight

(4) Documents against acceptance

Documents against acceptance collection is a collection method in which the collecting bank gives the commercial documents to the drawee after the drawee accepts the usance bill and the drawee pays the bill at the due date.

D/A collection is characterized by the transfer of ownership of the goods before the payment of the goods. If the importer fails to pay for the goods after the draft is due, the collecting bank shall not bear any responsibilities, and the exporter shall bear the loss of both the goods and the payment. As a result, exporters are generally very cautious about this approach and do not use it very often.

In this way of collection, the exporter shall open a usance draft after shipment and deliver it together with the full set of shipping documents to the bank for collection. When the collecting bank presents the draft and documents to the importer, the importer accepts the usance draft, and the collecting bank delivers the full set of shipping documents to the importer, and presents the importer for payment when the draft is due. Its business procedures are shown in figure 9.13.

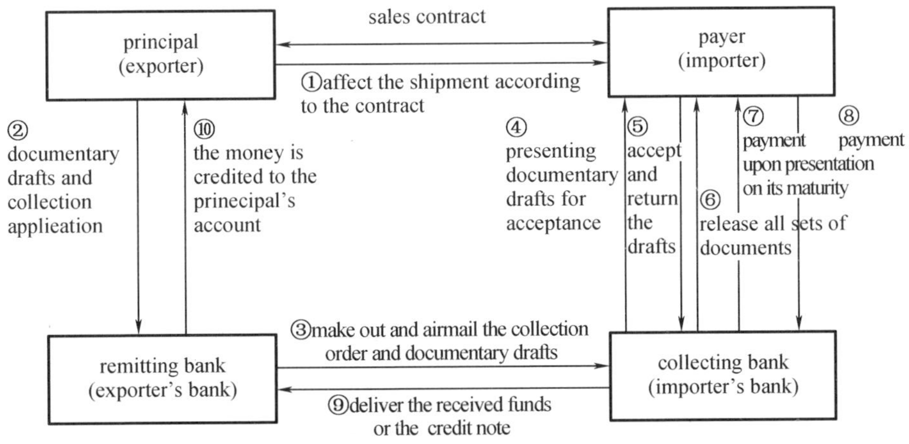

Figure 9.13 Procedure of D/A after sight

Both D/A and D/P after sight belong to forward collection. Since the exporter draws a usance draft, the importer should accept the draft at sight and pay the draft when it is due. The difference between them lies in the condition of presenting documents: D/A means to deliver documents after acceptance and pay at maturity; while D/P after sight requires acceptance at first, and the delivery of documents is based on the payment at maturity. The comparison of three different ways of delivering documents in documentary collection is shown in table 9.2.

Table 9.2 Comparison of three different ways of delivering documents in documentary collection

Items	D/P at sight	D/P after sight	D/A
Bills to be issued	Sight draft, or no draft	Usance draft	Usance draft
Acceptance	No	Necessary	Necessary
Conditions of delivering documents	Redeeming documents upon payment	Redeeming documents upon payment	Redeeming documents upon acceptance
Risks involved in export	It is a commercial credit and can be used to control the property right. The exporter can receive the payment quickly so as to avoid the backlog of funds, therefore faces little risks	It is a commercial credit and can be used to control the property right. The exporter can collect the money when the bill is due. The exporter will be faced with the backlog of capitals, and small risks	It belongs to commercial credit and cannot be used to control the property right. The exporter can collect the money when the bill is due. The exporter will be faced with the backlog of capitals, and certain risks of losing both money and goods

(5) The influence of different delivery methods on importers and exporters

Different ways of delivering documents have different effects on both sides of import and export. D/P at sight, followed by D/P after sight and finally D/A is the most ideal method for exporters.

Using D/P at sight, the exporter always controls the documents before the importer makes a payment, so as to control the goods. He will neither fail to receive the payment for the goods nor lose the goods, which is conducive to reducing the risks. At the same time, exporters can quickly receive the payment so as to avoid the backlog of funds, which is conducive to improving the efficiency of using funds.

D/P after is similar to D/P at sight in terms of risk control, but payment cannot be collected until the draft is due and the importer pays for the goods. Therefore, the problem of fund backlog exists in different degrees, which is not conducive to the efficient use of funds.

D/A is similar to D/P after sight in terms of collection time and capital occupation, what's more, the importer after the delivery of documents may be bankrupt or unable to pay for the goods, or unreasonably refuse to pay, delay the payment, etc. So it is unfavorable for exporters, either in terms of risks or the use of capitals.

(6) Trust receipt (T/R)

In the case D/P after sight, if the due date of the draft is later than the arrival date of the goods, i. e. , the goods have arrived at the destination or the port of destination before the deadline of the draft, the importer may collect the commercial documents from the collecting bank after paying for the goods in advance (the interest between the maturity date of the draft and the payment date shall be deducted) or borrow the bill from the collecting bank and provide the trust receipt at the same time.

A trust receipt is a certificate issued by the importer when he admits to lending a full set of commercial documents from the collecting bank in the way of trust. It shows that the borrower is willing to take delivery of the goods, declare customs, store the goods, insure the goods or sell them as the principal of the collecting bank, and acknowledges that the ownership of the goods still belongs to the collecting bank, and the money after the goods are sold will be given to the collecting bank when the bill is due. The importer borrows the shipping documents in advance against the trust receipt, picks up the goods first, pays off the goods when the draft is due, and retrieves the trust receipt. Lending documents from the bank on trust receipt is a kind of financing provided by the bank to the importer.

The exporter may, on its own initiative, authorize the collecting bank to lend documents to the importer on the basis of the trust receipt submitted by the importer, i. e. , D/P after sight against trust receipt. If the importer refuses to pay when the draft is due in the future, it has nothing to do with the collecting bank and the exporter shall bear all the risks arising therefrom. If the collecting bank allows the importer with good credit standing to borrow the shipping documents against the trust receipt and take delivery of the goods in advance. The collecting bank voluntarily lends the bill to the importer. If the collecting bank cannot collect the payment when the bill is due, the collecting bank will bear the corresponding risks and responsibilities.

Case 9.2 In a collection business, the remitting bank states in the collection instructions that "DOCS TO BE RELEASED ONLY AGAINST ACCEPTANCE" and "PAYMENT ON DUE DATE TO BE GUARANTEED BY × × BANK. tested tlx to this effect required." After handling D/A, the collecting bank sends the collecting bank the acceptance advice, which clearly indicates that "THE BIL ACCEPTED BY DRAWEE" was due on August 6, 2008. Soon after, when the remitting bank enquires about acceptance, the collecting bank replies by telegraphy again that "DOCS HAVE BEEN ACCEPTED BY DRAWEE TO MATURE ON 080806". In the above acceptance advice and the reply to the enquiry, the collecting bank does not indicate payment under guarantee, nor does it send any telex of promising guarantee, and the remitting bank has not raised any objection. When the acceptance bill is due, the importer refuses to pay for the goods, and the collecting bank issues a notice of dishonor to the remitting bank. The remitting bank considers that the collection instruction requires the release of documents against a guarantee for payment due from the collecting bank, and that the collecting bank has released the documents to the payer and therefore demands immediate payment. But the collecting bank believes that the release of documents is based on the acceptance of the payer and it has no obligation to guarantee the payment due.

Analysis: The focus of this case is the responsibility shouldered by the collecting bank when it fails to fully carry out collection instructions. The collecting bank considers that, in accordance with the general principles of international laws, the collecting bank should reply to the remitting bank if is unable to make the guaranteed payment required by the collection bank. Releasing the documents to the payer without consulting the remitting bank seriously breaches the contract, for which the remitting bank shall be responsible. The collecting bank holds that the collection instruction requires the release of documents by acceptance, and releasing documents happens only after the acceptance by the payer. As to the instruction for collection, which requires a guarantee from the collecting bank, and at the same time requires confirmation by a tested telex, which is in fact not given by the collecting bank. And the relevant acceptance advice and correspondence clearly notify the remitting bank that the payer has accepted. But the remitting bank fails to raise any objections. Consequently, the collecting bank thinks it should not undertake any guarantee responsibilities. According to relevant rules for collection, upon receipt of collection documents from a remitting bank, the collecting bank must act in accordance with the instructions in the collection instructions and *the uniform rules for collection* (URC522). The inability or unwillingness to perform such instructions shall be replied to the remitting bank without delay. Nevertheless, the collecting bank does not do so and only informs the remitting bank the release of the documents against acceptance when being inquired by the remitting bank. As a result, the collecting bank violates URC522 regulations in this case. However, it cannot be concluded that the collecting bank should assume responsibilities.

The remitting bank not only instructs the collecting bank to guarantee payment at maturity, but also requests the collecting bank to confirm it by a tested telegram. Although the collecting bank neither explicitly notifies the remitting bank that it refuses to accept the instruction, nor does it inform the remitting bank that it complies with the instruction in a tested telegram as requested by the remitting bank. The collecting bank fails to make any response to the two closely related instructions from the remitting bank, and the confirmation by a tested telegram could not be done by tacit declaration. Taken together, the instructions from the remitting bank could not be accepted in an implied way. Therefore, the fact that the collecting bank has not replied should not be taken as evidence that the collecting bank has accepted the instructions from the remitting bank on payment guarantee when it is due.

Case 9. 3 A company exports three batches of goods respectively, and the contract stipulates payment terms as follows: D/P at sight, D/P at 30 days after sight and D/A at 30 days after sight. Suppose the delivery of documents by the bank takes 7 days and the collection date is August 1. What is the day of presentation, the day of acceptance, the day of payment and the day of delivering documents excluding the reasonable working hours of the bank?

Tips for analysis: if the reasonable working hours of the bank are not taken into account, the dates are shown in table 9.3.

Table 9.3 Dates

Way of collection	Presentation day	Acceptance day	Payment day	Day of delivering documents
D/P at sight	August 8	–	August 8	August 8
D/P at 30 days after sight	August 8	August 8	September 7	September 7
D/A at 30 days after sight	August 8	August 8	September 7	August 8

Case 9.4 collection clause in the contract

(1) D/P at sight

Upon the first presentation the buyers shall pay against documentary draft at sight drawn by the sellers. The shipping documents are to be delivered against payment only.

(2) D/P after sight

The buyers shall duly accept the documentary draft drawn by the sellers at ×× days after sight upon the first presentation and make a payment on its maturity. The shipping documents are to be delivered against payment only.

(3) D/A

The buyers shall duly accept the documentary draft drawn by the sellers at ×× days after sight upon the first presentation and make a payment on its maturity. The shipping documents are to be delivered against acceptance.

Case 9.5 An export contract has been concluded between a foreign trade enterprise of our country and company A of a country. The payment term is 45 days after sight of D/P. When the bill of exchange and the attached documents are sent to the collecting bank at the place of import by the remitting bank, company A timely completes the acceptance procedure on the bill of exchange. When the goods arrive at the port of destination, eager to use the goods company A issues trust receipt (T/R) to borrow the documents from the collecting bank to take delivery of the goods for resale. When the draft comes due, A is unable to pay due to the poor management. The collecting bank notifies the remitting bank on the grounds that the drawee refuses to pay, and suggests that our foreign trade enterprise directly asks for payment from A.

Analysis: The collecting bank lends the documents to the importer by the trust receipt without the authorization of the principal, therefore shall be responsible for the loss when the importer is insolvent upon expiration. So our export enterprise cannot accept the advice from the collecting bank, but should instruct the collecting bank to make payment through the remitting bank.

【Task】

In the case of the subtask, Nam Kwong company adopts the documentary collection method when handling the collection and settlement business, and the condition of presentation is D/P at sight. After shipping the goods according to the contract, Nam Kwong company shall draw a sight draft together with the full set of documents to the Jiangsu branch of Bank of China (remitting bank). The remitting bank shall send the collection order and the full set of documents to Bank of China, Hong Kong branch (collecting bank). It then shall present the draft to Namhwa company, who then shall redeem the documents at sight after payment. If the D/P after sight condition is used by Nam Kwong company, the collecting bank shall first make a presentation to Nanhwa company for acceptance of the draft, then make a presentation for payment on the date stipulated in the contract, and deliver the documents to Namhwa company after receiving the payment. If the condition of delivering documents used by Nam Kwong company is D/A, the collecting bank should first present the bill to Namhwa company for acceptance. After acceptance, Namhwa company can obtain the shipping documents and take delivery of the goods against the bill. The collecting bank will present the bill to Namhwa company for payment on the payment date stipulated in the contract and collect the payment.

When Namhwa company collects the goods by D/P at sight, it shall prepare a draft at sight, the contents of which shall be as follows:

Exchange for USD 100 000.00 Nanjing, August 4, 2008

D/P At the sight of this First of Exchange (Second of the same tenor and date being unpaid), Pay to the order of Bank of China, Hong Kong Branch.

The sum of SAY US DOLLARS ONE HUNDRED THOUSAND ONLY

To: Hong Kong Nanhwa International
Trading Co. Ltd., Hong Kong

For: Jiangsu Nam Kwong International
Trading Corp., Nanjing
(Signature)

Task 9.3 Settlement by letter of credit

【Task for analysis】

In international settlement, L/C is a major method of settlement widely used. L/C business has remarkable characteristics. It has a set of business operation procedures that can provide protection for both the importer and the exporter against risks. It involves multiple parties, which share a certain relationship with one another. Letter of credit itself has a standard format and content, and can be divided into different types. Different letters of credit have different characteristics and applications.

Task 9.3.1 The concept and characteristics of letter of credit

【Case for demonstration】

On August 1, 2008, Jiangsu Nam Kwong International Trading Corp. JNK signed a contract with Hong Kong Nanhwa International Trading Co., Ltd. to import a batch of wool fabrics with the contract value of HK ＄1 000 000.00. Nam Kwong company applied to Jiangsu branch of Bank of China for opening a letter of credit. The issuing bank accepted the application, issued the L/C according to the application after receiving the deposit, and sent it to Bank of China, Hong Kong branch (advising bank). After confirming the apparent authenticity of the L/C, the advising bank notified Nanhwa company of the contents. After checking the L/C, Nanhwa company shipped the goods and drew a draft and submitted it together with the documents required by the L/C to Bank of China Hong Kong branch (negotiating bank) for negotiation. After checking the documents, the negotiating bank paid to Nanhwa company and sent the draft and shipping documents to the issuing bank for reimbursement. The issuing bank checked the documents before making the payment to the negotiating bank, and then notified Nam Kwong company to make payment. Nam Kwong company made the payment to the issuing bank and took delivery of the goods with the relevant documents. So far, the two companies completed a settlement business through the letter of credit.

【Questions for discussion】

Based on the lead-in case, understand the basic knowledge of L/C business and think about the following questions:

(1) What is a letter of credit?

(2) What are the characteristics of settlement by L/C?

【Relevant knowledge】

(1) The concept of L/C

A letter of credit is an undertaking issued by the bank of the importer (issuing bank) to the exporter (beneficiary) at the request of the importer (applicant) to pay a certain amount of money on the premise that the exporter provides the goods documents and drafts as stipulated. In short, a letter of credit is a written document issued by a bank that conditionally promises to pay.

(2) Features of letter of credit

①A letter of credit is a kind of bank credit

This is the fundamental difference between the letter of credit and other methods of settlement. The issuing bank guarantees the payment with its own credit, and bears the primary responsibility for payment after the L/C is issued.

②A letter of credit is a self-sufficient document

Letter of credit is an independent contract in legal sense, which constitutes the contractual relationship between all parties concerned. The most important feature of its independence is that it has nothing to do with any contract. The issuance of the letter of credit is based on the sales contract. However, once the letter of credit is issued, it becomes another contract independent of the sales contract and is not bound by the sales contract.

③A letter of credit is a kind of pure documentary business

Article 5 of the UCP600 states: "the bank deals with the documents, not with the goods, services or other acts involved in the documents." In other words, L/C business is a pure document business, which deals with documents rather than goods or services related to documents.

(3) Bills of exchange in L/C business

In L/C business, commercial drafts drawn by the exporter are often used. In all L/C transactions, commercial drafts are drawn by the exporter, although "your draft" (the bank's draft) is often required. There are generally 12 items to be filled in the draft. How to fill them is listed as follows:

Column 1: drawn under. Fill in the name and address of the issuing bank.

Column 2: L/C No.

Column 3: the date of issuing L/C (dated).

Column 4: payable with interest @ % per annum. To be filled in by the settlement bank.

Column 5: exchange for. There are two columns on the bill of exchange with the same record, the shorter one is to be filled with an amount in figures and the longer one is to be filled with an amount in words. Drafts generally do not exceed the amount specified in the credit.

Column 6: the sum of. It should be filled from the top frame, so as to leave no gaps in case someone deliberately tampers with the amount of the draft. The amount in words consists of two parts, one is the currency name and the other is the currency amount.

Column 7: NO. The number of invoices in the documents made in this transaction is to be filled.

Column 8: payment term (at... sight).

Column 9: pay to the order of. Under the conditions of payment by L/C, the name and address of the bank should be filled in the column of the payee of the draft, generally the name and address of the negotiating bank.

Column 10: date of presentation of the draft. It refers to the date on which the beneficiary delivers the draft to the negotiating bank. It is to be filled by the bank.

Column 11: payer. The drawee of the draft and the drawee of the contract are not exactly the same. This item should be filled strictly in accordance with the requirements of the letter of credit. The name and address of the applicant or the issuer of the letter of credit should be filled in.

Column 12: drawer. In practice, the name of the drawer is in the bottom right corner, corresponding to the payer.

(4) Advantages and disadvantages of settlement in L/C

①Advantages

When the payment is settled by L/C, the beneficiary's (exporter's) collection is guaranteed, especially when the exporter does not know the importer very well, the advantage of L/C becomes more prominent. At the same time, the letter of credit makes the financial burden of both sides more balanced. For the exporter, the documents can be sold to the bank of the exporting country immediately after the shipment for collecting payment, and the letter of credit can be used as package loan, so the financial burden is much smaller than that with cash on delivery and collection. For importers, they usually only need to pay part of the deposit when opening the L/C, and only pay the full amount when they get the documents. Their financial burden is much lighter compared to the prepayment.

②Disadvantages

Letter of credit also has some disadvantages. First, it is easy to commit fraud. As the letter of credit is a self-sufficient document, and the relevant bank only deals with the documents, if the beneficiary forges a document consistent with the true one or makes a false document with no goods at all, then the importer will become the victim. Although in theory, importers can claim compensation from exporters under sales contracts or even resort to law, cross-border disputes are often difficult to resolve. Second, the procedures of letter of credit are complicated with many links, which not only consumes much time, but also cost more money. The procedures, such as document examination also need strong technical expertise, which increases the cost of business.

Case 9.6 An export company in China reached an export contract with a foreign importer, which stipulated that the settlement should be made by letter of credit. After delivering the goods and presenting the documents according to the letter of credit opened abroad, our export company received the notification that the importer went bankrupt and therefore became unable to pay for the goods. Can our export company collect the payment back?

Analysis: Under the way of L/C, the issuing bank guarantees payment with its own credit and undertakes the first payment responsibility after the L/C is issued. As long as the beneficiary provides qualified documents according to the requirements of the L/C, whether the negotiating bank rejects the negotiation or the paying bank rejects the payment, or the applicant goes bankrupt, the issuing bank's payment obligation is determined and unavoidable, and it must bear the payment obligation. Therefore, our company can obtain payment from the issuing bank on the condition that the documents presented are meeting the requirements.

【Tasks for implementation】

In this sub-task case, Nam Kwong company carries out contract payment and settlement through a letter of credit. After Bank of China Jiangsu branch (issuing bank) accepts the application of Nam Kwong company to open the L/C, and after Nanhwa company has provided the cargo documents and drafts as required, it promises to pay the amount of the L/C to Nanhwa company. This letter of credit is the written document of conditional acceptance of payment issued by Jiangsu branch of Bank of China. In this settlement business, the Jiangsu branch of Bank of China guarantees the payment with its own credit and becomes the first payer, that is, the commercial credit of Nam Kwong company is converted into bank credit. The letter of credit is issued in accordance with the import contract between Nam Kwong company and Nanhwa company. After the letter of credit is issued, it becomes another contract independent of the import contract. No matter how the sales contract is performed, the payment responsibility of the issuing bank will not be affected. In this settlement business, the bank deals with documents. As long as the documents comply with credit terms, and with each other, the Jiangsu branch of Bank of China must pay. It can be seen that L/C business is a pure document business.

Task 9.3.2 The business procedures of a letter of credit

【Questions for discussion】

A letter of credit must go through many procedures and links from the beginning of the importer's application to the end of the whole settlement procedure. Although there are some differences in the business process of different types of letters of credit, the general procedure is the same. Mastering a set of operating procedures of letter of credit is a basic skill in the daily business operations of international traders. Based on the above case in the subtask, please think the following questions:

(1) What are the general operating procedures of L/C business?

(2) What is the specific content of each process?

【Relevant knowledge】

A complete L/C business, from the beginning to the end, generally runs through the following major links of signing contracts, applying for L/C, advice, negotiation, claim, reimbursement, payment and redemption. The general procedure of letter of credit is shown in figure 9.14.

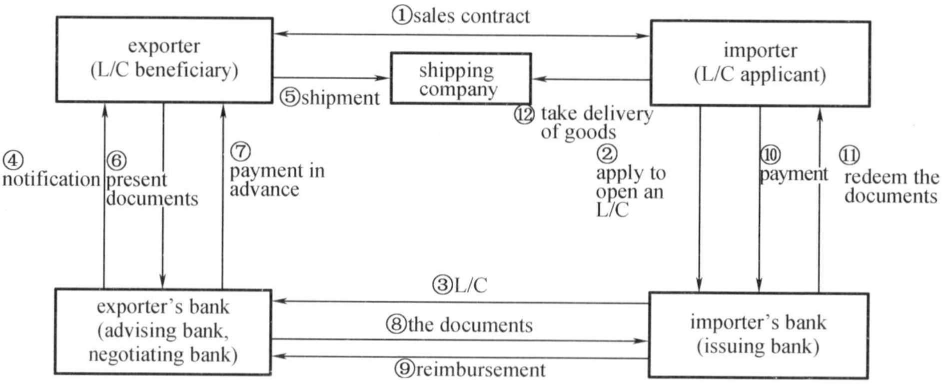

Figure 9.14 Basic business process of L/C

(1) The importer applies for L/C

The importer and the exporter sign a trade contract, in which it is agreed that the business shall be settled by L/C and other items like the type, amount, payment term, expiry date, the opening date of L/C shall also be specified.

According to the provisions of the trade contract, the importer fills in and submits documentary credit application to the issuing bank (usually the local bank), provides a deposit or guarantee, and applies for opening an L/C. The application for letter of credit is the legal document between the applicant and the issuing bank, and also the basis for issuing the letter of credit. The completeness and clarity of its contents are very important. The issuing instructions, the letter of credit itself and the amendment instructions of L/C and the amendment itself must be complete and clear. The instruction for opening an L/C is the application for letter of credit, which will take effect only after it is signed by the applicant and the bank.

When applying for an L/C, the applicant shall bear all the charges required by the domestic and foreign banks. A certain percentage of the margin or other collateral shall be paid to the issuing bank, ranging from a few percents to several tens of percent of the amount of the credit. The amount of the margin shall be determined by the issuing bank and is related to the credit standing of the applicant and market conditions. For customers with good credit standing, banks will grant the limit for issuing credit, and within the specified limit the customers can be exempted from the margin.

(2) The issuing bank issues the letter of credit

After receiving the application for an L/C, the issuing bank should carry out the examination and inspection before the L/C is opened. Strict inspection and careful opening of the L/C are aimed at reducing the potential risks. The investigation and examination include the following aspects:

①The application and the letter of guarantee for opening an L/C.

②The applicant's credit standing, current business status, financial status, economic strength and previous credit records.

③Valid certificates shall be provided when the bank opens an L/C for the importer, such as import payment verification, import license, import registration certificate and other registration documents.

After accepting the application for opening the L/C from the importer, the opening bank charges the margin and issues the letter of credit according to the application, sends the letter of credit by airmail or by cable to the correspondent bank or the agent bank (advising bank, negotiating bank) in the place where the exporter is located and advises or transmits the letter of credit to the beneficiary (exporter) through them.

(3) The advising bank advises the letter of credit

Upon receipt of the L/C, the exporter's bank shall check whether the test key or the authorized signature is correct, and then carefully examine the terms of the L/C so as to make sure they are complete and clear before informing or passing to the beneficiary the advice of credit in an accurate and timely manner as required by the L/C.

(4) The exporter examines the L/C, delivers the goods, presents the document

After receiving the L/C, the beneficiary (exporter) shall carefully examine whether the content of the L/C is in conformity with the terms and conditions of the contract, and notify the applicant (importer) to amend the L/C if there is any inconformity. In order to ensure that the beneficiary (exporter) fulfills his/her obligations under the L/C and the trade contract at the same time, the beneficiary must examine the L/C in strict accordance with the contract when accepting the L/C so as to eliminate the potential risks when the L/C is presented. In China, the advising bank basically does not examine the letter of credit. The letter of credit shall be examined by the exporter itself. The items examined are generally as follows:

①Whether the credit is a valid credit duly advised by the advising bank.

②The type of letter of credit.

③Whether the L/C is confirmed.

④The applicant and the beneficiary.

⑤The currency and the amount of the letter of credit.

⑥The credit period and the description of the goods.

⑦The place of the expiry of the letter of credit.

⑧The time of shipment, transshipment and partial shipment clauses and validity.

⑨The terms of payment of the L/C and the documents submitted.

⑩Other terms and special terms printed on the L/C.

The beneficiary shall, after confirming the correctness of the credit, make the shipment according to the stipulations of the credit, issue documentary draft (if necessary), prepare the full set of documents required by the credit and send them to the local bank (negotiating bank) for negotiation together with the letter of credit within the presentation period and validity period stipulated in the credit.

(5) The negotiation bank examines the documents for negotiation, sends them and claims for reimbursement

The negotiating bank, after receiving the bill of lading and checking it against the L/C to confirm the consistency of the documents and the credit, pays the exporter after deducting the discount interest and the commission fee from the amount of the bill, which is called negotiation of credit. The negotiating bank must examine all documents with reasonable care to determine whether they appear to conform to the terms and conditions of the credit. If there are any discrepancies, the negotiation bank may ask the beneficiary to modify the documents. In case of failure to amend, the negotiating bank shall telex the issuing bank for any discrepancy or mark the discrepancy on the letter, requesting the issuing bank to contact the applicant and reply whether the applicant accepts the discrepant documents. If the applicant accepts discrepancies, the bank may negotiate and send the documents. Discrepancy means that documents under the credit show one or more non-compliance with the terms or conditions of the credit.

After negotiation, the negotiating bank forwards the bill of lading together with the drafts and the proof of claim to the issuing bank or its nominated paying bank for payment. There are generally four types of claims stipulated in a credit: cash on demand, active debit, authorized debit and claim from the reimbursing bank.

(6) The issuing bank examines documents and makes reimbursement

Upon receipt of the bill of lading, the issuing bank or its nominated paying bank shall make payment to the negotiating bank upon verification of conformity of the documents with the credit. The issuing bank shall fully examine the documents in accordance with the terms of the credit with reasonable care and determine whether reimburse the confirming bank or the nominated bank according to the practice applicable to this credit (UCP500 or UCP600). In case of discrepancy in presentation, the issuing bank shall have the right to refuse to accept the discrepant documents and to pay the amount of the L/C to the other party within the stipulated time limit, such as the L/C with overdue shipment date.

UCP500 stipulates that the issuing bank shall determine whether documents presented are in consistence with the credit requirements within a reasonable period of time, but no more than 7 banking days (counting from the next day after the date of receipt). UCP600 eliminates the premise of a reasonable time by shortening 7 working days to "5 working days", consequently the stipulations become more clear. In case of dishonor, the issuing bank shall raise each discrepancy in one time, not in stages, and shall not make unreasonable demands on documents presented by the presenter. When the issuing bank decides to refuse the payment, it must give the presenter a separate notice of dishonor.

(7) The applicant makes the payment, retires documents and takes delivery of goods

After receiving documents and making the payment, the issuing bank shall immediately notify the issuing applicant (importer) of taking delivery of goods against documents retired. The importer shall, upon receipt of the issuing bank's notice, examine the documents prior to payment and, after verifying the documents, pay the full amount to the issuing bank as soon as possible to redeem the full set of documents and surrenders of the bill of lading. If the goods are not in conformity with the documents, the applicant has no right to claim against the issuing bank. If there is any problem in the examination of the documents, the importer shall explain to the issuing bank the reason for dishonor, but shall not ask the bank to compensate for the poor quality of the goods. If the applicant refuses to pay, the issuing bank shall bear its own losses and have no right of recourse against the reimbursed amount.

(8) The content of the application for a letter of credit

An application for opening an L/C usually consists of two parts.

①On the front is the content of the letter of credit

It is a detailed instruction from the importer to the issuing bank. The letter of credit should be filled completely according to the content of the trade contract. The contract is the basis of the letter of credit and the basis for the applicant to apply for the letter of credit and the beneficiary to examine the letter of credit. The specific contents include: documents to be presented; the amount and method of payment; beneficiary's name and address; validity or expiry date of the credit; description of goods, shipping details, whether confirmation is required, etc.

②On the back is the applicant's declaration or warranty made to the issuing bank

It is a legal contract between the importer and the issuing bank to clarify the rights and obligations between the applicant and the issuing bank. In order to reduce the capital risks, most issuing banks require the applicant to pay part of the deposit when applying for an L/C.

(9) The amendment of letter of credit

The beneficiary (exporter) shall request an amendment to the L/C if the beneficiary and/or the bank find during the examination that the terms of the L/C are unacceptable, or they are inconsistent with the contract or the L/C contain incomplete terms after the L/C is issued. Sometimes, the importer may make a request for modification due to the change of situation. The amendment instructions of the credit shall also be clear and complete, and the amendment commission shall be borne by the party requesting the amendment.

If the importer proposes an amendment, the issuing bank shall, with its approval, notify the advising bank by amendment advice or cable, and then the advising bank shall notify the exporter (beneficiary). If the beneficiary accepts the amendment, the amendment takes effect. If the beneficiary refuses to accept it, the amendment shall be invalid and the original terms of the credit shall prevail. If the amendment notice involves more than two clauses, the exporter can only accept or reject all of them, not part of them.

In case of requesting the amendment, the exporter shall first obtain the approval of the importer and the issuing bank, and then the importer shall go through the amendment formalities through the issuing bank before it becomes effective.

The bank shall prepare notification of amendment on the basis of the application for amendment, and generally notify the exporter by TELEX or SWIFT through the same advising bank, and shall not directly notify the exporter (beneficiary) or entrust another bank to inform the amendment of the letter of credit. A copy of the amendment notice shall be attached to the L/C for reference according to the amendment date.

Case 9.7 The Hong Kong and Shanghai banking corporation notifies the export company of the L/C through Bank of China, Dalian branch. Due to the urgent delivery of the amendment, it chooses the notice of the amendment from the Dalian office of the Hong Kong and Shanghai Banking Corporation Limited (HSBC) to modify the specification of the goods. As the amendment is not advised to the beneficiary in time, the beneficiary ships the goods according to the original specifications and makes negotiation, consequently, the opening bank refuses to pay.

Analysis: According to article 11b of UCP500: if a bank notifies a beneficiary of a credit by using the services of another bank (advising bank), it must also use the services of the same bank to notify any amendment. Therefore, this responsibility should be borne by the issuing bank. Furthermore, the amendment is made without the consent of the beneficiary, so the original letter of credit is still valid and the issuing bank must not refuse to pay for the goods.

(10) Document discrepancies in the examination of L/C

When examining documents, the negotiating bank may encounter discrepancies in the following aspects: credit expired; late shipment; unclean bill of lading; the presentation of the documents beyond the stipulated time limit after the shipping documents are issued; short shipment; credit amount excessed; under insured; description of goods on invoice differs from that of the credit; marks and numbers differ between document; goods shipped on deck; incorrect endorsement in bills of lading, insurance documents and bills of exchange; absence of documents called for under the credit; insurance documents presented are of lower order than required by the credit; weights differ between documents; unacceptable type of bill of lading, e. g., charter party, house bills; the currency on the insurance policy is not specified in the letter of credit; absence of signatures, where required, on documents presented; bill of exchange drawn on the wrong party; bill of exchange drawn payable on an undeterminable date; the risks covered are less than those specified in the credit; absence of "freight paid" statement on bills of lading where the credit covers a cost and freight (CFR) or cost insurance and freight (CIF) shipment; shipment made between ports other than those stated in the credit; insurance dated later than the date on the shipping documents; no evidence of goods actually "shipped on board"; the amounts shown in the invoice differs from that in the bill of exchange; documents inconsistent with each other.

(11) The confirmation of the letter of credit

Upon receipt of the credit forwarded by the advising bank, the beneficiary may request the issuing bank to seek confirmation of the credit from a bank familiar to the beneficiary if he/she considers that the issuing bank has a bad credit standing or knows little about its credit standing. At the invitation of the issuing bank, the bank adding the word "confirmed" to the letter of credit is the confirming bank. It is usually an advising bank or other reputable banks in the exporting country.

Sometimes, when an issuing bank entrusts an advising bank to advise a credit, it simultaneously requests the advising bank to add confirmation to the credit. If there is an agreement previously made between the two banks or consent from the advising bank, the advising bank is the confirming bank. After confirming the credit by the advising bank or other banks, the confirming bank shall accept the same responsibilities as the issuing bank. Banks that are invited to confirm the credit should pay attention to avoiding risks, such as only the letter of credit by the issuing bank with good credit standing and the letter of credit with certain financial strength will be insured; add confirmation of any clause in the credit which is not adverse to the beneficiary's gathering payment.

Case 9.8 Our export enterprise has received an irrevocable documentary letter of credit from abroad, which is notified and confirmed by a foreign bank located in China. After the shipment of the goods, when our export enterprise is about to hand over the relevant documents to the foreign bank for negotiation, it is informed by the foreign bank that since the issuing bank has declared bankruptcy, it would not bear the responsibility of negotiation or payment of the L/C and it requires the exporter to change the previous settlement method to collection for export. What should our export company do about it?

Analysis: Our exporter should deliver the goods as stipulated and deliver the documents to the confirming foreign bank for payment. In accordance with *the uniform customs and practice for documentary credits*, once a credit is confirmed, the confirming bank is the first payer as is the issuing bank and is liable to the beneficiary for guaranteeing payment, which cannot be revoked without the consent of the beneficiary. The confirming bank must negotiate and pay for all required documents presented to it by the beneficiary within the validity of the credit.

【Tasks for implementation】

In the case of the subtask, Jiangsu Nam Kwong International Trading Corp. conducts contract payment and settlement through letter of credit. It's signing the contract of importing wool cloth with Hong Kong Nanhwa International Trading Co., Ltd. signals the beginning of this settlement business, which includes a complete L/C business process. The first step is to apply for an L/C, that is, Nam Kwong company applies to Jiangsu branch (issuing bank) of Bank of China for an L/C. The second step is to open an L/C, that is, Jiangsu branch of Bank of China issues the credit to Hong Kong branch of Bank of China (advising bank). The third step is the notification, that is, Bank of China Hong Kong branch notifies Nanhwa company of the letter of credit. The fourth step is to examine the credit, deliver the goods and deliver the documents, that is, after examining the letter of credit, Nanhwa company arranges the shipment and draws drafts, and hands over the relevant documents to Bank of China Hong Kong branch (negotiating bank) for negotiation. The fifth step is negotiation and claim, that is, Bank of China Hong Kong branch verifies the documents and makes payment to Nanhwa company, and sends the draft and shipping documents to Bank of China Jiangsu branch for claiming the payment. The sixth step is reimbursement, that is, Bank of China, Jiangsu branch checks the documents and makes the payment to the negotiating bank, and then notifies Nam Kwong company of paying for the documents. The seventh step is to take delivery of goods against documents retired, that is, Nam Kwong company pays the issuing bank for the documents and takes delivery of the goods according to the relevant documents.

When settling by L/C, Nanhwa company shall draw a bill of exchange with the negotiating bank, assuming, L/C date: August 1, 2008; L/C No.: SN01234; invoice No.: 0808/4108; issuing date on the bill of exchange: August 8, 2008; payment term: 30 days after sight, the contents of the draft shall be:

Drawn under Bank of China, Jiangsu Branch., Nanjing

L/C No. SN01234

Dated August 1, 2008

No. 0808/4108　Exchange for HKD1 000 000.00　Hong Kong, August 8, 2008

At thirty days after sight of this FIRST of Exchange (the Second of the same tenor and date being unpaid), Pay to the order of Bank of China, Hong Kong Branch

The sum of HONGKONG DOLLAR ONE MILLION ONLY

To: Jiangsu Nam Kwong International Trading Corp., Nanjing

For: Hong Kong Nanhwa International Trading Co. Ltd., Hong Kong

(Signed)

Task 9.3.3 Parties to a letter of credit

【Questions for discussion】

In international trade settlement, L/C business is comparatively complicated, involving multiple parties, who share a close relationship between rights and obligations. To be clear about the main parties involved in a letter of credit is the very foundation for international traders to get familiar with and master credit business. Therefore it is necessary for them to correctly grasp the relationship between those parties. Based on the case in the subtask, please think the following questions:

(1) What are the principal parties involved in a letter of credit?

(2) What kind of legal relationship exists between these parties?

【Relevant knowledge】

Generally speaking, the parties involved in a letter of credit can be divided into basic parties and other parties. Among them, basic parties include an applicant, an issuing bank, a beneficiary and an advising bank, and other parties include a negotiating bank, a reimbursing bank, a confirming bank and a paying bank. Other parties are collectively referred to as nominated banks and are specifically designated by the issuing bank in the credit.

(1) The applicant

The applicant, also known as the opener, is the person who applies to a bank for a letter of credit, usually the importer. The applicant (importer) applies to the local bank (usually the opening bank) for a letter of credit in accordance with the contract. The applicant is bound by two contracts: the sales contract with the beneficiary (exporter) and the business agency contract with the issuing bank (application for opening an L/C).

(2) The issuing bank

The issuing bank, or the opening bank, is the bank that opens the letter of credit as entrusted by the applicant, generally in the country of the importer. The issuing bank is bound by three contracts, namely, the payment agency contract with the applicant, the credit with the beneficiary, and the agency agreement with the advising bank or the negotiating bank. The issuing bank is the most important party in the L/C business. Its reputation and business experience constitute the main factors considered by the other parties to take part in the L/C business.

(3) The beneficiary

The beneficiary refers to the person who is entitled to use the letter of credit, shall provide documents in conformity with the requirements of the letter of credit, and can demand payment from the issuing bank or the paying bank as specified in the credit, generally, the exporter, and also the drawer. Beneficiary is bound by two contracts, namely the trade contract with the applicant and the letter of credit with the issuing bank.

(4) The advising bank

The advising bank, or the notifying bank, refers to the bank entrusted by the issuing bank to forward the credit to the beneficiary, usually the bank in the exporting country. The advising bank is entrusted by the issuing bank to handle the relevant L/C business and its behavior is bound by its agency contract with the issuing bank. The advising bank shall only certify the apparent authenticity of the credit and shall not be liable for negotiation or commitment to the beneficiary and shall be entitled to charge the issuing bank for advising the credit or amendment. The advising bank shall only certify the apparent authenticity of the credit and shall not be liable for negotiation or commitment to the beneficiary and shall be entitled to charge the issuing bank for advising the credit or amendment. Its specific responsibility is mainly to verify the authenticity of the letter of credit, and to clarify doubts in a timely manner.

(5) The negotiating bank

The negotiating bank is a bank, which is authorized by the issuing bank to purchase documents presented by the beneficiary in accordance with the stipulations of the credit, discounts the draft, and claims the advance payment from the paying bank or the reimbursing bank specified in the credit, usually in the exporting country. The issuing bank may designate a negotiating bank in the credit, which may be the advising bank or the confirming bank or another bank in the exporting country.

(6) The paying bank

The paying bank is the bank nominated by the issuing bank to make payment under the credit or act as the payer of the draft. The paying bank is generally the issuing bank or another bank entrusted by the issuing bank to make the payment. After payment, the paying bank has no right of recourse against the beneficiary or his predecessors, which involves more risks, thus the commission fee is higher than negotiation. The paying bank is designated by the issuing bank and has not made any commitment to the credit itself. Therefore, it also has the right to refuse the payment.

(7) The confirming bank

The confirming bank is the bank that guarantees payment on the letter of credit upon the request of the issuing bank, usually the advising bank. Sometimes the issuing bank asks another bank (usually a bank with a good reputation in the exporting country) to add confirmation to make the letter of credit more acceptable. If the bank accepts the invitation by adding a clause of guarantee or a confirmation note to the letter of credit, it becomes a confirming bank. In practice, the advising bank, the confirming bank and the negotiating bank may be the same bank.

(8) The reimbursing bank

The reimbursing bank is a third country bank designated in the credit to pay advances on behalf of the issuing bank to the negotiating bank or the paying bank. The reimbursing bank is the correspondent bank of the issuing bank, generally the joint bank or the agent bank of the clearing center of L/C settlement currency, and only assuming the obligation of payment. The reimbursing bank has no rights or obligations with the issuer or the beneficiary. In practice, the reimbursing bank may be the issuing bank.

【Tasks for implementation】

In the case of the previous subtask, Nam Kwong company uses the letter of credit to settle the import payment with Nanhwa company. In the settlement business, Nam Kwong company applies to Jiangsu branch of Bank of China for opening a letter of credit. Then Jiangsu branch of Bank of China sends the letter of credit to Bank of China, Hong Kong branch, which notifies Nanhwa company of the contents of the letter of credit. Nanhwa company presents the documents to Bank of China Hong Kong branch and obtains the negotiation payment. Bank of China Hong Kong branch then sends the documentary drafts to Bank of China, Jiangsu branch for claiming the payment. After payment Jiangsu branch of Bank of China notifies Nam Kwong company of taking delivery of goods against documents retired. Therefore, Nam Kwong company is the applicant, Bank of China Jiangsu branch is the issuing bank and the paying bank, Bank of China Hong Kong branch is the advising bank and the negotiating bank, and Nanhwa company is the beneficiary.

Task 9.3.4 The main content of the letter of credit

【Case for demonstration】

The following is an example of a letter of credit in SWIFT format for you to know the basic style and content of an L/C.

BASIC HEADER F 01 BKCHCNBJA5XX 9056 375784
APPL. HEADER O 700 1340990118 BPSMPTPLAXXX 2682 088146 9901182140 N
+ BANCO PINTO AND SOOTO MAYOR, LISBOA
+ PORTUGAL
(BANK NO: 1218000) + LISBON CODEX, PORTUGAL
:MT:700 ——— ISSUE OF A DOCUMENTARY CREDIT ———

SEQUENCE OF TOTAL	:27: 1/1
FORM OF DOCUMENTARY CREDIT	:40A: IRREVOCABLE
DOCUMENTARY CREDIT NUMBER	:20: 058230CDI11711LC
DATE OF ISSUE	:31C: 080118
DATE AND PLACE OF EXPIRY	:31D: 990220 QINGDAO
APPLICANT	:50: SAINT BILL LIMITADA RUA DE PEDROUCOS, 98 - A 1200—287 LISBOA PORTUGAL
BENEFICIARY	:59: DASHAN METALS + MINERALS - IMPORT + EXPORT CORPORATION 21 YUNHAI ROAD, QINGDAO CHINA
CURRENCY CODE, AMOUNT	:32B: USD20659.20
MAXIMUM CREDIT AMOUNT	:39B: NOT EXCEEDING
AVAILABLE WITH…BY…	:41A: BKCHCNBJ51C BY PAYMENT + BANK OF CHINA, QINGDAO BRANCH
(BANK NO: 0044105)	+ QINGDAO CHINA
PARTIAL SHIPMENT	:43P: NOT ALLOWED
TRANSSHIPMENT	:43T: ALLOWED
LOADING/DISPATCH/TAKING/FROM	:44A: QINGDAO
FOR TRANSPORTATION TO …	:44B: LISBON BY SEAFREIGHT
LATEST DATE OF SHIPMENT	:44C:080211
DESCRIPT OF GOODS/SERVICES	:45A:

+12000 PAIRS DOUBLE STAR BRAND MEN'S RUBBER SHOES AS PER PROF. IN VOICES

DD 07.11.17 AND 07.11.25
+CIF LISBON
DOCUMENTS REQUIRED : 46A:
+ SIGNED COMMERCIAL INVOICE (ORIGINAL AND 4 COPIES), VISAED BYTHE CHAMBER OF COMMERCE CERTIFYING GOODS ORIGIN
+FULL SET(3/3)OF CLEAN ON BOAED OCEAN BILLS OF LADING , TO THE ORDER OF BANCO PINTO + SOTTO MAYOR , NOTIFYING BUYERS , THEIR NAME AND ADDRESS FULLY MENTIONED AND STATING FREIGHT PAID
+PACKING LIST
+INSURANCE POLICY/CERTIFICATE TO THE ORDER OF BANCO PINTO + SOTTO MAYOR OR TO ORDER AND BLANK ENDORSED, COVERING GOODS FOR THE INVOICE VALUE PLUS 10 PCT AGAINST THE RISKS OF ICC (A), ISC (CARGO) AND IWC (CARGO)
CHARGES : 71B: ALL BANKING CHGS OUTSIDE PORTUGAL ARE FOR BENEF ACCT
PERIOD FOR PRESENTATIONS : 48: 8 DAYS
CONFIRMATION INSTRUCTION : 49: CONFIRM
INSTRUCTION TO BANK : 78: PROVIDED DOCS ARE STRICTLY IN GOOD ORDER WE WILL CREDIT YR ACCT WITH AN AMERICAN BANK AT YR OPTION AFTER INSTRUCTIONS IN FIELD 72 HAVE BEEN COMPLIED WITH
SENDER TO RECEIVER INFO : 72: AVAILABLE BY YR PYMT AT 5 FULL WORKING DAYS AFTER YR SWIFT ADVICE TO US STATING YOU CONSIDER DOCS IN ORDER AND EXACT AMT OF NEGOTIATION PLS SEND US DOCS IN 2 SEPARATE LOTS

【Questions for discussion】

Based on the lead-in case, please consider the following question: what is the main content of a letter of credit?

【Relevant knowledge】

There is no uniform form of letters of credit used by banks in various countries in the world. The content varies according to different types of the letter of credit, but the basic content is the same. The International Chamber of Commerce has been working on the standardization of letters of credit format. In 1970, it adopted *the Standard Format for Issuing Documentary Letters of Credit* and recommended it to banks in various countries. The content of a letter of credit mainly includes the following items.

(1) About L/C

①Type of credit

It refers to the nature of the letter of credit. UCP500 states: "all letters of credit shall expressly indicate whether they are revocable or irrevocable, and in the absence of such indication the credit shall be deemed irrevocable." However, UCP600 only recognizes irrevocable letter of credit and deletes the revocable letter of credit.

②L/C number

It is the L/C number of the issuing bank. The issuing bank numbers the credit to be issued and this number will appear in the documents of the beneficiary to indicate the relationship between the documents and the credit.

③Date and place of issue

The place of issuing an L/C refers to the location of the issuing bank and the date of issuance refers to the date of issuing the credit.

④Amount of credit

It is the maximum limit of the issuing bank's liability for payment. The amount of the letter of credit shall be expressed in both letters and numbers, and the currency shall be expressed in the currency code established by the International Organization for Standardization (such as USD, GBP, EUR, etc.). If terms like about, approximately, circa, etc. are added before the amount, the L/C will allow an increase or a decrease of 10%.

⑤Date and place of expiry

The validity of the L/C is the deadline for the issuing bank to undertake its obligation of the conditional payment. All letters of credit shall have a period of validity within which the beneficiary must present the documents and exercise his/her rights. Beyond the deadline, the issuing bank is no longer liable for payment. The place of maturity is the place of presentation, which is the place where documents must be presented on or before the due date, usually the place of the bank designated by the issuing bank, preferably the place of the bank of the exporting country.

⑥Issuing bank

It is usually marked first in the letter of credit and should be given in full name with detailed address.

⑦Notifying bank

Fill in the name and address of the bank advising the credit to the beneficiary.

⑧Applicant

A letter of credit is a payment instrument agreed upon by both the seller and the buyer. The applicant should be the importer of the goods. The credit should have the full name and the full address of the applicant.

⑨Beneficiary

He is the only person entitled to draw on the credit, usually the exporter. The credit should have the full name and the full address of the beneficiary.

⑩Documents presentation period

It is the deadline for the beneficiary to withdraw money against the presentation of documents. After this period, the issuing bank is no longer liable for payment. Expiry date is generally the deadline for the presentation of documents by the beneficiary to the exporting bank (the negotiating bank or the paying bank).

(2) About draft

①Drawer.

②Drawee.

③Tenor.

④Drawn clause.

(3) About documents

This item describes the name, number of copies and specific requirements of the document, which constitutes the most important part of the letter of credit. Documents shall be listed in order of the commercial invoice, the transportation document, the insurance document and other documents. Documents required under a credit usually include:

①Commercial invoice.

②Bill of lading.

③Cargo receipt.

④Insurance policy.

⑤Packing list.

⑥Certificate of origin.

⑦Inspection certificate.

⑧Certificate of quality.

⑨Other documents.

(4) About goods

①Commodity name, article number, specification. The name of the goods should be as short and popular as possible, and the description of the goods should not list too many details.

②Quantity and packing.

③Unit price etc. Article 30 of the UCP600 provides that about, approximately, circa or similar terms may be used prior to the quantity and/or unit price of the goods with a 10 percent increase or decrease on both.

(5) About shipment

①Port of shipment.

It is the place where the consignor delivers the goods to the carrier or his/her agent, requiring that the full name be used. The L/C should not stipulate shipment from one port.

②Port of destination.

The port of destination must be clear. Avoid abbreviations or ambiguities and use the full name when writing it.

③Latest date of shipment.

Export goods must be shipped before this date, otherwise, there will be an "in conformity between the documents and the credit" and the bank will refuse to pay.

④Partial shipment (not) allowed.

Choose between "ALLOWED" and "NOT ALLOWED". If there is no specific statement in the credit, partial shipment is deemed to be allowed.

⑤Transshipment (not) allowed.

Choose "ALLOWED" or "NOT ALLOWED". Choose "ALLOWED" or "NOT ALLOWED". If there is no indication in the credit, transshipment is deemed to be allowed.

⑥Mode of transportation.

It refers to sea, land, air or parcel transport, container transport, pallet transport.

(6) Other items

①Instructions to negotiating bank.

②Undertaking clause. The issuing bank states its obligation to pay by this clause.

③Method of reimbursement.

④Method of dispatching documents.

⑤Subject to UCP Clause. This declaration is applicable to UCP500 or UCP600. This is a very important statement, which has a decisive impact on the acceptability of the letter of credit.

⑥Special terms.

⑦Opening bank's signature. The letter of credit opened by letter requires the authorized signatory of the opening bank to countersign while the letter of credit opened by cable need the test key.

(7) the soft clause of L/C

"The soft clause" in L/C business, also called the "trap clause" (pitfall clause) in our country, refers to the clause added in an irrevocable letter of credit, which actually causes the applicant to control the whole transaction and makes the beneficiary in the position of being controlled. However, the payment commitment of the issuing bank under the L/C is uncertain, and the issuing bank can take advantage of this clause at any time to unilaterally relieve its obligation of guaranteeing payment. A letter of credit with such clauses is essentially a disguised revocable letter of credit, which can easily lead to non-conformity between the documents and the credit and encounter dishonor by the issuing bank.

The "soft clauses" of letters of credit can be mainly classified into the following types:

①The letter of credit is temporarily ineffective. For example, the letter of credit is not yet effective until the notice of import license is issued, or the letter of credit shall not take effect until the sample is confirmed by the applicant.

② The shipping company, the name of the vessel, the port of destination, the port of shipment or the examiner, and the date of shipment shall be subject to the approval of the applicant and shall be further notified by the issuing bank in the form of the amendment letter.

③The issuer shall provide the quality certificate, the receipt of the goods received or issue the shipping instructions, whose signature shall be verified by the issuing bank or in accordance with the document of the issuing bank.

④the commercial invoice and the quality confirmation issued by the beneficiary should be signed or countersigned by the applicant or his/her designated person, whose signature should be consistent with the specimen or the notes filed by the issuing bank.

(8) The forms of letters of credit

There are two forms of letters of credit, namely letters of credit to open by airmail and letters of credit to open by cable.

①To open by airmail

Letters of credit to open by airmail refer to those issued by the issuing bank in the form of printed letter. Letters of credit in this form have relatively comprehensive contents. After the L/C is opened, it will be sent to the advising bank by airmail. This form is a traditional method of opening a letter of credit, which is rarely used nowadays.

②To open by cable

The letter of credit to open by cable means that the issuing bank shall communicate the terms and conditions of the L/C to the advising bank by various telecommunication methods such as cable, telex, fax, SWIFT, etc. In practice, most letters of credit are opened by Telex, SWIFT. Letters of credit issued by Telex cost more, have to go through cumbersome procedures and lack uniformity in terms and sentences, therefore are easy to cause misunderstandings. Letters of credit opened by SWIFT are issued or notified through the SWIFT system. It is characterized by standardization, immobilization, uniform format, fast and safe transmission, low cost, and convenience of use, therefore it is widely used in international trade. Letters of credit to open by cable can be divided into brief cable and full cable.

a. Brief cable

The issuing bank simply notifies the establishment of the letter of credit and sends the main contents of the L/C such as L/C number, beneficiary, issuer, name of goods, quantity, price, time of shipment and validity of the L/C to the advising bank in advance, while detailed terms will be forwarded to the advising bank by separate air. This brief cable letter of credit features simple contents but is legally invalid. Since it is not a valid letter of credit, it cannot be used as the basis for presentation and negotiation.

b. Full cable

Full cable refers to the letter of credit with detailed and complete contents of the message. The issuing bank opens the full cable letter of credit by telecommunication and transmits all terms of the letter of credit to the advising bank. The full cable letter of credit has complete contents and therefore is the basis for presentation and negotiation. The contents of the full cable letter of credit are shown in table 9.4.

Table 9.4 Contents of the full cable letter of credit

(MT 700 issue of a documentary credit)

M/O	27	Sequence of total	1n/1n
M	40A	Form of documentary credit	24x
M	20	Documentary credit number	16x
O	23	Reference to pre-advice	16x
O	31C	Date of issue	6n

Table 9.4(continued)

M	31D	Date and place of expiry	6n29x
O	51a	Applicant bank	A or D
M	50	Applicant	4 × 35x
M	59	Beneficiary	[/34] 4 × 35x
M	32B	Currency code, amount	3a15number
O	39A	Percentage credit amount tolerance	2n/2n
O	39B	Maximum credit amount	13x
O	39C	Additional amounts covered	4 × 35x
M	41a	Available with…by…	A or D
O	42C	Drafts at…	3 × 35x
O	42a	Drawee	A or D
O	42M	Mixed payment details	4 × 35x
O	42P	Deferred payment details	4 × 35x
O	43P	Partial shipments	1 × 35x
O	43T	Transshipment	1 × 35x
O	44A	Loading on board/dispatch/taking in charge at/form	1 × 65x
O	44B	For transportation to …	1 × 65x
O	44C	Latest date of shipment	6n
O	44D	Shipment period	6n65x
O	45A	Description of goods and/or services	100 × 65x
O	46A	Documents required	100 × 65x
O	47A	Additional conditions	100 × 65x
O	71B	Charges	6 × 35x
O	48	Period for presentation	4 × 35x
M	49	Confirmation instructions	7x
O	53a	Reimbursement bank	A or D
O	78	Instruction to the paying/accepting/negotiating bank	12 × 65x
O	57a	"Advise through" bank	A、B or D
O	72	Sender to receiver information	6 × 35x

【Tasks for implementation】

In the case of the previous subtask, Nam Kwong company uses letter of credit to settle the import payment with Nanhwa company. In this settlement business, Jiangsu branch of Bank of China opens a letter of credit after the application of Nam Kwong company. The contents of the letter of credit mainly include the following aspects:

(1) The name of issuing bank

Jiangsu branch of Bank of China, shall be followed with a detailed address.

(2) Form of credit

The letter of credit shall clearly indicate that it is irrevocable.

(3) L/C number and date of issue

The letter of credit shall be numbered by Jiangsu branch of Bank of China and dated August 1, 2008.

(4) The applicant

Jiangsu Nam Kwong International Trading Corp., should be given in the full name and followed by its detailed address.

(5) The beneficiary

Hong Kong Nanhwa International Trading Co., Ltd., should be given in the full name and with the detailed address.

(6) The advising bank

Bank of China, Hong Kong branch, should be added with the detailed address.

(7) Amount of the credit

The credit amount is the contract amount, which is HK $1 000 000.00.

(8) Term of validity

This should be filled out by Jiangsu branch of Bank of China based on the application for letter of credit by Nam Kwong company.

(9) Description of goods

The goods in this case are wool fabrics. The key contents such as name, quantity, package, price and contract number should be filled out by Jiangsu branch of Bank of China according to the application for letter of credit by Nam Kwong company.

(10) Transportation

Items like place of departure, port of destination, time of shipment, partial shipment and transshipment are to be filled out by Jiangsu branch of Bank of China according to the application for letter of credit by Nam Kwong company.

(11) Documents required

Documents required under the L/C, including bills of exchange, commercial invoices, packing lists, ocean bills of lading, insurance policies, certificates of origin, commodity inspection certificates and other certificates, shall be filled out by Jiangsu branch of Bank of China according to the application form of Nam Kwong company for opening the L/C.

(12) Warranty clause

The Jiangsu branch of Bank of China states its payment obligations under the terms of guarantee.

(13) Signature or test key

Bank of China, Jiangsu branch, will encrypt the L/C issued by cable.

(14) Subject to UCP clause

Jiangsu branch of Bank of China declares in the letter of credit that UCP600 is applicable.

Task 9.3.5 The main types of letters of credit

【Questions for discussion】

Letters of credit can be classified into different categories from different perspectives. Different types of L/C have different characteristics and are used differently in practice. It is also very important for international traders to be familiar with the main types of L/C. Based on the lead-in case and the case of the previous subtask, please consider the following questions:

1. What are the main categories of letters of credit?
2. How are they used in practice?

【Relevant knowledge】

There are many types of letters of credit divided from different angles. A letter of credit can have the characteristics of various kinds of letter of credit. Letters of credit commonly used internationally can be divided into the following categories according to their purposes, natures, payment terms, circulation, transferability, repeated use and use for special trade settlement,

(1) According to whether the draft under L/C is accompanied by shipping documents

Clean credit is a letter of credit payable by the issuing bank only against draft (clean draft) without documents attached. The earliest credit in history was a clean L/C. It is mainly used for prepayment, travel and personal consumption. The beneficiary only needs to sign a draft when drawing money and no other documents are required.

Documentary credit is a letter of credit paid by the issuing bank against documentary drafts or against shipping documents only. Most letters of credit used in international trade are documentary L/C.

(2) According to the responsibilities of the issuing bank

Irrevocable letter of credit means a letter of credit, which once opened, cannot be unilaterally canceled or amended by the issuing bank within the validity period without the consent of the beneficiary and the parties concerned. An irrevocable letter of credit constitutes a definite guarantee of payment. The issuing bank must perform its obligation of payment as long as the beneficiary provides documents in conformity to the terms of the credit, thus favorable to the beneficiary. Letters of credit usually used in international trade are irrevocable. A credit must specify whether it is revocable or irrevocable, and if there is no specific indication, it will be considered irrevocable.

Revocable L/C means a letter of credit that can be canceled by its issuing bank at any time without the prior consent of the beneficiary or the relevant parties. Cancellation of credit is conditional, that is, the applicant's liability to the issuing bank terminates only if the advising bank has not accepted the documents when receiving the notice of cancellation or amendment. The issuing bank is still liable to reimburse the documents that have been negotiated prior to the arrival of the cancellation notice. It fails to guarantee the benefits of the beneficiary, so exporters generally do not accept it. Because of this, UCP600 cancels the irrevocable letter of credit.

(3) According to whether additional confirmation is available

Confirmed letter of credit means that in addition to the payment commitment of the issuing bank, another bank (confirming bank) shall guarantee the issuing bank's payment responsibility again at the request of the issuing bank or the beneficiary. After adding its confirmation to the credit, the confirming bank cannot amend or cancel the confirmation without the consent of all the parties concerned. Since both the issuing bank and the confirming bank bear the primary responsibility of payment, the beneficiary obtains double assurance, which enhances the security of receiving payment.

Unconfirmed L/C refers to the letter of credit in which only the issuing bank has an obligation to guarantee payment. Its reliability depends entirely on the credit standing of the issuing bank. Since a confirmed L/C requires a double charge from the beneficiary, and the issuing bank is generally unwilling to ask another bank for confirmation of its own L/C, the advising bank is also reluctant to ask the issuing bank to open a confirmed L/C unless the credit standing of the issuing bank is extremely poor. At present, the letter of credit used by countries all over the world is unconfirmed.

(4) According to the payment method of the letter of credit

Sight payment credit refers to a letter of credit in which the issuing bank or the paying bank performs the obligation of payment immediately after receiving the shipping documents conforming to the terms of the credit. Some of these letters of credit do not require the issuing and presentation of bills of exchange, payment can be made only upon presentation of documents and some require presentation of drafts before payment. This kind of letter of credit is a typical letter of credit payable at sight.

Usance credit is a letter of credit in which the issuing bank or the paying bank does not pay immediately upon receipt of the shipping documents conforming to the terms of the credit, but pays according to the date specified on the credit or the drafts. Usually, for the beneficiary, obtaining the usance bill accepted by the bank is equivalent to receiving the payment for the goods, for which the beneficiary can get a discount. There are two kinds of usance L/C, one is acceptance L/C and the other is deferred payment L/C.

Acceptance credit is a letter of credit accepted and paid at the due date of the draft by the nominated bank upon the beneficiary draws and presents a usance draft to the nominated bank. It's actually a usance letter of credit for a draft. When the beneficiary receives the draft accepted by the bank, the bank assumes its irrevocable commitment to pay at usance. The accepted draft can be discounted without recourse, and the beneficiary may obtain cash for it at any time.

Deferred payment credit refers to a letter of credit in which the issuing bank or the paying bank does not perform the payment obligation immediately after receiving the shipping documents conforming to the terms of the letter of credit, but waits until the due date stipulated in the letter of credit. It is a letter of credit payable at usance without a draft. The paying bank will generally provide a deferred payment undertaking to guarantee payment when due. Its business is similar to D/P, where the bank, upon receipt of the documents, delivers them to the applicant, who then makes payment on the due date. The exporter's payment is secured by the undertaking made either from the issuing bank or from the issuing bank and the confirming bank to pay when due in the credit.

(5) According to whether the beneficiary's right to the letter of credit is transferable

Transferable L/C is a letter of credit in which part or all of the rights can be transferred to another person (i. e., the second beneficiary) by the advising bank authorized by the issuing bank at the request of the beneficiary. The first beneficiary is usually the middleman who signs the contract with the importer, and the second beneficiary is usually the actual supplier. In order to earn the profit margin, the middleman transfers the letter of credit to the actual supplier, who handles the shipping procedures. After the transfer of the L/C, shipment shall be effected by the second beneficiary. A credit may be transferred only if the issuing bank clearly indicates "transferable" in the credit. Transferable L/C can only be transferred once, i. e., it can only be transferred by the first beneficiary to the second beneficiary, and the second beneficiary shall not require the transfer of the L/C to the third beneficiary. If the L/C allows partial shipment, the first beneficiary may assign the credit into several parts to several persons, or transfer parts of the credit and keep the rest part of the credit for his own use. The new letter of credit shall be consistent with the original letter of credit in terms of the terms and conditions stipulated in the credit, except for the following aspects: the applicant can be changed; the amount of the letter of credit and the unit price of the goods can be reduced; the expiry date, delivery date and latest shipment date may be advanced or postponed; the proportion of goods insured can be increased.

Non-transferable L/C is a letter of credit under which the beneficiary cannot transfer its rights to another person. Any letter of credit without being marked with "transferable" is deemed to be non-transferable. In practice, irrevocable and non-transferable letters of credit are commonly used.

Case 9.9 clauses for settlement by L/C in a contract

(1) Payment by L/C at sight

The buyer shall open through a bank acceptable to the seller an irrevocable sight letter of credit to reach the seller ×× days before the month of shipment, valid until the 15th day after the month of shipment for negotiation in China.

(2) Payment terms of usance L/C

The buyer shall open through a bank acceptable to the seller an irrevocable letter of credit payable 45 days after sight to reach the seller ×× days before the month of shipment, valid for negotiation in China until the 15th day after the month of shipment.

【Tasks for implementation】

In the case of the previous subtask, Nam Kwong company uses letter of credit to settle the import payment with Nanhwa company. In this settlement business, Jiangsu branch of Bank of China opens a letter of credit after the application of Nam Kwong company. The letter of credit uses documentary drafts, therefore is a documentary credit. In the case, it is not specified whether the letter of credit is revocable or irrevocable; as a result, this letter of credit is considered irrevocable. And it is also not specified whether the credit is confirmed or not, so the credit can be considered unconfirmed. In this case, the payment term of the draft in the letter of credit is not clearly indicated. As Bank of China, Hong Kong branch will make the payment to Nanhwa company immediately after examining the documents for correctness, this letter of credit is a sight letter of credit. It is not specified in the case whether the credit is marked "transferable", so the credit is considered non-transferable.

Task 9.4 Settlement by bank guarantee and standby letter of credit

【Task for analysis】

In an international settlement, bank guarantee and standby letter of credit can also be used for international settlement in addition to the three major settlement methods. When applying a bank guarantee, it is necessary for us to understand its parties, main contents and business process. When using standby letter of credit, we should know its main contents, types and business procedures.

Task 9.4.1 The definition of bank guarantee and its parties

【Case for demonstration】

On August 1, 2008, Jiangsu Nam Kwong International Trading Corp. signed an import contract with Hong Kong Nanhwa International Trading Co., Ltd. for a batch of wool fabrics with the contract value of HK $1 000 000.00. Nam Kwong company applies for a bank guarantee from Jiangsu branch of Bank of China (the guarantor bank). After a detailed examination of the credit standing and property status of Nam Kwong company, the guarantor bank accepts the application, issues a bank guarantee and sends it to Bank of China, Hong Kong branch (the advising bank). The advising bank notifies Nanhwa company (the beneficiary) of the contents of the guarantee. If Nam Kwong company defaults and fails to make payment to Nanhwa company, Nanhwa company shall claim compensation from the guarantor bank through the advising bank. Jiangsu branch of Bank of China shall compensate Nanhwa company according to the bank guarantee and then shall claim against Nam Kwong company for compensation. Nam Kwong company shall pay compensation to the guarantor bank. At this point, the two companies have completed a settlement business through the bank guarantee.

【Questions for discussion】

Based on the lead-in case, please try to have a basic understand of the bank guarantee business and think about the following questions:

(1) What is a bank guarantee?

(2) What are the characteristics of settlements by bank guarantee?

(3) What are the main parties?

【Relevant Knowledge】

(1) The definition of bank guarantee

Banker's letter of guarantee, also known as bank guarantee, abbreviated as L/G, is a written credit guarantee issued to a third party (the beneficiary) by banks, insurance companies, guarantee companies or individuals (guarantors) at the request of the applicant to undertake the liability of payment of a debt or the fulfillment of an obligation in the event of default by the party primarily responsible.

A bank guarantee has two basic functions, one is to guarantee the payment of the contract, the other is to compensate the injured party and punish the responsible person when the breach occurs. By substituting or supplementing commercial credit with bank credit, bank guarantee features better credit and strong flexibility. Therefore, it is widely used in many fields of international settlements, such as trade payment, project contracting, rent payment, capital lending, compensation trade, processing with supplied materials, etc.

(2) The characteristics of bank guarantee

①The payment liability of the guarantor with a conditional guarantee is secondary

When using a guarantee, usually the beneficiary (creditor) should first request payment from the applicant (debtor), and only when the debtor does not pay can the guarantee be used to demand payment from the guarantor, so in theory, the guarantor's payment liability is secondary. However, in case of L/C, the whole situation is different. Once the L/C is issued, the issuing bank has the primary responsibility for payment, and the beneficiary should request payment from the issuing bank instead of presenting the documents to the applicant. Therefore, the issuing bank has the primary responsibility for payment.

②The payment is made only if a default occurs

The letter of credit is used to complete the payment under the sales contract. Normally, the payment under the letter of credit is bound to happen. A letter of guarantee is the opposite of a letter of credit. The beneficiary will claim under the letter of guarantee only when the applicant breaches the contract (e. g., the applicant neither performs the contract nor makes the compensation as agreed), so the payment under the letter of guarantee may not occur.

③A letter of guarantee is issued only to provide a credit guarantee

The guarantor/issuer issues the guarantee out of confidence in the applicant's ability to perform the contract. The purpose of the guarantee is not to pay compensation at all, but merely to provide a credit guarantee. Therefore, the applicant is generally not required to pay a deposit, but only required to offer a pledge or provide a counter guarantee.

(3) Parties to a bank guarantee

There are many parties involved in the bank guarantee business, among which there are three basic parties, namely the applicant, the beneficiary and the guarantee bank. Sometimes, depending on the specific circumstances of the guarantee, other parties may also be involved, such as the advising bank (the transmitting bank), the confirming bank, the counter-guaranteeing bank and the reissuing bank.

①The applicant

The applicant is also called the principal or the guaranteed, that is, the party who applies to the bank and entrusts the bank to issue the guarantee. The applicant usually applies for the letter of guarantee according to the contract or in order to improve his/her credit standing, whose main responsibility is: perform his/her obligations in strict accordance with the contract between him/her and the beneficiary of the guarantee to avoid claims under guarantee; in case of a claim, the applicant shall reimburse the guarantor bank immediately for all payments made by the guarantor bank to the beneficiary; bear all costs and interests under guarantee; provide counter-guarantee or property mortgage as required by the guarantor bank when necessary. For the applicant, the claim conditions of the guarantee should prevent the beneficiary from withdrawing the money if the conditions are not met.

②The beneficiary

The creditor of the basic contract, is the party who receives the guarantee and has the right to claim against the guarantor bank in accordance with the provisions of the guarantee. The beneficiary is one enjoying all the security rights under the letter of guarantee, whose main responsibilities and rights are: fulfill the contract with the applicant; if the applicant fails to perform his/her obligations under the contract, the beneficiary may make a claim to the guarantor bank through the letter of guarantee and obtain the payment; in case of a claim, the proof of claim or relevant documents as requested shall be presented in accordance with the provisions of the guarantee.

③The guarantor bank

A guarantor bank is a bank that issues a letter of guarantee to the beneficiary as entrusted by the applicant. The guarantor bank shall issue a letter of guarantee to the beneficiary at the request of the applicant and on the condition that the applicant provides a certain guarantee. Before issuing a guarantee, the guarantee bank shall have the right to make a comprehensive review of the guarantee contents, the credit standing, the performance capability and the operation style of the applicant to decide whether to issue a guarantee. The main responsibility of the guarantor bank is to compensate the beneficiary according to the payment terms specified in the guarantee when the beneficiary makes a claim under the contract. The guarantor bank shall have the right to require the applicant to provide a counter security, to charge the applicant a service fee and to claim compensation from the applicant or the counter guarantor after having made the compensation to the beneficiary. The guarantor bank shall have the right to dispose of the security deposit or collateral if the applicant is unable to immediately reimburse the amount already paid by the guarantor bank; if the compensation is still not complete after disposal, the guarantor bank shall reserve the right to recover from the applicant the rest amount.

④The advising bank

The advising bank, also known as the transmitting bank, is the bank notifying or delivering the guarantee to the beneficiary as entrusted by the guarantor bank, usually in the place where the beneficiary is located. The main responsibility of the advising bank is to check the apparent authenticity of the guarantee, such as check the seal or the test key of the guarantor bank, inform the beneficiary timely in strict accordance with the requirements and instructions of the guarantor bank; promptly communicate to the guaranty bank. If, for some reason, the guarantee fails to be notified or delivered to the beneficiary, the advising bank shall promptly communicate this to the guarantor bank. After the notifying the letter of guarantee, the advising bank shall have the right to charge the guarantor bank or the applicant or the beneficiary for the delivery of the guarantee, and shall not bear any liability for the correctness of the contents, the delay or any loss of the guarantee in the course of mailing.

⑤The confirming bank

A confirming bank is a bank that confirms the letter of guarantee. At the request of the guarantor bank, the confirming bank, with its outstanding reputation, shall, in addition to the promise of payment already made by the guarantor bank, undertake to perform the obligation of payment in case of unreasonable refusal or inability to pay by the guarantor bank. The confirming bank shall reimburse the beneficiary only when the guarantor bank fails to fulfill the payment obligation as stipulated in the guarantee, and shall have the right to claim compensation from the guarantor bank after payment. So in this way, double guarantees are available to beneficiaries. The beneficiary has two choices: one is to have the original guarantee confirmed by a large international bank or a domestic bank, so that a guarantee has two guarantors; the other is to require the domestic bank to issue another letter of guarantee, then there appear the counter guarantor bank and the reissuing bank.

⑥The counter guarantor bank

A counter-guarantor bank is a bank entrusted by the applicant to issue instructions for opening a letter of guarantee. The applicant turns to the support of the domestic bank and requires the domestic bank to entrust its correspondent bank in the place of the beneficiary to issue a letter of guarantee, and at the same time makes a promise to pay the entrusted bank immediately when the claim is made. The trustee bank in the place of the beneficiary becomes the de facto guarantor bank. The counter-guarantee bank is the third party bank that has business relations with the applicant. It has the responsibility to compensate the guarantor bank or the reissuing bank and has the right to claim compensation from the applicant.

⑦Reissuing bank

The reissuing bank is the bank that accepts the request from the original guarantor bank and issues the guarantee to the beneficiary with the original guarantor bank as the applicant and itself as the guarantor bank, generally the bank in the place where the beneficiary is located. After opening the letter of guarantee, the issuing bank becomes the new guarantor bank, the original guarantor bank becomes the instructing bank. In case of compensation, the beneficiary can only claim compensation from the reissuing bank, and the reissuing bank has the right to claim reimbursement from the original guarantor bank after payment.

【Task】

In the case of this sub-task, Nam Kwong company issues a bank guarantee to settle the contract payment. In the settlement business, Bank of China, Jiangsu branch, at the request of Nam Kwong company, opens to Nanhwa company a bank guarantee, which is a written credit guarantee issued by Bank of China, Jiangsu branch to guarantee its liability for contractual obligations in case of default by Nam Kwong company which is primarily responsible for Nanhwa company. Nanhwa company shall ask Nam Kwong company for payment first. Only when Nam Kwong company fails to pay, Nanhwa company can ask Bank of China, Jiangsu branch for payment by letter of guarantee. Therefore, Bank of China, Jiangsu branch assumes the secondary responsibility for payment. This letter of guarantee involves four parties, Nam Kwong company as the applicant, Nanhwa company as the beneficiary, Bank of China Jiangsu branch as the guarantor bank, and Bank of China Hong Kong branch as the notifying bank.

Task 9.4.2 Contents and procedures of a bank guarantee

【Case for demonstration】

Figure 9.15 is an example of a bank guarantee for you to know its main contents.

Advance payment guarantee

TO:________(beneficiary)　　　Date:

No.:

Dear sirs:

This guarantee is hereby issued as the advance payment guarantee of ________ (Applicant) (hereinafter called the supplier) for ________ (the name of the contract and its number) to ________ (the name of the beneficiary) (hereinafter called the buyer).

Whereas the buyer has agreed to advance to the supplier an amount of ________ (say ________ only) whereas the buyer has required the supplier to furnish a guarantee with an amount equal to the above said advance payment for performance of his obligations under the contract, and the ________ (the name of Guarantor) at the request of the supplier and in consideration of the buyer's agreeing to make the above said advance to the supplier, has agreed to furnish the required guarantee.

Now therefore the guarantor hereby guarantees that the supplier shall utilize the above said advance for the purpose of the contract and if he fails and commits default in fulfillment of any of his obligation for which the advance payment is made it shall entitle the buyer to be paid not exceeding the above-mentioned amount.

Against notice in writing of any default which the guarantor should be given by the buyer stating that the supplier has failed to fulfill its obligation to the buyer and upon such first demand payment shall be made by the guarantor of the sum then due under this guarantee without any obligation.

The sum of this guarantee shall be automatically and proportionally reduced in step of the progress of the contract and the guarantor's obligation under this guarantee shall not in any case exceeding the sum of ________ (say ________ only).

This guarantee shall become effective from the date of receipt of the above said advance by the supplier and valid until ________(the date of expiry). Upon expiry, please return this guarantee to us for cancellation.

This advance payment guarantee is subject to uniform rules for demand guarantee (ICC Publication No. 458).

Best regards.

For and on behalf of

ABC Bank

Authorized Signature (s)

Figure 9.15 Sample bank guarantee

【Questions for discussion】

Based on the above sample bank guarantee, please try to understand its main contents and think about the following questions:

(1) What are the basic contents of a bank guarantee?

(2) What are its basic business procedures?

【Relevant knowledge】

(1) The form and the contents of a bank guarantee

The form of the guarantee is the written terms of the guarantee, which demonstrates the responsibilities and obligations of the guarantor under the guarantee and the scope of his/her responsibilities. Different forms reflect different levels of risks and different compensation or payment commitments of the guarantor under a certain guarantee category. Due to the different legal norms and customary practices in different countries, there is no uniform for various types of guarantees. However, the principle of issuing a letter of guarantee is the same, that is, the bank guarantee shall be issued according to the provisions of the transaction contract, and the contents shall be complete, rigorous, fair and clear without excessive details. Generally speaking, the basic contents of a bank guarantee mainly include the following aspects.

①Names and addresses of the parties concerned

The letter of guarantee shall indicate the full names and the detailed addresses of the principal parties, i. e., the applicant, the beneficiary, the guarantor bank and the advising bank, etc., among which the address of the guarantor bank is particularly important because it involves the application of the law of the guarantee, and the place of presentation by the beneficiary and the place of maturity of the guarantee itself are also very important. In addition, the beneficiary's name and address must be correct. Otherwise, the advising bank or the reissuing bank cannot timely make notification or reissue.

②The nature of letters of guarantee

It refers to the classification of guarantees, such as tender guarantee, performance guarantee, etc. Different types of guarantees have different responsibilities and obligations.

③The main contents of the basic contract for the issue of a letter of guarantee

Since the responsibilities and obligations of both parties to the transaction are established according to the transaction contract, which is the subject matter guaranteed by the bank guarantee, so the guarantee must specify the contents of the transaction contract, such as the contract number, the signing date, the contracting parties, whether there is any modification, etc.

④The amount of the L/G and the name of the currency

The amount guaranteed is the limitation of the guarantor's liability and is usually the maximum amount claimed by the beneficiary. The amount of the guarantee can be a specific number, or can be expressed with a percentage of the amount of the transaction contract. Generally, the name of the currency should be clearly indicated. The amount in numbers and that in words should be complete and consistent with each other. Unless otherwise stated in the letter of guarantee, the guaranteed amount shall not be reduced by the partial performance of the contract.

⑤The validity and expiry date of the L/G

The validity period of the letter of guarantee refers to the deadline for the beneficiary's claim to be served on the guarantor bank and the expiry date of the guarantee is the deadline for the guarantor bank to release its guarantee liability. Generally speaking, after the expiration, the guarantor's liability is relieved. If a claim is made by the beneficiary, the claim shall be delivered in written form to the guarantor bank on or before the validity date specified in the letter of guarantee. Upon receipt, the guarantor bank shall promptly notify the applicant of the contents of the claim and all documents received without any delay.

⑥The conditions and methods for the claim of a L/G

A claim condition is a condition for judging whether or not there is a breach of contract and for a claim to be made. Claim methods refer to the means (e. g. , by letter or cable) and the route (whether through the advising bank) by which the beneficiary makes a claim to the guarantor bank. Only when one party fails to perform or breaches the terms of the contract can the other party withdraw money by the letter of guarantee. A method commonly adopted nowadays is to make payment against the documents or the supporting documents submitted by the beneficiary in accordance with the stipulations of the letter of guarantee. The claim conditions are directly related to the interests of both the applicant and the beneficiary and therefore must be carefully considered by all parties.

⑦Guarantee amount deduction clause

The letter of guarantee shall specify that the sum of the L/G may be reduced by a specified amount or a predetermined amount on a specified date or after presentation to the guarantor bank of a document specified in the guarantee.

⑧The number and the date of the issue of the L/G

The purpose of the guaranteed number is to facilitate the internal management of the bank. The issuing date of the guarantee is generally the effective date of the guarantee, which is conducive to clarifying the guarantee liability of the bank.

⑨The liability of the L/G

This is the main content and the core of a bank guarantee. The guarantee shall specify the responsibilities and rights of the applicant, the beneficiary, the guarantor bank and other parties, especially the guarantee liability committed by the guarantor bank. The liability of the guarantor bank to the beneficiary shall be limited to the terms and conditions specified in the guarantee.

⑩Other terms

It includes confirmation, amendment, cancellation and arbitration related to the letter of guarantee.

According to *the Uniform Rules for Demand Guarantees ICC Publication No.* 458 (UGD458) established by the International Chamber of Commerce, the main contents of a bank guarantee include the parties concerned (name and address); the basis for issuing the letter of guarantee; the amount of the guarantee and the clause of diminishing amount; terms of payment.

(2) The method of issuing a bank guarantee

In the bank guarantee business, the letter of guarantee is usually issued in two ways: direct issue and reissue.

①Direct issue

Also known as direct guarantee, refers to the way in which the guarantor bank directly issues a letter of guarantee to the beneficiary at the applicant's request, thus directly assuming responsibilities to the beneficiary.

②Reissue

Also known as indirect guarantee, is a settlement method where the bank in the applicant's place, according to the relevant provisions of the tender document or the contract and the usual practice and legal requirements of the beneficiary's country, entrusts another bank (usually the bank in the place of the beneficiary, i. e., the guarantor bank), which shall bear the responsibility of payment to the beneficiary, to issue a letter of guarantee on its behalf in the form of a counter-guarantee as requested.

(3) The business procedure of a bank guarantee

During the validity period of the guarantee, the guarantor bank assumes a contingent liability under guarantee until the expiry of the guarantee. In general, a bank guarantee business needs to go through the following links.

①The applicant applies to the bank for a letter of guarantee

The applicant shall fill in the application form for issuing the letter of guarantee or sign the entrustment guarantee agreement with the guarantor bank, submit a certain amount of margin or other forms of counter-guarantee as collateral, and submit relevant business reference documents (such as bidding documents, contracts, relevant contracts, agreements, etc.). The letter of guarantee constitutes the written contract of the relationship between the applicant and the guarantor bank, and also forms the legal basis for the guarantor bank to issue the letter of guarantee. The purpose of the client applying for issuing the letter of guarantee is to consolidate its responsibility and commitment to perform the contract, and at the same time to guarantee to the bank issuing the letter of guarantee that it will compensate the bank in full amount after the bank makes reimbursement against the letter of guarantee. The applicant shall carefully read the relevant provisions of the contract, fill in the application form according to the specific requirements of the contract and calculate the amount of guarantee and the length of validity accurately and meticulously.

②Verification by the guarantor bank

In order to protect its own interests, the bank will examine and verify the credit standing and the financial status of the applicant, the collateral and the counter-guarantee measures, the feasibility and benefits of the items of the basic contract, the application for the letter of guarantee or the entrusted guarantee agreement, the form of the letter of guarantee, etc. On the basis of a careful examination, the bank decides whether to accept the application or not.

③The guarantor bank issues a letter of guarantee

After reviewing and approving the relevant information provided by the applicant and the credit standing of the applicant, the guarantor bank may issue the letter of guarantee directly or re-issue the letter of guarantee against C/G from another bank, and collect the guarantee deposit from the applicant according to the prescribed rate. In order to avoid being involved in complicated disputes and maintain its own reputation, the guarantor bank shall attach great importance to the claim clauses of the guarantee when issuing the guarantee, and pay special attention to the documentation of the claim conditions of the guarantee. In addition, the guarantor bank shall indicate the validity date in the guarantee. In daily business, the letter of guarantee can be issued by cable or by letter, which is the same as the letter of credit. After issuing the letter of guarantee, the guarantor bank usually entrusts the bank in the place where the beneficiary is located to notify the letter of guarantee, or the principal may notify the beneficiary directly.

④Amendment of the letter of guarantee

The guarantee may be modified within the validity period. Amendments to the guarantee shall be made only by the unanimous consent of the parties concerned and shall be deemed null and void in case of unilateral modification by any party alone. When the applicant and the beneficiary have reached an agreement on the amendment of the guarantee, the applicant shall submit a written application to the guarantor bank and affix its official seal, indicating the number, the date, the amount of the original guarantee and the detailed terms under the request for amendment and the resulting liability terms, at the same time should issue the position paper where the beneficiary requests or agrees to the amendment for the reference of the guarantor bank. After the guarantor bank has examined the application and agreed to the amendment, its responsible person in charge shall sign and send the amendment letter.

⑤Claims under the letter of guarantee

The guarantor bank shall assume the primary liability for payment independently and shall compensate the beneficiary up to the amount of the guarantee on the basis of the claim documents submitted by the beneficiary in accordance with the requirements of the guarantee. Within the validity period of the guarantee, the guarantor bank shall conduct a strict examination on the claim in accordance with the claim clauses of the guarantee upon the receipt of the claim documents and relevant supporting documents submitted by the beneficiary and make timely payment after confirming that the claim documents and relevant supporting documents are in full compliance with the claim clauses of the guarantee so as to fulfill its responsibilities in the letter of guarantee. The guarantor bank may immediately exercise its right to claim for compensation from the applicant or the counter guarantor of the guarantee after the payment.

⑥Cancellation of the letter of guarantee

The guarantee becomes null and void upon expiration, and the guarantor bank's guarantee liability is discharged immediately. Thereafter the guarantor bank is no longer responsible for any claims that may arise and the guarantee may be cancelled. In such a case, the guarantor bank shall immediately go through the cancellation procedures and require the beneficiary to return the guarantee to the guarantor bank in accordance with the relevant provisions of the guarantee, and the beneficiary shall sign a document expressly waiving all rights under guarantee. In addition, the full payment of the balance under guarantee also means the end of the guarantee and the guarantor bank can go through the cancelation procedures accordingly. The cancellation of guarantee means the end of the operation procedure of a guaranteed business.

(4) A comparison between a bank guarantee and a documentary credit

There are many similarities and obvious differences between a bank guarantee and a documentary credit, two ways of settlement.

①The similarities

a. Both are commitments made by banks

Both the bank guarantee and the documentary letter of credit are conditional payment guarantee or commitment issued by the bank to the beneficiary at the request of the applicant. Both of them belong to the bank credit, and both are used to substitute or supplement the commercial credit as the bank credit, so that the beneficiary can avoid or reduce the loss caused by the applicant's non-performance.

b. Both are independent

The bank guarantee and the documentary credit are generated from the basic contract between the applicant and the beneficiary, but are independent from the basic contract. The claim for compensation shall be in accordance with the terms of the letter of guarantee or the letter of credit. In addition, the bank guarantee and the documentary letter of credit are also independent from the contract between the applicant and the bank. The bank cannot refuse to pay or compensate the beneficiary on the grounds that the applicant has not fulfilled his obligations.

c. Both are documentary businesses

Under the independent bank guarantee and the documentary letter of credit, the bank decides whether to perform the payment or compensation liability according to the documents presented by the beneficiary, and the bank does not have to concern itself with the actual performance of the contractual obligations by the two parties.

d. The bank's responsibility for checking documents is limited to apparent compliance

Under the bank guarantee and the documentary credit, the bank is only responsible for checking the apparent authenticity of beneficiary's documents. The bank's liability is limited to good faith and reasonable care, and it is not responsible for acts beyond its control, such as the authenticity and legal effects of documents, delay or loss in delivery.

②The differences

a. They have different scopes for application and use

The documentary credit is usually only applicable to the purchase and sale of goods and generally exists as a means of international trade settlement. While a bank guarantee is not only applicable to trade in goods, but also to any other kind of economic transaction. It is not only a means of settlement, but also a means to ensure the fulfillment of certain obligations under the contract.

b. Banks assume different liabilities for payment

In case of a credit, the bank assumes the primary responsibility for payment. If the beneficiary requests payment, he/she shall present the documents to the issuing bank or its nominated bank, not to the applicant. While in case of a bank guarantee, depending on the undertaking and terms of the guarantee itself, the bank is liable for either primary (independent guarantee) or secondary (accessory guarantee) payment. The applicant shall first make payment to the beneficiary or fulfill other obligations and only when the applicant fails to make payment or fulfill the contractual obligations, the beneficiary can demand payment from the guarantor bank by the letter of guarantee. In practice, when a claim is made by the beneficiary, it is usually followed by an investigation by the guarantor bank, which shall confirm that the applicant has not fulfilled his/her contractual obligations before the payment is made. Therefore, in the letter of guarantee the guarantor bank's liability for payment is generally secondary.

c. The preconditions are different

The letter of credit is mainly used for the normal performance of contracts for the international sale of goods. When the seller, after the shipment of the goods, submits documents in conformity with the terms of the credit to the bank for payment, such payment is bound to occur. The main function of a bank guarantee is to guarantee, under which the guarantor bank assumes a contingent payment responsibility. When the transaction goes on normally and the parties concerned strictly perform the contract, the bank guarantee does not need to be used. It is only when the applicant defaults that the beneficiary will demand compensation from the guarantor bank against the letter of guarantee. Therefore, payment against the guarantee is not inevitable in every transaction.

d. The basis of payment is different

Under the documentary letter of credit, the bank will only pay against the commercial documents in conformity with the letter of credit. If the documents are inconsistent with the credit, the bank will refuse to pay. The bank only concerns about the documents, not the facts. While under the bank guarantee, the guarantor bank's payment is based on the "facts" rather than the "documents" of the applicant's failure to perform the basic contractual obligations. When the beneficiary claims compensation from the guarantor bank, it is necessary for him/her to submit to the bank the evidence or documents of the applicant's breach of contract. The bank needs to investigate and collect evidence and prove the facts before paying to the beneficiary.

e. Banks take different risks

Under documentary credits, the issuing bank requires the applicant to submit a certain amount of margin in advance and pays against the compliant shipping documents submitted by the beneficiary, so the credit risk is relatively small. However, the guarantor bank under the bank guarantee does not have the shipping documents, and is more likely to encounter unreasonable claims by the beneficiary, so the bank may bear a greater credit risk.

f. Applicable conventions are different

Letters of credit have a unified international practice, namely UCP500 or UCP600, which has a profound effect, consequently, the parties are subject to international practice in the process of implementation. But legal norms on guarantees vary from country to country, and the existing international practice on guarantees, UDG458, has a relatively small impact and is therefore more difficult to implement.

In addition, there are differences between the bank guarantee and the documentary credit in financing, revocability, transferability, etc. The bank guarantee has no financing function, is irrevocable, the beneficiary's right to lodge claims is generally non-transferable.

【Tasks for implementation】

The bank guarantee in this sub-task is an advance payment guarantee, which includes the name and the address of the beneficiary, the applicant and the guarantor bank; the number and the issuing date of the guarantee; the nature of the guarantee; the name and the number of the basic contract; the amount of the guarantee and the name of the currency; the guarantee liability of the guarantee; the conditions and methods of claims for the guarantee; the validity and the expiry date of the guarantee; the guarantee amount deduction clause and its applicable practice, etc.

In the case of the previous subtask, Nam Kwong company issued a bank guarantee to settle the contract payment. This settlement business reflects a complete bank guarantee business process, which includes: Nam Kwong company applies to issue a letter of guarantee; Bank of China, Jiangsu branch (the guarantor bank) makes a review; the guarantor bank issues the bank guarantee and sends it to Bank of China, Hong Kong branch (the advising bank); the notifying bank notifies Nanhwa company (the beneficiary) of the contents of the guarantee; after the default of Nam Kwong company, the beneficiary shall claim compensation from the guarantor bank through the advising bank; the guarantor bank shall compensate Nanhwa company according to the bank guarantee; the guarantor bank shall claim compensation from Nam Kwong company after reimbursement, and recover the guarantee (cancellation) from Nam Kwong company after compensation.

Task 9.4.3 The concept and the classification of standby letters of credit

【Cases for demonstration】

On August 1, 2008, Nam Kwong company entered into an import contract with Nanhwa company for a batch of wool fabrics with the contract value of KH $1 000 000.00. Nam Kwong company applies to Bank of China, Jiangsu branch (the issuing bank) for the issuance of a standby letter of credit. After verification, the issuing bank accepts the application and issues the standby letter of credit and sends it to Bank of China, Hong Kong branch (the advising bank). The advising bank advises Nanhwa company of the contents of the standby letter of credit. If Nam Kwong company fulfills its payment obligations under the contract, the issuing bank shall not have to fulfill its payment obligations for issuing the standby letter of credit, and its guarantee liability shall be discharged when the standby letter of credit expires. If Nam Kwong company fails to perform the contract when due, Nanhwa company may, in accordance with the provisions of the standby letter of credit, submit the relevant documents to the issuing bank for compensation. After receiving the documents, the issuing bank shall pay to Nanhwa company if the documents comply with the stipulations of the credit after examination. After the payment Jiangsu branch of Bank of China then lodges a claim against Nam Kwong company. Nam Kwong company then repays the amount of the standby letter of credit. Till now, the two companies have completed a settlement business through the standby letter of credit.

【Questions for discussion】

Based on the lead-in case, please try to understand the basic situation of the standby letter of credit business, and consider the following questions:

(1) What is a standby letter of credit?

(2) Who are the main parties?

(3) What kind of categories can they be classified into?

【Relevant knowledge】

(1) The concept of a standby letter of credit

A stand-by letter of credit (SL/C), also known as a guarantee L/C, is a guarantee payment voucher issued by the issuing bank to the beneficiary at the request of the applicant to guarantee the fulfillment of the obligations by the applicant with its own bank credit. That is, the issuing bank warrants to the beneficiary that it shall be conditionally liable for the repayment when the applicant fails to fulfill the prescribed obligations.

The purpose of a standby letter of credit is basically the same as a bank guarantee. It can be used not only for the payment of complete sets of equipment, large machinery means of transport and the payment of rent, but also for the performance guarantee of common import and export trade, international bidding, international financing, processing and assembling, compensation trade and technical trade.

(2) Characteristics of a standby letter of credit

A standby letter of credit is a bank credit in which the issuing bank assumes an independent and primary responsibility for payment to the beneficiary. If the applicant breaches the contract, the issuing bank shall pay the amount specified in the credit against the beneficiary's declaration in conformity with the credit, which is submitted within the validity of the credit. The beneficiary shall not require payment from the issuing bank if the applicant fulfills the contract as scheduled. It can be seen that the standby letter of credit plays the same role as the bank guarantee. According to ISP98, the standby letter of credit, when issued, is an irrevocable, independent, documentary and binding commitment, characterized in three respects.

①A standby letter of credit is an irrevocable letter of credit

The issuing bank assumes the primary payment liability and its obligations shall not be amended or cancelled by the issuing bank itself, unless otherwise stated in the standby letter of credit or agreed by the other parties.

②A standby letter of credit is a guarantee with apparent independence

Like a commercial letter of credit, a standby letter of credit is an independent document, which, once issued, is independent from the basic contract on which it is based. The issuing bank's performance of its obligations under the credit shall not be conditioned on the underlying contract.

③A stand by letter of credit also has the characteristics of documentation

Under the standby letter of credit, payment by the issuing bank is subject to an examination of the apparent condition of the documents required by the standby letter of credit. The issuing bank shall make payment to the beneficiary if the documents presented by the beneficiary meet the terms and conditions of the credit.

(3) The principal parties to the standby letter of credit

①Applicant

An applicant is a person who applies to a bank for a standby letter of credit for himself/herself or for another person. The applicant shall normally provide guarantee and be obligated to pay the opening charge.

②Beneficiary

The beneficiary is the nominated person who is eligible for obtaining payment under the standby letter of credit. Upon receipt of the L/C, the beneficiary may arrange shipment or perform other acts of fulfilling the contract. If the applicant fails to fulfill its obligations as committed or in accordance with the underlying contract, the beneficiary may make a claim against the issuing bank or the confirming party by presenting the claim and the documents in compliance with the standby letter of credit.

③Issuing bank

An issuing bank is a bank entrusted by an applicant to issue a standby letter of credit. The issuing bank is obliged to open the L/C in accordance with the instructions of the application and undertakes to pay the beneficiary first. The issuing bank may claim compensation from the applicant after reimbursement, and may obtain compensation from the guarantee if the applicant fails to pay or is unable to pay. If the issuing bank fails to fulfill its obligation to examine the documents carefully and makes payment to the beneficiary by mistake, it loses the right to claim against the applicant.

④Confirmer

The confirmer is the guarantor undertaking to pay the credit by his commitment to the issuing bank and his/her own guarantee, under the direction of the issuing bank. The issuing bank usually requests confirmation from the advising bank. The advising bank is not obliged to confirm and shall promptly notify the applicant if confirmation is not provided. The confirmer is independent and has the same status as the issuing bank, that is, it bears the same obligations and responsibilities to the beneficiary as the issuing bank.

⑤Advising bank

An advising bank refers to the bank designated by the issuing bank to forward the standby letter of credit to the beneficiary. The advising bank shall have the right not to notify the beneficiary, but shall promptly let the issuing bank know it. Upon acceptance of the notice, the advising bank shall verify the apparent authenticity of the standby letter of credit and immediately notify the beneficiary of the standby letter of credit. The advising bank shall have the right to obtain remuneration from the issuing bank. A standby letter of credit may also be sent by the issuing bank or the applicant directly to the beneficiary.

⑥Nominated person

When issuing a standby letter of credit, the issuing bank may designate another person to give notification, accept the presentation, make a confirmation, negotiate, pay, undertake deferred payment obligations or accept the draft.

(4) Categories of standby letters of credit

Standby letters of credit are widely used, convenient and flexible, and their opening amount has already exceeded that of commercial letters of credit. Having become an alternative form of bank guarantee, it can be used not only as a substitute for tender guarantee, performance guarantee, advance payment guarantee and quality maintenance guarantee, but also as payment guarantee, loan guarantee and counter-guarantee guarantee. In the 1980s and 1990s, standby letters of credit were equated with independent guarantees. The standby letter of credit is issued because of the loss of the beneficiary caused by the applicant's breach of contract, as a result the issuing bank reimburses the beneficiary against the amount of the standby letter of credit. This kind of standby letter of credit is called the standby letter of credit for payment in breach of contract. With the development of stand-by L/C business, stand-by letters of credit for direct payment without involving breach of contract have appeared. This type of credit guarantees one basic payment obligation with which the issuing bank pays at maturity no matter whether it involves a breach of contract or not.

【Tasks for implementation】

In the case of this sub-task, Nam Kwong company settles the contract payment by issuing a standby letter of credit. In this settlement business, Bank of China, Jiangsu branch, shall open a standby letter of credit at the request of Nam Kwong company. If Nam Kwong company fails to fulfill the contract at the due date, Nanhwa company may claim compensation from the issuing bank, which assumes the primary responsibility for payment. This responsibility is independent from the trade contract between Nam Kwong company and Nanhwa company. If Nam Kwong company has fulfilled its contractual obligations, the issuing bank will no longer be obliged to pay. Therefore, the issuing bank's payment liability may not occur. There are four parties involved, namely Nam Kwong company as the applicant, Bank of China Jiangsu branch as the issuing bank, Nanhwa company as the beneficiary and Bank of China Hong Kong branch as the advising bank. This standby letter of credit is a performance standby letter of credit established by Bank of China, Jiangsu branch, to guarantee the payment obligations of Nam Kwong company under the trade contract.

Task 9.4.4 Contents and procedures of the standby letter of credit

【Cases for demonstration】

Here is a sample of a standby letter of credit for you to get a glimpse of its main contents.

The irrevocable standby letter of credit

From: Union Bank of Switzerland , Zurich

To: Bank of China, Jiangsu Branch, Nanjing, China

Test for: USD100 000.00

Attn: Your L/C Dept.

Zurich, August 1, 2008 Our Ref: KAUT/VOJ/301 - 57939

Irrevocable standby letter of credit No. 301 - 57939

Dear Sirs:

We hereby open our irrevocable standby letter of credit No. 301 - 57939 in favour of China National Chemicals Import & Export Corporation, Jiangsu branch, Nanjing, China on behalf of Welman Trading S. A. Geneva, Switzerland up to the aggregate amount of USD 100 000.00 available against:

Beneficiary's draft drawn on us at sight and bearing the clause drawn under Union Bank of Switzerland Irrevocable Standby Letter of Credit No. 301 - 57939 accompanied by beneficiary's duly signed statements:

1. That the goods have been delivered in accordance with the purchase order.

2. That the full set of following shipping documents have been airmailed direct to Messrs. Levinumessillik Ve Dis Ticaret A. S. , Oney Hani Kat 5, Karakoy, Turkey by registered express letter:

- original invoice with 5 copies addressed to Welman Trading S. A. Geneva.
- packing list with one copy.
- generalised certificate of origin with one copy.
- an original insurance policy covering insurance against all risks from warehouse to warehouse.
- inspection certificate.
- full set of B/L issued to the order and indicating as "notify address: Levinumessillik Ve Dis Ticaret A. S. , Istanbul, Turkey" .

3. That messrs Welman Trading S. A. Geneva, Switzerland failed to pay the invoice amount on the due date, I. E. 90 days following the date of the respective Bill of Lading.

Important:

This standby L/C is not a documentary one and does not cover payment of documents nor documentary collection.

It may exclusively be utilized by the beneficiary in case the invoice should not be paid on due 90 days from date of B/L.

Such claim must be presented in comformity with the above terms, including the statements prescribed above.

Shipping documents may not be sent to us, nor handled as a documentary collection.

Validity: Until Jan. 16, 2009 at your counter.

Figure 9.16 Sample standby letter of credit

Covering: the due payment of the invoice relative to the supply of 1 000 kg Pathelocyanine Blue Bags 4382 in accordance with contract No. 91 bgstrboo 23 dated September 9, 2008.

Special instructions:

1. Kindly advise beneficiary of this credit, adding your confirmation.

2. In the event of any drawing being made hereunder, we authorize the negotiation of this credit at your counter. Payment will be affected by us 3 Zurich banking days after the date of your duly tested telex advice to us confirming that docs. In confirmity with the terms of this credit have been received and forwarded to us by registered airmail.

3. Your telex/negotiation advice as under 2. above must be in our hands not later than Dec. 31,2008.

This credit is subject to UCP600.

We hereby agree with drawers, endorsers and bonafide holders of drafts drawn under and in compliance with the terms of this credit that they will be duly honoured on due presentation of drawee.

This message represents the operative instrument. No mail confirmations will follow.

Yours Truly

Union Bank of Switzerland , Zurich

Authorized Signature (s)

Figure 9.16(contiuned)

【Questions for discussion】

Based on the above sample, please consider the following questions:

(1) What are the basic contents of a standby letter of credit?

(2) What are its basic business procedures?

【Relevant knowledge】

(1) The basic contents of a standby letter of credit

The contents of a standby letter of credit are similar to those of a documentary letter of credit, but the requirements for documents under a standby L/C are much simpler than those under a documentary L/C. Its contents generally include the following parts:

①The full number of the standby letter of credit and the date of opening.

②The name and detailed address of all parties, including the issuing bank, the applicant, the beneficiary and the advising bank, etc.

③The date, number and main content of the basic contract.

④The amount and the type of currency of the standby letter of credit.

⑤The type of the standby letter of credit with a statement of its irrevocable nature.

⑥The validity of the standby letter of credit, including the commencement date and the expiry date.

⑦Demands on papers or documents required by the beneficiary and their way of presentation at the time of claim.

⑧A statement for responsibility guarantee in the standby letter of credit.

⑨The proper law of the standby letter of credit, that is, in case of any dispute under the standby letter of credit, which arbitration institution shall arbitrate and which laws and practices shall be applied, etc.

(2) The business procedures of a standby letter of credit

Although the standby letter of credit is essentially a kind of bank guarantee, it still has the nature of the letter of credit, and its business procedures are basically the same as those of the documentary letter of credit. Generally speaking, the business of a standby letter of credit goes through the following steps.

①The applicant shall, in accordance with the provisions of the basic contract, apply to the bank for the issuance of the standby letter of credit and pay the opening charge, margin and provide other guarantees.

②After a careful examination, the issuing bank shall issue the standby letter of credit and notify or forward the standby L/C to the beneficiary through the advising bank.

③After obtaining the letter of credit, the beneficiary shall deliver the goods or perform other acts of fulfilling the contract. If the applicant fulfills his/her obligations under the basic contract, the standby letter of credit will automatically become null and void, and the issuing bank will not have to fulfill its obligation to pay against its issuance of the standby letter of credit, consequently, its guarantee liability will be discharged when the standby L/C expires, and the beneficiary shall return the standby letter of credit to the issuing bank. Till now, all the trading procedures of the standby L/C are completed. This is how a standby L/C works in most normal circumstances.

④If the applicant fails to perform his/her obligations as committed or in accordance with the underlying contract, the beneficiary may, in accordance with the provisions of the standby letter of credit, submit the claim documents and the relevant documents in conformity with the standby letter of credit to the issuing bank or the confirming party for compensation.

⑤After receiving the documents for claim, the issuing bank shall pay the beneficiary unconditionally if the documents are examined to be in conformity with the stipulations of the credit.

⑥After making reimbursement to the beneficiary, the issuing bank may claim compensation from the applicant, who is obliged to repay.

The business procedures of a standby letter of credit are shown in figure 9.17.

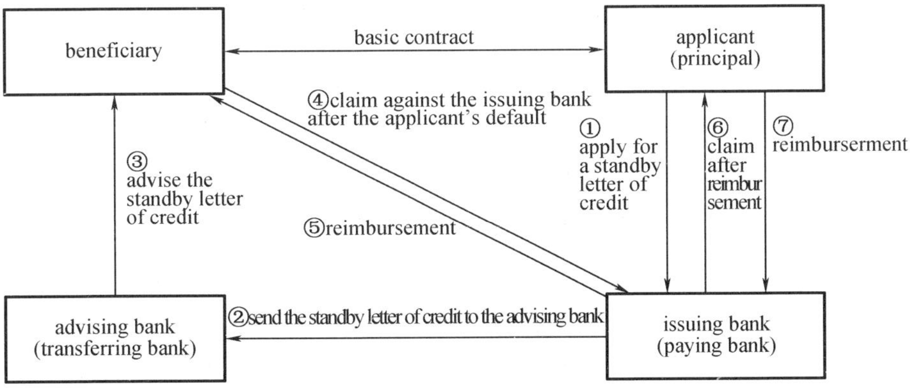

Figure 9.17 Business procedures of a standby letter of credit

【Tasks for implementation】

The standby letter of credit in this sub-task is a performance standby letter of credit, whose contents include: the number and the issuing date of the standby letter of credit; the name and the address of the issuing bank, the applicant, the beneficiary and the advising bank; the amount and the currency of the standby letter of credit; a statement of its irrevocable nature; the validity of the standby letter of credit; demands on papers or documents required by the beneficiary and their way of presentation upon claim; the date, the number and the main contents of the basic contract; the statement on the liability warranty in the standby letter of credit; applicable practices of the standby letter of credit, etc.

In the case of the previous sub-task, Nam Kwong company opened a standby letter of credit to pay for the contract. This settlement business reflects a complete standby L/C business process, which includes: Nam Kwong company applies for a standby L/C; Bank of China, Jiangsu branch company(the issuing bank), issues the standby L/C and forwards it to Bank of China, Hong Kong branch (the advising bank); the advising bank notifies Nanhwa company(the beneficiary) of the contents of the standby L/C; If Nam Kwong company breaches the contract, the beneficiary shall claim compensation against the issuing bank; the issuing bank then reimburses Nanhwa company in accordance with the standby L/C; after the payment, the issuing bank shall claim against Nam Kwong company, which shall return the standby L/C to the issuing bank after repayment.

References

[1]郭晓晶,秦社华,丁辉关,等.国际汇兑与结算[M].北京:高等教育出版社,2012.
[2]郭晓晶,秦雷.国际汇兑与结算[M].2版.北京:高等教育出版社,2014.